Jesus
in the Drama
of Salvation

Jesus
in the Drama
of Salvation

TOWARD A BIBLICAL
DOCTRINE OF REDEMPTION

RAYMUND SCHWAGER

Translated by
James G. Williams and Paul Haddon

A Herder & Herder Book
The Crossroad Publishing Company
New York

The Crossroad Publishing Company
370 Lexington Avenue, New York, NY 10017

Original edition: *Jesus im Heilsdrama:*
Entwurf einer biblischen Erlösungslehre.

English translation © 1999 by The Crossroad Publishing Company

Printed in the United States of America

Library of Congress Cataloging-in-Publication Data

    [Jesus im Heilsdrama. English.]
    Jesus in the drama of salvation : toward a biblical doctrine of
redemption / Raymund Schwager ; translated by James G. Williams and
Paul Haddon.
      p. cm.
    Includes bibliographical references and index.
    ISBN 0-8245-1796-2 (pbk.)
    1. Jesus Christ – Person and offices. 2. Redemption – Biblical
teaching. I. Title.
BT202.S375713 1999
232′.3 – dc21
                          98-52207

1   2   3   4   5   6   7   8   9   10   04   03   02   01   00   99

CONTENTS

Part Three
SYSTEMATIC CONSIDERATIONS
Page 159

PREFACE

This work continues the investigation of the doctrine of redemption that I began with *Must There Be Scapegoats?* In that study, thanks to René Girard's theory, both the doctrine of redemption and many specific exegetical questions could be placed in a new light. The fruitfulness of that first attempt was also sustained, in my view, in my collection of essays on the history of the doctrine of redemption (*Der wunderbare Tausch* [The marvelous exchange]). At the same time, however, these essays made it clear that numerous exegetical issues and questions of biblical theology required further clarification. Many criticisms of *Must There Be Scapegoats?* also indicated that this was necessary. So a renewed and deepened approach to the biblical problematic suggested itself to me.

Two basic concerns should be expressed first of all. One is the discussion and debate with the historical-critical method. This question of method stems from the inner problematic of the New Testament itself, while it is simultaneously a result of the criticism of the Enlightenment idea of the autonomous moral subject as worked out in the thought of Girard under the heading of "the Romantic lie." G. Wenz has also set forth a similar criticism concerning the moral subject in his recently published *Geschichte der Versöhnungslehre in der evangelischen Theologie der Neuzeit* (History of the doctrine of reconciliation in modern evangelical theology).

The second concern is the attempt to connect the exegetical and biblical questions with a systematic consideration of the doctrine of redemption. For this difficult task M. Corbin's investigations of Anselm of Canterbury offered great assistance. Corbin was able to show convincingly that the bishop of Canterbury sought likewise to master biblical problems with a systematically sketched doctrine of redemption, and that even until today his attempt remains misunderstood and unappropriated.

The dramatic exegesis that I am attempting here is indebted, on the one hand, to the "Theodramatik" (God-drama) of Hans Urs von Balthasar, even if I depart from it at points. On the other hand, it continues a modest attempt at a dramatic theology which I first broached in *Das dramatische Kirchenverständnis bei Ignatius von Loyola* (1970) (Ignatius of Loyola's dramatic understanding of the church). I have also developed this dramatic approach in an extended narrative or "novel" about Jesus, *Jesus of Nazareth: How He Understood His Life* (Crossroad, 1998).

Part One

Paradox and Drama

Everyday human experience seems to be filled with absurdities, tensions, and contradictions. There is much that even strenuous intellectual effort will never completely sort out. New occurrences often stand in opposition to our familiar images. No world known to us is fully free from contradiction, and paradoxes can never be completely eliminated by the ordering activity of the human mind. In worldviews and religions especially, such opposing images are frequently found. As these embrace all the dimensions of human life, tensions which arise within them cannot be adjusted and harmonized at a higher level. "Religious experiences seem to drive those who testify to them to choose paradoxical formulations to describe them, i.e., to name things together which are logically incompatible."[1] Religious language is therefore also a language of complex pictures and many-layered metaphors.

But it is not only the empirical sciences and philosophy which cannot acquiesce to contradictions: Christian theology also seeks coherence and consistency. "However much religious testimony continues to call upon the paradoxical character of religious experience ('God is day–night, heat–cold,' or, in Christian terms, God is savior and judge together, people are sinners and justified at the same time), so much more should the focus of the one testifying be not only on establishing paradoxes of this sort, but also on understanding them. One should not remain dumb before them, but attempt to bring the content of this experience to expression in one's speech."[2] If faith were simply to acquiesce to paradoxes and contradictory experiences, then our ordering and critical reason would have to resign its function, and religious utterances would no longer be distinguishable from every sort of myth.

One of the great tasks of Christian theology from the beginning was therefore to interpret biblical texts which were paradoxical and apparently opposed to one another. This was done by bringing them into a horizon of understanding which was as comprehensive as possible. Thus no logical contradictions would appear in the language, even if paradox-

---

1. Schaeffler (1987), 329.
2. Ibid.

1

ical images inevitably remained. For example, against the background of strict Jewish monotheism, the New Testament utterances about the Son of God and the Holy Spirit created great difficulties. Did not the new faith lead toward a regression into polytheism? Also the description of Christ as suffering servant and the one on high, the preexistent Son of God, only avoided formal contradictions with great difficulty. The long, painful theological process which led to the dogmas of the Trinity and of Christ arose out of this set of problems. Even if completely satisfying and final solutions to these questions were not reached, and indeed could never be reached, linguistic clarification was achieved. Human reason, penetrating into the articles of faith, was thereby able to distinguish between actual logical contradictions and a mystery surpassing all contradictions.

God's Goodness and Anger

However, there is a theological debate which has been much longer, more entangled, and without an ecclesiastically recognized outcome until now: the debate concerning the paradoxical images of God's love and God's justice or anger. St Paul's theology of the cross turned entirely on this question. Because the apostle did not come to any easily grasped answer, this issue arose again in the postapostolic period with greater force.

Marcion, expelled from the Roman community in the year 144, was the first to be profoundly moved by the Pauline doctrine of justification of the sinner by pure grace, but he was unable to reconcile other biblical utterances with this doctrine, especially the proclamation of God's anger (hell). He therefore adopted gnostic imagery and separated the God of pure love, the God of Jesus Christ, from the Old Testament creator God, whom he understood as a God of anger and of a justice which weighs heavily on humankind. This division in the way of representing God led also to a division of the New Testament writings. Marcion did not find complete support for his doctrine anywhere in the New Testament, so he came to the view that the disciples of Jesus themselves had not correctly understood the message of their master and had therefore in their later proclamation mixed in images of the Old Testament demiurge. Only the purified Pauline letters and a thoroughly cleansed Gospel of Luke were recognized as the true message of Jesus. The church led by the bishops could obviously not adopt the radical treatment which Marcion deemed necessary. But, as they themselves could propose no comprehensive answer which would convince Marcion and his followers, the outcome was the founding of a counter-church, which for a time was a genuine rival to the apostolic church and differed from the latter especially in its canon of holy Scriptures and its doctrine of God.

Irenaeus, bishop of Lyons, was the first leader and thinker to meet the challenge of Marcion and the other gnostics. He presented a comprehensive theological answer which depended on the official canon of the bishops' church. From this canon he showed convincingly that, according to the judgment of all the Scriptures, the father of Jesus Christ is identical with the Old Testament creator God. He unraveled many difficult Old Testament passages with his great idea of the divine economy of salvation, inspired by the Greek philosophy of education.[3] According to this economy, God spoke at each phase of his saving dealings in a way that they corresponded to the current times and to the situation of humankind.[4] Irenaeus also understood Marcion's central theme of divine love and justice within the framework of the economy of salvation, even though it must be said that he did not achieve a satisfactory solution on this point. On the contrary, he intensified the biblical problem by demonstrating an increase in severity from the Old to the New Testament, in accordance with his idea of a divine plan of education.[5]

The anger of God according to Irenaeus is no blind passion, but the punitive justice which belongs to education, and to that extent it is reconcilable with the God of goodness. The problem lies therefore less in the Old Testament, as Marcion thought, than in the New, for here punishment — as befits a higher level of perfection — is much stricter.[6] Irenaeus saw clearly that in its central parts the Old Testament acknowledges only an early and violent death as the highest form of judgment and punishment, whereas in the New Testament sinners are threatened with hell. To that extent his intensification of the problematic and his rejection of Marcion's violent solution are fully justified. But in his writings there is hardly any mention of the justification of the sinner by pure grace. He teaches rather that goodness and severity come to people according to their deserts. He thus leaves the central biblical question entirely open: how is it that weak people, faced with the high demands of Jesus' teaching, can stand the test of God's justice? For that reason the tension remains unresolved between God's goodness and God's justice which threatens eternal damnation.

The great Alexandrian theologians Clement and Origen took up the central Greek ideas on education — as had Irenaeus — but they gave them an entirely different twist by distinguishing between utterances

---

3. See Jäger (1954, 1955).
4. See Schwager, "Der Gott des Alten Testaments und der Gott des Gekreuzigten," in Schwager (1986), 15–20.
5. Irenaeus, *Against Heresies* IV.28.2.
6. Ibid., IV.28.1.

about God's nature and utterances about the educational activity of
God. In the biblical language about God's unity, goodness, and mercy,
which, as they understand it, is largely in agreement with the best insights of Greek philosophy, they saw utterances about God himself,
whereas they interpreted the doctrine of divine judgment and divine
punishment in the sense of educational measures to deal with hard-
hearted creatures. Clement says, "[But] as children by their teacher or
their father, so will we be punished by providence. God does not take revenge (revenge is retaliation by evil) but punishes for the benefit of those
who are punished, in their totality and as individuals."[7] But, if the divine
punishment never has a retaliatory character, but always seeks only to
benefit the totality and individuals through educational measures, then
eternal punishment is no longer thinkable, for such a thing can certainly
never benefit individuals. For this reason Origen, at least in his well-
known style of posing questions, rejected the eternal punishment of hell
and taught that not only the hardest-hearted sinners but also the devil
and demons would finally be reconciled with God after a very long process of purification in the next world.[8] In this way, Christian theology
succeeded for the first time in resolving to some extent the contradiction
between the biblical utterances about God's goodness and anger without
weakening divine justice. Origen took the freedom of creatures very seriously and took into account that creatures who are extremely hardened
in evil "will be restored through particularly heavy punishments which
last long and are to be borne as it were for aeons in a very difficult
process of purification."[9] It is true that this doctrine of universal reconciliation (*apoktastasis*) was condemned together with other teachings
of Origen by an edict of the Emperor Justinian in 543 and by the third
Council of Constantinople in 553. But since other Greek fathers in addition to Clement and Origen equally defended universal reconciliation,[10]
without being for that reason thrown under ecclesiastical suspicion, this
solution has always played a part in the Eastern church.

The question was seen in an entirely different way in the Western
church, under the dominating influence of St Augustine. Already in his
youth the problem of good and evil had very much moved the future
bishop of Hippo, and he believed at first that he had found a solution in
the Manichaean postulate of two eternal principles (one good and one
evil). After his conversion, Augustine at first shared the church doctrine
as understood by Irenaeus, without finally settling on it. Particularly in

---

7. Clement of Alex., *Strom.* VII 102. See also *Strom.* VI 46; VII 16.
8. Origen, *De princ.* I 6.1.3; II 6.5.
9. Ibid., I 6.3.
10. So, for example, Gregory of Nyssa, extremely honored in the Eastern church; see
Schwager, "Zur 'physischen' Erlebnislehre Gregors von Nyssa," in Schwager (1986), 92.

interpreting Romans 9, he finally developed his doctrine of predestination, which held firmly to the idea of a punitive justice by maintaining that all humankind, because of the sin of Adam and Eve, belong to the *massa damnata* (condemned mass) and thus rightly deserve eternal punishment. This thought fell completely within the sphere of his new idea of a predestining God. According to this idea, God's eternal, incomprehensible goodness shows itself in the choosing of one part of humankind, without any merit on their part and for no observable reason, whereas the other segment, also without any reason, is sentenced to suffer the punishment of hell and to exhibit the eternal (punitive) justice of God within creation. According to the later Augustine, both incomprehensible goodness and relentless severity belong to the eternal God. For humankind the apparently unresolvable opposition is "resolved" in that some people ultimately experience only the goodness and others — without any possibility of escape — only the relentless judgment. Augustine was inspired to formulate this abysmal judgment by biblical texts, but these were not decisive, for Origen discussed the identical utterances very thoroughly and came to a completely different solution.[11] According to him, "to harden the heart" and "to save" are not two different activities of God, but both spring from the one benevolence, and the difference proceeds only from the different degree of readiness, grounded in the freedom of the creature, to take up goodness.[12] Augustine, referring to Pharaoh's hardened heart (see Exod. 7–11), came to a completely different doctrine from Origen's. His personal experience played a part in this, and on the other hand he had a theological-aesthetic sensitivity in his perception of reality which was clearly different from that of Origen. For Augustine the opposition of good and evil was necessary so that the comprehensive perfection of God in the beauty of creation could fully shine forth in every respect.[13] This view of the world, which sees evil in inner tension with good and which must correspond to a deep human perception, makes it in some measure understandable why the problematical doctrine of predestination was tolerable and even almost self-evident, not only to Augustine but also to Western Christianity over a very long period.

A partially new understanding of God's goodness and justice, although within the oppressive framework of the doctrine of predestination, was worked out by Anselm of Canterbury. His doctrine of redemption was entirely misunderstood for a long time, but in reality it was outstanding for its depth. M. Corbin has most clearly worked out

---

11. Origen, *De princ.* III 1.7–24.
12. Ibid., III 1.11.
13. Augustine *De civ.* XI 18.

the inner coherence in the difficult thought-world of the bishop of Canterbury.[14] He extended interpretations of Anselm offered by K. Barth and H. U. v. Balthasar by painstaking and comprehensive analyses of individual texts, and he did this in a way that is unlikely to be surpassed in the foreseeable future. In his *Proslogion,* Anselm sets out for the first time that the divine goodness is so great that greater than it cannot be thought, and that it is identical with the highest form of justice. In *Cur Deus Homo* he moves in the opposite direction and shows step by step that divine justice, insofar as it is thought through logically and independently of human wishes, is identical with a mercy greater than which cannot be thought. In order to advance this insight, Anselm pursues a mode of thought which seems superficially to be very time-bound. This has mostly led his interpreters into error, but after closer analysis it can be seen to be identical with that language of the Old and New Testaments, which themselves seem at first sight to speak of God's justice and judgment in a human, all too human way. Anselm succeeds in reaching the true biblical message by confronting the biblical passages about justice — through the mouth of his conversation partner Boso — with the other series of passages that deal with God's incomprehensible goodness, and this in a way that carefully avoids any premature compromise between the two series. He relentlessly deepens the discussion of justice until it is able to embrace the utterances about goodness in their entirety. If the unity of the two testaments stands at the center of Irenaeus's thought, Anselm's preoccupation is the harmonious agreement between the different qualities of God, which is achieved by purifying each one from all human representations and thinking of it in such a way that it cannot be thought as greater. Anselm assumes that the thought-world of his conversation partner is characterized primarily only by biblical images and does not reflect a full understanding of the faith. He also expects of his believing readers a conversion of their way of thinking, a conversion which he sees as so radical that it can be compared with the conversion of a nonbeliever to Christian belief.[15] Because the deeper coherence in Anselm's thought was for centuries barely seen, and because his images were taken for his true thought instead of only the starting point of a long process of purification of ideas, the history of the subsequent working out of his doctrine of redemption had little or no connection with his actual thinking. Semipagan concepts of God's anger and of an offense against God's honor entered under Anselm's name into the history of Christian piety.

---

14. M. Corbin, "La Nouveauté de l'Incarnation. Introduction à l'Epistola et au *Cur Deus Homo,* in *L'oeuvre de S. Anselme de Cantorbéry* (1988), 3:11–163.
15. Ibid., 32–41.

Another theologian who has an eminent place in the history of Western theology, Martin Luther, also spoke about God's anger. On a superficial reading, the reformer can give the impression of speaking about God in all too human terms. But by means of his strictly christological exegesis he gave a deeper sense to the biblical concept of anger, and he thereby opened up a new way of seeing the relationship of the different qualities of God to one another. By justice he understands what justifies sinners and what is therefore essentially identical with God's goodness. He places this over against anger, and he interprets both of God's ways of working from his new picture of the crucified one. According to Luther, Christ during his passion was assailed in his innermost soul and had to withstand the struggle with evil in place of us. He experienced the full weight of the divine anger, prior to being delivered from Satan and the experience of hell by his heavenly Father. But this anger was only one of the two works of God, and in fact a "strange" one, in which the true work of salvation was hidden, to be revealed in the resurrection of the crucified, in the sending of the Holy Spirit, and in the preaching of the justification of sinners.

Through the distinction between God's own and strange work and through the christological interpretation of goodness and anger, Luther introduced a pioneering innovation into Western theology. But this gain remained overshadowed by the Augustinian legacy of the doctrine of predestination, which the reformer took over without any real critique. He even deepened the shadow left by Augustine by not clearly holding to Augustine's view of Adam's freedom of choice and by thus situating the problem of the eternal damnation of sinners in God himself. Luther was therefore forced to distinguish between the God of revelation (*deus revelatus*) and a hidden God (*deus absconditus*). While the former is a God of goodness under the clothing of anger, the latter remains entirely incomprehensible to humankind, for goodness and anger can no longer be distinguished in this hidden God. The reformer made this threatening countenance of God bearable for the faithful who followed him by teaching them to hold on completely to the God revealed in the crucified one — which was more a way of getting around this worrisome problem than a solution to it.

Karl Barth was the first to make a decisive breakthrough, and finally to free Western theology from the "darkness" of the Augustinian doctrine of predestination. Because he understood the Christian revelation in the full sense as the self-revelation of God, there remained for him no other hidden God behind the revealed Father. According to Barth, God in his entirety is the one who has shown himself on the cross and in the resurrection of Christ. Thanks to this christological understanding of revelation, Barth was able not only to unlock the full significance of

Luther's interpretation of God's goodness and anger, but also to deepen the reformer's christological exegesis. Christ is the center of the whole history of salvation insofar as the Old Testament themes of promise and rejection come together in him.

Cain as well as Abel, Esau as well as Jacob, Saul as well as David are models of Christ, because one line points to the rejected one on the cross and the other to the one elected by God. Israel and the church relate to each other as the crucified one to the risen one. Now, since the one Christ is both the rejected one and the elected one and the two roles can be distinguished in him but not separated, for that reason the distinction between Cain and Abel becomes simply one of their function in salvation history rather than a way of speaking of eternal salvation or damnation. As sinners, all people stand like Cain and like the crucified one under judgment, and in Christ all are elected like Abel and like the risen one. Thanks to this fresh interpretation of the doctrine of predestination as a doctrine of election, Barth was able, out of the problematic of the Western tradition, to come near to the hopeful Eastern view of Origen.

However even the great Basel theologian left one problem unresolved. Because he understood the eternal choice of God exclusively from the standpoint of the crucified and risen one, he had to interpret the anger of God which was revealed on the cross as an element in this choice. Furthermore, as he gave clear priority to the election over the creation in the course of his strictly christological exegesis, he could no longer interpret the aspect of anger in the eternal choice in terms of a refusal by creatures. Rather, he had to attribute it to an original initiative of God.[16] This eternal anger remains not only hard to understand, it also introduces an ambivalent element into Barth's picture of God. Certainly, any suspicion of the diabolical is eliminated in that God's election clearly embraces and overcomes anger, but the sign of the cross remains in a certain twilight, because it reveals not only God's enormous love of the sinner, but also God's everlasting anger, which existed long before any fault of humankind.

Hans Urs von Balthasar, who already during his years of study was disturbed by the theological opposition between the Eastern tradition (Origen) and Western tradition (Augustine), integrated Barth's great doctrine of election into Catholic theology and at the same time gave it a new alignment by his *Theodramatik* (God-drama). The goodness, justice, and anger of God are set for him in the framework of the process of salvation history that is played out in the field of tension between uncreated and created freedom. In Balthasar's doctrine of redemption,

16. Barth (1932–67) 2/2:131; see ibid., 4/1:48f.

Christ is also burdened with the sin of the whole world (and hence with God's anger), but people hold a more definite position of esteem because of their freedom of choice as covenant partners in the divine drama of salvation. According to Balthasar, anger is a reaction of God to failure on the part of human beings, but this freedom is not, as with Irenaeus, delivered up helpless to judgment. Because the Son of God, in loving obedience, experienced fully the total abandonment and distance of sinners from God, he was able, as it were, to infiltrate sin-entrapped creaturely freedom. Even the hardest-hearted sinners are never alone in their distance from God, but Christ has come close to them through his journey to the cross and into the underworld. The Christian message of redemption consequently contains the well-founded hope, without replacing creaturely freedom, that the crucified one can finally reach all people and that not one will be lost.[17]

The "God-drama" illuminates the twilight in Barth's theology, for it is able both to distinguish clearly the qualities of God and to give them an intrinsic order. This affirmation of divine goodness refers directly to the essential nature of God unveiled in revelation, whereas the biblical language of just punishment and anger announces the divine reaction to those creatures who have fallen into sin through a free decision. The two affirmations are thus of unequal value, for the divine love encompasses the justice that punishes and gets angry, and reveals, by the way in which the punishment on the cross is undergone in the Son's surrender, its incomprehensible and unfathomable goodness. Nevertheless, the "God-drama" itself remains not quite free of a final ambiguity in its interpretation of the divine anger: it is not able to make sufficiently clear how the God of love for our enemies, whom Jesus proclaimed in the Sermon on the Mount, can ever become an angry God. It is expected of people that they should love their enemies without any previous satisfaction given, and this noble challenge is expressly based on the perfection of God: "You should be perfect therefore as your heavenly Father is perfect" (Matt. 5:48). Should the Father of Jesus Christ be thought of as an angry God, if men and women, who have to model themselves on God's perfection, may not confront each other with the demand for retaliation? The proclamation of Jesus and his message of the kingdom of God at hand play a subordinate role in the *Theodramatik*. The same is true — and mostly in an even greater measure — of the different Protestant theologies of the cross.

The theology of the Enlightenment period had already reacted against this one-sidedness by trying to develop a doctrine of reconciliation built entirely on the New Testament image of the kingdom of God. Every

---

17. See Balthasar (1973–83) 4:223–93; see also Balthasar, 1986 and 1987.

variation of ethico-political theology followed in pursuit of this aim. Also contemporary liberation theology, inspired above all by the great Old Testament picture of the exodus and by Jesus' behavior toward the poor and the outcasts, places the message of God's kingdom as a kingdom of justice at the center. Important biblical themes are thereby brought to expression, which are at risk of disappearing in a theology of the cross, but the danger arises that the message about judgment and the redeemer's death do not receive the necessary emphasis. The old tension, never quite resolved, between God's goodness and God's angry justice, shows itself again in the different, to some extent contradictory, tendencies and currents of recent theology.

In contemporary exegesis also, the same problem emerges in slightly altered form. Critical research gives two different, even contradictory, answers to the question about the New Testament proclamation of salvation, the one proceeding only from God's goodness, the other emphasizing the death of Christ the redeemer.[18] The question, as H. Schürmann indicates, becomes unavoidable: Is Jesus supposed to have had another message of salvation than the one the church formulated early on and still today proclaims? Did Jesus proclaim liberation through the kingdom of God, whereas the church's doctrine of redemption developed in another direction?[19] P. Fiedler has stated the systematic consequences of this grave exegetical issue:

> Does God really grant forgiveness unconditionally, as Jesus consistently proclaimed, or is it only because of Jesus' death? A "both ...and" answer has to be excluded. In the first case, depending on one's attitude to Jesus, one can consider his "offer of grace" and the claim implied therein as completed in the death on the cross or as finally ratified by God after Easter — despite the apparent failure. In the second case, the dilemma persists: If one is not to insist that Jesus proclaimed to his hearers the message of salvation with this inbuilt contradiction — clearly unworthy of him — one can only assume that he died because of an error concerning the working out of salvation by God, which he should finally have seen.[20]

Schürmann rejects the dilemma as Fiedler feels obliged to formulate it; he is therefore not content with a description of the exegetical opinions, but attempts a solution himself. However, in doing this, he only touches on the problem of judgment, and he entirely passes over the

---

18. See Schürmann (1983), 11–12.
19. Ibid., 12.
20. Fiedler (1976), 280–81.

question of hell. His work, which is otherwise very valuable, does not therefore take the problematic of God's goodness and anger forward in a definitive way. But it does show that every attempt which starts with only one pole, with the proclamation of the kingdom or with the cross and resurrection, falls short of its task.

Drama and Theological Reasoning

This brief historical overview has shown that it is not easy to clarify the paradox of God's goodness and justice or anger or explain in depth the central question of redemption. Nor is there any generally accepted philosophical analysis available which would promise any greater assistance. The set of exegetical problems, finally, makes it very clear that every systematic approach which depends on one starting point must necessarily prove unsatisfactory.

In order to avoid a restrictive one-sided systematic theology, a theology of narrative has been proposed. In a discussion concerning the modern understanding of history, J. B. Metz started from the thesis that the Christian proclamation of redemption must be considered within the framework of the history of human freedom and suffering. But this history should not be placed under the heading of a universal theory of emancipation. That way leads to mistaking the root of evil and falling under the spell of an "irrational mechanism of excuse and/or guilt-suppression."[21] Instead, it should be seen as the history of guilt. If one really takes seriously such a history, with its many incomprehensible sufferings, then it necessarily leads every attempt at a reasoned soteriology into crisis. This is why Metz makes a determined plea "for a theology of redemption which is anchored in memory and narrative,"[22] which no longer seeks to capture and contain the principle of evil within a theory.

The danger, perceived by Metz, that a carefully reasoned theology will fail to do justice to the concrete history, with its many experiences of suffering, is a very real one. It is also very true that the "mechanism of excuse and guilt-suppression" plays an important role — and not only in modern emancipation theories and philosophies of history, as O. Marquard has shown,[23] but also in history itself. Over and over again, people have failed to see, or not wanted to see, the guilt at their own door, have deflected it toward others, and have thus interpreted and at the same time falsified both their own life histories and the history of nations. From the great work of Poliakov on anti-Semitism, for example, it appears with almost frightening clarity how often in the course of

21. Metz (1973a), 177.
22. Ibid., 182.
23. Marquard (1973).

Christian history guilt has been unjustifiably displaced onto the Jews,[24] and the case of the Jews is no isolated special case. Poliakov himself, through a still more comprehensive investigation, has demonstrated the working of a "diabolical causality,"[25] which consists in nothing less than this mechanism of (unconscious) displacement of guilt, and which has been at work throughout history. We must therefore concur with Metz's plea for history to be understood as a history of suffering and for us to consider continually the hidden guilt in it. Nevertheless, there are arguments which must be raised against his rejection of a reasoned doctrine of redemption. As narratives are in themselves capable of being continued indefinitely, a purely narrative theology runs into the dilemma of either abandoning itself to a narrative thread which leads on endlessly, dissolving the Christian memory of events into a sea of other narrations — and there are already examples of this — or limiting itself, without any particular justification, to the biblical narratives. In the latter case, faith would no longer be rationally accountable because, as Boso in the dialogues of Anselm established, it would be based on "pictures" which are "painted on clouds" and which lack a "firm, rational foundation."[26] A purely narrative doctrine of redemption, unsupported by a corresponding line of reasoning, can thus be no alternative to a systematic theology,[27] even if this latter continually runs the danger of failing to do justice to the concrete history of suffering.

In some ways similar to a narrative doctrine of redemption is a theology which takes drama as its model. But this is clearly differentiated from a narrative-based doctrine in that it is able to integrate a genuine line of reasoning. Balthasar has already convincingly demonstrated in his *Theodramatik* that the categories of drama, when they are used with care, are appropriate to Christian theology. The theological line of reasoning can be developed out of drama, since drama does not advance without end in epic manner, but expresses itself in conflict and its corresponding resolution. In the case of biblical drama, moreover, we are not dealing with just any conflict. The event of the cross proves so radical, and the subsequent dénouement or solution (Easter) so overpowering, that "greater than these cannot be thought." Theological drama is consequently able to integrate a line of reasoning, just as Anselm of Canterbury designed and evolved one for his doctrine of redemption.

---

24. Poliakov (1977–87).
25. Poliakov (1980, 1985).
26. Anselm, *Cur deus homo* I 4.
27. In saying this I am not disputing that narrative research, whose acceptance Güttgemanns (1970), 232–50, has energetically promoted, can make a valuable contribution to a better understanding of biblical narratives.

The church fathers long ago worked with the idea that Christian truth has to prove itself as true, and that this proof must take place in an act of self-interpretation. Christian believers who reflect on this cannot, of course, critically question God's proof of himself from some autonomous standpoint, but they are able to perceive in it an ever greater totality, surpassing all human conception.[28] Anselm of Canterbury himself stands in this tradition. In his thought, the difference between "natural" theology, which is focused on God as the "highest being" (*summum ens, summum bonum*), and Christian reflection, which is determined by the message of the cross, was worked out systematically for the first time through a new reflection of thinking on itself (*id quo maius cogitari nequit*).[29] Both forms of theological reflection have, of course, a lot in common with one another — and this has to be maintained against any one-sided theology of the cross. But they are not identical with each other. A theology of the "highest being" works entirely on the foundation of the analogy of being. Predicates such as goodness, justice, knowledge, and power are transferred over from human experience to God by analogy, so that in talk about God the words always mean something both similar and dissimilar to the immediate human sense. The difficulty with this analogous way of speaking is that the similarity and the dissimilarity cannot be separated out: in one and the same movement of thinking and speaking, the two must always be grasped at the same time. Analogous concepts can therefore never be fixed or rigid concepts. They remain only analogous when they are carried every time they are used by a movement of thought which holds on to both the similarity and the dissimilarity simultaneously, and which does not furtively disintegrate the state of flux by allowing the analogous concept to split up unnoticed into one univocal and two equivocal concepts. Such an analogous way of speaking is essential to Christian theology, but it also conceals great problems. The danger here lies not, as Barth thought, in ultimately subsuming God and creatures under a general idea of being, and thereby making of God an idol. To counter this leveling tendency, the radical dissimilarity in all analogous concepts can be emphasized, as was done especially by E. Przywara in dialogue with Barth. Nor does the specific danger arise from the opposite direction, namely, from the too great difference and the negative emphasis, which would render God incapable of speaking to our world, as E. Jüngel warns. Against this undertow toward noncommunication, it is possible to emphasize the continuing similarity at work in all analogous concepts. The problem is

---

28. See Balthasar (1976), 103–34. We will attempt a concrete realization of this kind of argumentation in the second and third part of this work.

29. "That than which greater cannot be thought." See the Introduction of M. Corbin in *Anselme de Cantorbéry* (1986), 1:209–24; (1988), 3:48–57.

rather that human thought by itself cannot find a resting point between similarity and dissimilarity, and hence, in the name of analogy, can tend toward a purely negative theology as well as toward a semimythology. In distinction to this indecisiveness of analogy, which easily shifts over into arbitrary decision, a theology developed like Anselm's under the formulation *id quo maius cogitari nequit* can lead forward from the linguistic antitheses in the statements of faith immediately under consideration. It then asks whether the lines of thought, at first contradictory, can be gradually deepened, so that they end up in a final unity and harmony, "higher than which nothing greater can be thought." In this way analogy holds to a clear direction and is saved from an unrestrained roaming hither and thither.

In order to reconcile God's goodness and justice with each other, Anselm's point of departure for his doctrine of redemption was the very human concepts of offense, honor, punishment, and satisfaction. These images were on the one hand immediately comprehensible, and on the other hand he was able through them to draw biblical utterances indirectly into the purifying process of his Christian thinking. These utterances, at first glance, speak of God in all too human terms. To reproduce the same procedure today would make no sense, as the immediate representations of his time are not the same as ours, and today's world is afflicted with tensions which differ in part from those of his age. But if the dominant representations and concerns of a given time are not drawn into the purifying process of a reflecting faith, then this latter easily becomes rootless, and it will offer solutions for problems which have not been accurately diagnosed, while those questions which actually concern people receive no further clarification. Anselm's method shows that a Christian theology which is to reach the furthest depths and heights must start from the dominant notions or representations of the age, and even from everyday images.

For contemporary theological reflection on redemption, the problems surrounding violence and the longing for peace should be given a special place. The experiences which go along with these are very intense and at the same time contradictory; they are also bound up with no specific culture or class of society. Whether you are rich or poor, whether you live in the North or South, the East or the West, everyone is confronted with the phenomenon of violence. All over the world, in which for the first time total self-destruction has become possible, the longing for peace is growing. But the problems surrounding violence run also through the whole Bible, from Cain and Abel through the wars of Israel to the two destructions of Jerusalem and from the slaying of the children in Bethlehem through the death on the cross to the wars in John's Apocalypse. Likewise it can be seen that the theme of peace takes up a sizeable part of the Old and New Testaments. Violence and the longing for peace are such universal experiences that they have a place in every religion and in every great philosophy. An important possibility for dialogue is thus opened up. Of course, the specifically Christian element cannot be fully expressed at this level alone, which is why it is necessary to have a radical deepening of the issues. The theme of violence must be sharpened by a discussion of the question of sin, the problematic of hell and the cross. The longing for peace must be purified and opened up by consideration of the message of the kingdom of God, the peace of Easter, and the perception of trinitarian love. Through this sharpening, purification, and broadening it will be possible to bring in the problematic of which we spoke at the outset, namely, the tension between God's goodness and his justice, which has been a continuing unresolved question throughout the long history of Eastern and Western theology.

Although we acknowledge a fundamental agreement with Anselm's way of thinking and arguing, our own way of proceeding differs from the dialogues in *Cur deus homo* in that we treat questions raised by the Bible at its own level, and initially only consider contemporary problems as background, whereas Anselm mainly chose the opposite way. Exegetical work has acquired nowadays such an importance that the questions arising from it must be approached directly. Conversely, however, it is strikingly clear that isolated exegetical work can, by itself, lead nowhere. Only when it integrates the great systematic articulations of questions will it be able to shed light on those problems which have always moved and to some extent even distressed believers.

The inclusion of modern historical-critical exegesis in systematic theology obviously raises countless complex questions. Must systematic reflection simply take over the findings of exegesis as principles on which to build? What to do when these findings are of a contradictory nature, which is actually the case in the question we are dealing with, as we have already briefly seen? To look for a meaningless common denominator among all the contradictory positions will certainly not lead us any further. Nor would it be helpful simply to write off historical criticism, as is nowadays not infrequently urged, for when we consider the varied history of Christianity, it is only too clear that everything possible can be projected onto Jesus. In spite of its partly contradictory findings, historical-critical research deserves our engagement with it, for it brings with it a long tradition not only of criticism, but also of counter-criticism (criticism of criticism). How it is concretely to be included in systematic reflection cannot be dealt with satisfactorily in the abstract. Hence in what follows we will continually bring in reflections on method while discussing individual problems of textual meaning.

Systematic theology is able to enter into discussion with critical exegesis because, as will be shown, historical judgment in very many cases depends not only on literary-critical analyses and those based on the history of traditions, but often much more strongly on the total picture that is formed of Jesus and his work. We will be concerned with this total picture and are for that reason less dependent on the majority or minority opinions in historical-critical research, particularly as such opinions can alter fairly quickly. But on important questions we can venture a judgment which emerges from dialogue with the exegesis of individual texts.

The way of proceeding will admittedly be somewhat complicated. In order to take the historical-critical exegesis of individual texts really seriously from the systematic viewpoint, the mediation of a dramatic exegesis is needed, which gathers together larger groups of texts under key words and coordinates them on the model of conflictual action. The following investigations will therefore move on three levels and advance from the historical-critical question through the historico-dramatic consideration to the systematic, so that at the same time the great problems of universal history remain continuously in view. In the second part, especially the first and second levels (individual exegesis and drama) will be discussed, while in the third part drama will be extended into systematic theology. The question will necessarily arise as to whether the attempted systematic formulation of the question rings true to the New Testament writings or whether it brings to these an alien perspective. Another pressing difficulty will be how God's saving dealings with humankind are connected with God's self-revelation as (triune) God.

The Old Testament Drama and Vengeance

In the writings of the New Testament not only are there hundreds of explicit quotations from the Old Testament; the whole language of the Gospels and of the apostolic letters is unintelligible without the background of the religious traditions of Israel. When, in the second century, the gnostics tried to distinguish and separate the Old Testament Yahweh from the God of Jesus Christ, the church instinctively reacted against such a violent attempt and, following this reaction, Irenaeus wrote his great theology against the heretics, based essentially on the unity of the two testaments.

The Unity of Old and New Testaments

The theology and exegesis of both the fathers and the Middle Ages followed Irenaeus in essentials. Even the great theological projects which diverged from the officially recognized tradition remained mostly faithful to the exegetical principle of the unity of the two testaments. Thus the exegesis of Joachim of Fiore, so influential from the point of view of the history of religion and culture, was based on the thinking of the "harmony of the Old and New Testaments," even if it understood this harmony differently from the ecclesiastical tradition. Similarly, Luther developed his new reforming theology at first fundamentally from the exegesis of the psalms and found the voice of Christ already speaking in the Old Testament. From this he learned to see the connection between the two testaments anew.

These brief historical pointers prove the position of importance given to the relationship between Old and New Testaments in systematic theology. This issue is even more important today, because historical-critical research has to some extent consciously broken the theological link between the two testaments, or at least made it very problematic. For our attempt at a historico-dramatic interpretation of Jesus' destiny it would therefore be highly desirable to begin with a comprehensive treatment of the Old Testament. However, for practical reasons we must limit ourselves to a few sketchy observations; to balance things to a certain degree, we will always briefly include flashbacks from the New Testament to the canonical writings and to the whole religious history of Israel before the appearance of the Christ.

Since the problematic of God's goodness and anger (justice) plays a central part in our investigation and since in the Old Testament there is frequent talk of God's vengeance and anger, we must at least make a brief study of this range of themes. This is all the more important as on the one hand contemporary exegesis has great difficulty here, and on the other hand images of "retribution" continue to be operative in the doctrine of redemption, images which hardly differ from the primitive sense of vengeance. This state of affairs proves that in using key words like "vengeance" and "retribution" we are touching on a complex of themes which must be very deeply anchored in the human soul and which both arouses moral reactions of rejection and also leads to the very center of the idea of God. Thanks to the most recent investigations into vengeance in archaic societies and at the beginnings of the juridical system, carried out by a French research group led by R. Verdier,[30] this difficult thematic area can today be seen somewhat more clearly as it appears in the biblical writings also. Many passages in the Old Testament, which at first seem offensive, are made easier to understand by these research findings, and it also becomes clearer why the idea of retribution has played and continues to play so great a role in the history of humankind. Consequently, it is also possible to put in more precise terms the question as to whether the cross of Christ should be interpreted within

---

30. Verdier (1980, 1984).

the framework of a universal divine scheme of retribution, or whether it actually breaches this scheme. For these important reasons, we cannot omit some treatment of the theme of vengeance in the Old Testament.

The System of Vengeance in Archaic Societies

In order to approach this set of problems in the correct way, it is essential to distinguish from the beginning between vengeance as passion (*vindicatif*) and society's system of vengeance (*vindicatoire*).[31] Where the system of vengeance is recognized, the injured party (or the group around the person) cannot obtain satisfaction in just any way they like; there are norms, stemming from sacred traditions, which decide how and when they may act. Nor is vengeance in the first place a "permission," but a sacred "duty" which has its rules, is carried out in a "ritual" fashion, and contributes decisively to the social identity of different groups. It plays its role as the middle of three realms of society. In the innermost circle belong those people with whom individuals identify themselves completely (the extended family, branch of the clan, etc.); in the middle realm are those who are considered of equal worth and with whom relations of exchange exist; finally in the third realm are included all strangers, who are considered different, of less worth, hostile, or even not fully human. Within the innermost circle, vengeance is most strictly prohibited. Here, offenses are overlooked or in extreme cases dealt with by exclusion from the community. With people of the third realm there are absolutely no regulations governing relationships; instead, one avoids such people by means of spatial separation, or one wages war on them. The middle realm, however, is the sphere of society which is regulated and settled by the system of vengeance.

Retribution is not carried out between individuals but always between primary groups. If someone is killed or harmed, then all the men belonging to the innermost circle are obliged to take action in revenge. The object is to compensate by retaliatory injury for the lowering of the value of human life experienced by one group. Since vengeance is essentially carried out among groups of equal status, it can even be understood as a form of "exchange" related to other forms of compensation. The "exchange" of women and goods and the "exchange" of injury and retaliatory injury constitute the one comprehensive social system by which tribal societies operate. In this system, each gift calls for a gift in return, and such a "gift" can also be injury, which is settled by an injury in return (vengeance). This is an exchange in which the equal worth of the two social entities is not determined by individual feeling but by traditional rules of society. That vengeance is in fact a social

---

31. See ibid. 1:15f., 24, 44, 75, 141; 4:12, 15, 48.

system and not a matter of private emotional reactions is most clearly shown by the fact that retribution by no means always strikes the guilty party. Not infrequently, the guilty one is expressly spared and in his place his brother, father, or uncle is killed. This is the sort of complete solidarity within the inner circle of the clan which vengeance creates. While it stabilizes the external relationships with groups of equal status, at the same time it gives individuals their identities through total identification with the other members of the vengeance group.

Among the studies that have emerged from the research group led by Verdier, there is one which sets out, by means of numerous examples, how the images of vengeance mentioned here were known also in the Old Testament.[32] In this work the emphasis is almost entirely on what Israel had in common with other societies. Its specific view of vengeance is hardly represented. In what follows, therefore, we will briefly sketch how the images of vengeance of primitive societies developed under the influence of faith in Yahweh and how a break was made at definite points with the transmitted sacred, social, and intellectual order.

Yahweh as the Only True Avenger

In the "Song of Moses" (Deut. 32:39–41) Yahweh says of himself that he is the only powerful and effective God, who kills and makes alive and who swears by himself that he takes the law into his own hands and imposes retribution on his enemies. The book of Deuteronomy certainly knows of countless regulations which oblige Israel also to make retribution for misdeeds and even in many cases to kill the law-breaker (see Deut. 12:1–26:19). But these regulations are always explicitly represented as God's commands, so that here also Yahweh is the real avenger. In the narrative parts of Israel's books it is further reported how Yahweh often ordered his people or individuals to practice retribution on enemies.[33] At first sight these images seem not to have been a peculiar feature of faith in Yahweh, since the system of vengeance was everywhere understood as a sacred order, guaranteed by the gods. However, on closer inspection it is impossible to overlook the differences.

Israel did not trace its sacred regulations back to a mythical original age; rather, it saw in them obligations which it had taken over in the course of history, when Yahweh entered into a covenant with his people at Sinai (Exod. 24:3, 7). Even if the actual content of countless regulations stemmed from long years of experience, which were similar to

---

32. A. LeMaire, "Vengeance et justice dans l'Ancien Testament," in Verdier (1984), 3:13–33.

33. See Num. 31:2–3; Deut. 20:16–18; Josh. 10:8–13; Jud. 11:29–36; 1 Sam. 15:1–33.

those of many other peoples, still faith in Yahweh understood the commands in a different way and saw in them the expression of the will of a personal God, who brings about new things in the course of history.

From the idea of the covenant, the conviction grew that all members of the people are ultimately of equal worth and must have equal access to the law.[34] It is the prophets who gave an especially harsh critique of the actual praxis of vengeance and of the law in Israel, because the law was often bent by the rich and powerful, and misdeeds against the poor, the widows, and the orphans were not requited sufficiently.[35] The representation of Yahweh as the true avenger, consequently, did not serve a global legitimization of the existing order of retribution, but was often directed precisely against it. In the divine "avenger," people saw the great advocate of the poor, the widows, and orphans, who did not accede to their rights before the powerful ones of the earth.[36] There were frequent prayers, therefore, begging for Yahweh's retributory and avenging intervention.[37]

In accordance with the ancient oriental ideology of kingship, dominant for example in Egypt, Assyria, or Babylon, even there the king had to care for the well-being of the whole nation and to lend support to the poor and oppressed. But since the king as the adoptive son of the divinity was seen also as the guarantor of world order, any criticism of unjust conditions could be made only within the framework of the inviolable order of things. Faith in Israel had a unique critical power, for the prophets turned their conviction of Yahweh as the true avenger in an extraordinary way against the representatives of the temporal sacred and legal order, against the kings, the princes, and the priests.[38] Faith did not make the existing order inviolable, but rather desacralized it (Jer. 7:1–15) and frequently stigmatized it as a brutal order of violence (Ezek. 22:3–13; Hos. 4:1ff.; Mic. 7:5ff.).

Universality is a further specific element in Israel's representation of vengeance (at least from the exile and postexilic times onward), for Yahweh is not only judge over the people; his retribution reaches as far as the neighboring peoples, indeed ultimately to all humankind.[39] In the studies of the research group led by Verdier, the system of vengeance, which regulates relationships between related tribes, is cancelled

---

34. Deut. 14:29; 24:17; 26:12–13; Isaiah 1:17; Jer. 22:3.

35. Isa. 1:23; 10:1–2; Jer. 7:5–7; 22:3; Ezek. 22:7, 12–13, 27–29; Hos. 5:1; Amos 4:1–7:15; 8:4–14.

36. Sir. 35:15–22; Isa. 25:4; 66:1; Jer. 15:10–15; 51:1–6; Mal. 3:5; Ps. 9:13; 94:1–6; 140.

37. Ps. 58; 79:10; 94:23; Jer. 15:15.

38. See Mic. 3:5–12; Isa. 28:7–15; Jer. 4:9; 21:11–14; 22:1–19; 23:9–24; Ezek. 11:1–4; 13:1–23; 21:17; 22:6; Hos. 5:1–7.

39. Isa. 26:21; 63:1–6; Jer. 49:1–52:7; Joel 4:1–21; Zech. 1:7–17; 12:1–9.

by war waged against strangers. But since, according to the faith of Israel, Yahweh is lord and avenger of all nations, the distinction does not apply here. In quarrels between individuals or in the struggles of nations, it is always Yahweh who exercises retribution. The image of divine vengeance becomes, thanks to Israel's monotheism, such a universal category that with its help it is possible to interpret both Israel's own history and that of the many nations. It enabled the prophets to postulate a connection between concrete acts of wrongdoing and important historical events. In this way they succeeded in integrating into their picture of Yahweh's dealings the great catastrophes and the brutal defeats. If Yahweh often appears to be like an easily aroused despot who rules the world with brutal severity, which Marcion and many after him found so offensive, it is not because the Jewish people expressed particularly primitive and vengeful feelings. The only thing that these shocking utterances betray is that Israel managed to speak of the bitter and brutal experiences of her faith in unvarnished manner and did not suppress even the darkest aspects of things.

If the teaching about retribution in Israel is seen against the background of the old sacred systems of vengeance, a new light is thrown on a point of scientific controversy. Klaus Koch has adduced lexical evidence that "the Old Testament possesses no single word for 'punishment,' "[40] and that the "words for 'evil deed, sin, crime' always also include the meaning 'disaster, destruction, ruin,' as conversely the verbs and nouns for 'upright behavior' include at the same time 'fortunate outcome.' "[41] On the basis of this evidence he concluded "that according to Israel's conception, sickness and poverty arise spontaneously from the evil deed, and health and well-being from the good deed."[42] For this reason he rejected the generally widespread notion that Israel possesses a doctrine of retribution in the usual sense. He held rather that faith in Yahweh was determined by the concept of a "fate-bearing sphere of action,"[43] according to which a good deed spontaneously generates good fortune and an evil deed equally produces disaster. This at first surprising thesis has also been questioned in part. For example, in the judgment of J. Scharbert: "The question about the belief in retribution in the Old Testament, which K. Koch thought it necessary to answer in the negative, is definitely to be given an affirmative answer."[44] The controversy might be resolved if the lexical discovery to which Koch refers was interpreted in the context of the sacred system of vengeance. In this system

---

40. K. Koch, (1972c), 164.
41. K. Koch (1972d), 433.
42. Ibid.
43. Ibid., 434.
44. J. Scharbert, "SLM im Alten Testament," in Koch (1972b), 322.

there is in fact no punishment, in the sense of a sanction imposed purely from outside on a misdeed. The regulations for vengeance belong rather to the very life of the tribe, as if to its bloodstream. Retribution arises spontaneously: the misdeed (harm) calls for a deed in return (return of harm), and the good deed demands a gift in return. The sacred system of exchange, retribution, and vengeance can explain far more simply and convincingly the peculiar features of Israel's language than does the somewhat mythical "fate-bearing sphere of action." Furthermore it provides an interpretative framework for all those observations which have been made in criticism of Koch.

The Critique of the Concept of Vengeance

Even if the representation of Yahweh as the only true and universal avenger of Israel had never been rejected and replaced with a different belief, there were nevertheless experiences which challenged the belief in retribution from various sides.

In view of the high demands of the law and the constant infringements of it that were not punished by the human order of things, belief in complete retribution by Yahweh would have had to count on so many acts of divine vengeance that any hopeful outlook on the future would have been stifled. There would have remained only the announcement of judgment, which in fact seems to have been the case with individual prophets. But since Yahweh was always experienced ultimately as a life-affirming God who wanted to give the people a future salvation despite all their mistakes, retribution for past deeds could in certain circumstances be set aside on account of the *priority of the future.* Yahweh was believed in as a God who is prepared to renounce vengeance and to forget and forgive past misdeeds to the extent that the people are prepared to turn away from them and to walk along new paths. Not the mechanism of retribution but a reorganization of the future was the highest demand of Israel's faith: "Do I have pleasure in the death of the guilty, says the Lord God, and not rather that he turn from his evil ways and live?" (Ezek. 18:23). Goodness and retribution did not belong in an equal way to the face of Yahweh as perceived by Israel. Even if the divine retribution seemed now and then to destroy all around it, faith in a goodness capable of forgiving all misdeeds clearly predominated: "Only for a moment I hid my face from you in overflowing wrath, but with everlasting love I have compassion on you, says the LORD, your redeemer" (Isa. 54:8; see also Hos. 11:8ff.; Tob. 13:1–12).

In spite of belief in the priority of divine goodness, there remained much suffering and poverty in the everyday life of Israel. In the later period especially, when the fate of the individual stood at the center of religious questioning, there were people who would not and could not, for that very reason, any longer understand their bitter fate as a meaningful act of divine retribution. Thus questions were raised which were aimed directly against the belief in retribution. These questions are put forth utterly relentlessly in the book of Job. The central section of Job consists of a continuous struggle between the rebellious voice of a suffering man and his so-called friends, who are in fact his worst enemies, because they attack him not externally but in the innermost being of his soul and attempt to bring him back under the yoke of belief in retribution with every kind of supposition, false suggestion, and indictment. However, Job defends himself against all the attacks, which are based on belief in the sacred social order, and resists even the subtle attempts to spy out some weakness in him in order to force him to give in. He stands therefore as a solitary figure in the history of Israel. Certainly, the prophets before him had had to learn through bitter experience that they were disowned by almost the entire people; but they could appeal to central aspects of the traditional faith in Yahweh in their message. By contrast, Job could neither hold on to the God of goodness, since he stood in the deepest distress, nor did he want to believe in the God of retribution, since it was precisely this retribution which seemed to him completely unjust. He could not rely on a human tradition against belief in God, since it was precisely this tradition which was used against him with great skill by his friends (=enemies). So he remained under the impression that he was being tortured by God himself. However, since he did not want to acknowledge a God of vengeance, there remained no alternative but to appeal to God himself against the image of God current up until then. Despite his complaints, however, he received from this God only a general answer, which failed to address his precise question.

A clearer answer to the penetrating question about retribution was already beginning to emerge prior to Job in the prophetic songs about the suffering servant of God. But this answer was so new for Israel that it remained uncomprehended for a long time. The author of the dramatic dialogue of the book of Job did not deal with it — indeed, we are not sure he knew about it. This answer was also not easy to understand. In the fourth song of the suffering servant, people look back on the one who has been rejected and killed and acknowledge that they interpreted his fate first of all from the viewpoint of the (traditional) belief in retribution, but then came to a completely different insight: "We thought he was stricken, smitten by God and afflicted. But he was wounded for our transgressions, he was bruised for our iniquities" (Isa. 53:4–5). In order to understand correctly the new insight which begins with the "but," it is necessary to look very carefully at the third song as well as at the whole context of the fourth song. Otherwise, it is possible to attribute the most sublime insight of Israel's faith to something which in the system of sacred vengeance of primitive societies was taken for granted, namely, that not only the guilty one, but equally another person from the primary group can be the object of the avenging deed. It would then be said that the suffering servant had to undergo the retributory vengeance not for his own misdeed but for those of others in his group. This interpretation is inadequate, because in the work of Deutero-Isaiah the personal bearing of the one who suffers, which plays absolutely no part in the sacred system of vengeance, is particularly emphasized and portrayed as surprising. The suffering servant did not defend himself, but offered his back and his cheeks to the blows of others (Isa. 50:5–6). When he was ill-treated, he did not open his mouth (to call for vengeance). He was led like a lamb to the slaughter (Isa. 53:7), and he took the sufferings of others upon him (Isa. 53:4). All of this he did, not out of resignation, but because God opened his ear every morning and thus enabled him to behave in this way (Isa. 50:4–5). The freedom from violence inspired by God is consequently the decisive new element displayed by the suffering servant. Thus his voluntary bearing of the retribution due to others takes on an entirely new meaning over against the old system of vengeance. In distinction to a society's scheme of compensation between tribes of equal status, the notion, the faith-inspired act of offering oneself on behalf of others comes to the fore.

However there remains a certain ambiguity in the songs of the stricken servant. Does their central message consist in the new and surprising way retribution was carried out? Or is it decisive here that God inspired the servant to nonviolence? In the first case, there would be no breakthrough from the old ideas of vengeance; they would simply have found a new and surprising variant. In the second case, however, God, as proclaimed in these songs, would have to have been understood unambiguously as a nonviolent God. On this assumption, the "retribution" which fell on the suffering servant would have to be understood in a new way. It would be the result, no longer of a direct act of will from God, but only the consequence of a (bad) human and social way of behavior.

This alternative possibility for interpretation has to remain open when looked at purely from the Old Testament itself. But upon it depends in large measure the final understanding of the relationship between God's anger and God's goodness. This same possible alternative will also play an important part in the interpretation of the fate of Jesus. From the Old Testament, therefore, there issues a warning to proceed very carefully in the interpretation of the New Testament texts. Since basic ideas of retribution belong to the very core of the sacred order and have thus shaped the language accordingly, it is important to take great care with the language as well as with the subject under consideration.

From the viewpoint of the Old Testament it is conceivable that the principle of retribution in the New Testament were merely refined; but it is equally possible that the system of vengeance was breached and that, at the linguistic level, old expressions were kept on but given a completely new meaning. Working from a few isolated utterances, we could hardly expect to find a satisfying answer to these complex problems. What must therefore be decisive is the way in which all the essential themes can be drawn into a systematic interpretation.

Part Two

DRAMA IN THE DESTINY OF JESUS

Jesus grew up in a world which was crucially determined by the Mosaic and prophetic tradition. But in his time there were very different religious tendencies within Judaism. The Pharisaic and Zealot movements were active at that time even in Galilee, and at least a small proportion of the people may have been influenced by apocalyptic expectations.

We are almost completely in the dark about the religious development that Jesus underwent during his years in Nazareth. Luke's Gospel only expresses the conviction that while in his youth, he grew step by step in wisdom (Luke 2:52). But little that is definite can be derived from this. Certainly, it is very unlikely that Jesus was conscious of his mission only from the time of his baptism onward. How could he have started his proclamation immediately? A longer process of maturation is suggested, and we may therefore share the assumption of H. Schürmann: "Jesus' parables would hardly all have been given in the few months in the few square kilometers around Capernaum; they were certainly no inspired intuitions of the moment, but well thought out 'memory-forms.' The kingdom-parable of the treasure in the field can in particular be read as an autobiographical reflection on an event in Nazareth: a man found a treasure which brought him to such a pitch of joy that he gave up everything he had in order to acquire the field (see Matt. 13:14)."[1]

It can be said not only with some probability, but with certainty that Jesus prepared for his public ministry in prayer. He withdrew immediately after the baptism to fast and pray in the wilderness (Mark 1:12ff. and parallels), and it is reported, among other important events, that he lingered deep in prayer (Luke 3:21; Mark 1:35; 6:46 and parallels; Mark 14:32–39 and parallels). These clear witnesses from the time of his public ministry seem to indicate that he prepared his future task in prayer during the many years in Nazareth. Here he may have experienced the nearness of God as a reality coming upon him in such a way that he began his public ministry not according to his own plans, but because he felt himself to be "destined" or "sent." He did not receive a

---

1. Schürmann (1983), 29.

doctrine in some school, which he then developed and passed on, but he proclaimed what was "sent" to him.

We can say, likewise with certain reservations, that the Baptist must have had a similar experience, since he did not preach some generally valid doctrine, but his message was sharply eschatological, directed toward the immediate future.[2] In the spirit of immediate expectation he predicted an imminent new divine action, more precisely as a judgment on Israel, in which he saw a condemned people.[3] It is unlikely that the Baptist acquired this harsh judgment on his own people through a comprehensive analysis of their general behavior. Because God's anger threatened, as he perceived in his prophetic manner, then Israel must be sinful, and in view of the threat of baptism by judgment and fire, only repentance and baptism by water offered a firm assurance of salvation.

If Jesus allowed himself to be baptized by John at the beginning of his public ministry, this means that he must have agreed with John's proclamation, at least on certain essential points. As his own message proves, he did not share the Baptist's preaching of an immediately imminent judgment as such, and so it must have been the conviction of a new divine action at hand which led him to make common cause with the Baptist. Agreement and difference are shown in his comparison of the Baptist's preaching of an *imminent judgment* with Jesus' own message of the *imminent kingdom of God*. The revelation after the baptism, in which he was filled with the spirit of God and addressed from heaven as God's beloved Son (Mark 1:9–11 and parallels), makes it clear that he himself had a decisive missionary task to fulfil at the outbreak of the new "kingdom." What actually happened to Jesus immediately after the baptism is disputed by historical-critical research, but this important scene with its deep meaning should not be overlooked in the course of the following reflections.

---

2. Becker (1972), 17.
3. Ibid., 33.

First Act:
The Dawning of the Kingdom of God

"The time is fulfilled and the kingdom of God is at hand" (Mark 1:15). This message constitutes an initial thematizing of the proclamation of Jesus in the synoptic Gospels. In the Old Testament Deutero-Isaiah speaks impressively of the kingship of God (Isa. 43:15; 44:6; 52:7). In the rabbinic tradition the formula "to take on oneself the yoke of God's kingship" meant the obligation to the Shema ("Hear, O Israel, the LORD [is] our God, the LORD is one") and to monotheism. In Jesus' environment the Zealots rallied around a program of Yahweh as king and the only Lord, which meant specifically resistance against the Romans. The whole message of Jesus, his proclamation of God, his interpretation of the law, and his call to conversion, were entirely within the broad framework of the dawning kingdom of God, which announced his new, unforeseeable action rather than describing the nature of God in general.

Jesus addressed that God as his Father who intended to set up his kingdom in the near future. The designation of "Father" for God was rare in the Old Testament. The reason for this was probably the desire to avoid mythological misunderstandings concerning physical procreation (god/goddess). Where nevertheless the Fatherhood of God was spoken of, this was in relation to an adopted son: Israel or its king (messiah) who was chosen out from among all the peoples and princes as son. In a few cases God was also called father because of his mercy and caring (Ps. 103:13; Isa. 63:16). The petition "Our Father in heaven" was used in the synagogue, which was dominated by the Pharisees, and this is comparable to some occurrences in the Gospels, particularly in the "Our Father" prayer (Matt. 6:9; see also Luke 11:2). The Gospels very frequently speak of God as father, but most notably Jesus himself addressed God thus and spoke of him as "my Father."[1] It is conspicuous that in one place in the Greek text the actual Aramaic word which Jesus used in prayer was preserved: "Abba, Father" (Mark 14:36; see also Rom. 8:15; Gal. 4:6).

The word "Abba" was originally baby-talk, used by small children to speak to their father. Later its uses were broadened somewhat, but it always kept its ring of familiarity and intimacy and was for that reason, as far as we know, never used by the Palestinian Jews to address God in prayer.[2] It is a fair inference that Jesus' use of the title indicates a new

---

1. In the Gospels this form of address is found 170 times in the mouth of Jesus, in the following distribution: Mark, 4 times; Luke, 15 times; Matt., 42 times; John, 109 times. See Jeremias (1966), 33f.

2. See ibid., 63.

experience of God, which must have been of great intimacy, and it was from this experience that the new proclamation arose.

Both in the message of the nearness of God and also in the language of Jesus' prayer, there can be seen a delicate but striking shift over against the religious experience of Israel. The two new keynotes may have influenced each other and become intermingled, as is seen, for example in the request to God: "Our Father ... your kingdom come" (Matt. 6:9ff.). In the Abba-experience there is revealed on the one hand the intimate and personal character of the kingdom of God; and this in turn makes it clear that Jesus' experience of prayer was not of a private or individualistic nature, but rather he perceived it in connection with his message and his mission. On the other hand, the new experience of prayer suggests the possibility that Jesus understood himself in a new way through this experience. The special nearness of God as Abba may have led to a corresponding awakening of the specific consciousness of sonship, as this is actually reported in the baptism narrative or in the shout of praise (Matt. 11:25–27 and parallels).

Linguistic characteristics of Jesus' message therefore show that in his experience of God, of history, and of himself we are confronted by something which deserves a deeper level of attention. He himself, it is true, made no great systematic utterances about it, but his parables, his own behavior, and the demands he made on people indicate how his new perception of God is to be understood. When we try to feel our way to getting closer to him and his message, a problem arises which is not sufficiently recognized in the everyday practice of contemporary exegesis. The historical-critical method was developed in conjunction with the philosophy of history of the Enlightenment. This latter recognizes human beings as the only agents of history, and so historical research is about showing how people mutually influence each other, distance themselves from each other, and fight one another. The course of history is explained in terms of the different forces in people, in society, and even, in part, in nature. Now if, in the case of Jesus, a quite different conviction emerges, namely, the belief that history is essentially determined by the actions of God and the nearness of his kingdom, then we have to ask whether contemporary critical methodology does not tend to eliminate in advance, or at least to make unclear, what for him was the central thing. The traditional method, which started from an already formulated understanding of the action of God, is in any case problematic, since it could be that the divine activity is thereby understood in a way modeled far too directly on the picture of human action, and hence it is treated more like mythology. As a third way, there only remains on the one hand to exercise great caution over the findings of the historical-critical method and, on the other, to seek out the inner coherence in whatever emerges as special in the life of Jesus. Discussion of his message and his destiny must become at the same time a discussion about historical methodology and about the question of the agents of history.

The Presence of the Time of Salvation

The message of the kingdom of God at hand was a joyful message. According to Luke, Jesus began his public ministry by declaring that the messianic announcement of Isaiah 61:1–2 was fulfilled, and thereby indirectly indicating himself as the one anointed by the spirit of the Lord, whose task is to bring good news to the poor, to announce liberation to captives, and to give sight to the blind (Luke 4:16–21). To the question of John's disciples, whether he was "the one who is to come," he answered, "The blind see, the lame walk, lepers are cleansed, and the deaf hear, the dead are raised, the poor receive good news" (Luke 7:22). Thus the Old Testament messianic words are related to his activity in the present. Critical exegesis gives differing judgments as to whether the narrative containing the question from John's disciples is original; but it is virtually undisputed that we have a genuine saying of Jesus in the logion of the blind, lame, deaf, and poor who experience healing and help.

The dawning of the time of salvation was becoming manifest not only in bodily healing, but above all in the overcoming of the power of evil. Jesus freed the possessed from their enslavement, and his saving activity was so clear that people could never deny it, but could at the most interpret it differently. Against the suspicion that he was working through the force of the highest demons against the other demons, Jesus proved that the accusation rests on the unfounded assumption of a voluntary act of self-destruction on the part of the demonic kingdom (Luke 11:14–23). He made his own claim over against this unsubstantiated assertion: "If I drive out demons by the finger of God, then the kingdom of God is come upon you" (Luke 11:20). The linguistic formulation of this saying is so striking and the situation it describes is so specific that it is unanimously recognized by critical exegesis as a genuine saying of Jesus (so Bultmann, 1964; Tödt, 1959; Kuhn, 1966; Bornkamm, 1968; E. Schweizer, 1976; Fiedler, 1976; Laufen, 1980). It stands in conjunction with another utterance which in practice no one disputes that it is from Jesus himself, and this speaks in a similar way about the already achieved overcoming of Satan: "I saw Satan fall like lightning from heaven. Behold, I have given you authority to tread on serpents and scorpions, and over all the enemy's power..." (Luke 10:18–19; see also Mark 3:27). According to the Jewish imagination, Satan was the great prosecutor of humankind (see Job 1:6–2:10; Zech. 3:1–2; Rev. 12:10). Through his fall from heaven, i.e., from the place where God is imagined to be, the element of prosecution was eliminated from the image of God. Jesus' vision of the fall of Satan is therefore materially connected with his new experience of God as heavenly Father, and it became efficacious in his exorcistic activity.

Because of his healing actions and the overcoming of evil forces, the time of Jesus was that time of salvation which had been expected for so long: "Blessed are you whose eyes see what you see. For I tell you that many prophets and kings desired to see what you see, and did not see it, and to hear what you hear, and did not hear it" (Luke 10:23–24). The messianic time of salvation was like a wedding. Jesus understood himself as bridegroom and his disciples were the wedding guests, who could not fast as long as the bridegroom was with them (Mark 2:19).

The words about the overcoming of Satan and the many diverse messianic images show that Jesus proclaimed the kingdom of God not merely as near at hand, but as *already dawning and present*. If he drove out demons, it was because the new time of salvation was already effective. He saw his own activity as inseparable from the coming of the kingdom of God. Although Jesus lived out of the faith-tradition of Israel, he sounded a note which had never rung out before.

The presence of salvation showed itself especially in the fact that as Jesus proclaimed his message, something actually happened. The effect he had was entirely different from that of other teachers: "for he taught them as one who had authority, and not as the scribes" (Mark 1:22). His message of salvation became a healing and liberating force. The sick became healthy; the possessed became free, and people on the margins of society experienced his loving attention. It was not the abstract content of what he said, but the total event of teaching, preaching, healing, and caring which affected people.

If one wishes to understand what is new in his message, it is not enough to compare his utterances with those of the Old Testament and of Jewish texts of the time. It is all-important that the event of his salvation-bearing proclamation remain constantly in view and the imagination try to capture the moments when the spark flew from him to his hearers. Only from such events, which took place once and for all and could have succeeded or failed, are his message and destiny understandable.

The Future as the Time of Salvation and Imminent Expectation

Jesus declared those blessed who are normally judged quite differently by humankind and considered unfortunate and battered creatures: "Blessed you poor, for to you belongs the kingdom of God. Blessed those who hunger now, for they will be satisfied. Blessed those who cry now, for they will laugh" (Luke 6:20ff.). Blessed are those unfortunate up until now, because the kingdom of God belongs to them and in it everything will be transformed. But this turnabout, as the beatitudes make clear, will happen only in the future. Besides the words and images that speak of the already present kingdom of God, there are countless others which point to the future. But how are the present and the future of the kingdom of God related to one another? "The attempts of the interpreters to deal with this question are numerous."[3] Even greater problems are raised by those words in which Jesus speaks of a kingdom of God *near in time*. What did he mean by this? Views here are very divergent, and discussion about it has marked almost the entire recent history of research.

All proposals for a solution come to terms in one way or another with the "thoroughgoing [*konsequent*] eschatology" of J. Weiss and A. Schweitzer. According to this, Jesus himself understood the kingdom of God as completely otherworldly, and meant by its nearness a cosmic catastrophe soon to come and a new beginning which would break out from heaven. Schweitzer even thought he could show that Jesus, at the time of sending out his disciples, was convinced that they would suffer persecution for a short time, but that before their return the kingdom would break out and he himself would be raised up on the clouds of heaven as Son of Man. After being disappointed in this expectation, he became certain that he had the authority to bring about the eschatological sufferings and that he alone was to suffer. Hence he felt compelled to go to Jerusalem in order to die at the hands of the authorities and to achieve a death of atonement for others, an atonement which the participants in the kingdom must complete.[4] In this way he tried to force the arrival of the kingdom of God.

This "thoroughgoing eschatology" was at first utterly rejected, and then from the First World War onward it found a certain responsive echo. Bultmann followed Schweitzer in thinking that Jesus expected a great eschatological drama, in keeping with apocalyptic assumptions of the time.[5] Certainly, in contrast to Jewish apocalyptical speculation, he dismissed all concrete representations of the kingdom of God, but he held on to its speedy and visible coming. For that reason Bultmann can say: "It goes without saying that Jesus was deceived about the imminent end of the world — just as the prophets had been."[6]

Many have followed Bultmann's opinion that Jesus was mistaken in his imminent expectation. Later research was influenced above all by the fact that there are no apocalyptic speculations in the Gospels. Thus, for

---

3. Bornkamm (1968), 83.
4. A. Schweitzer (1933), 435.
5. Bultmann (1926), 36.
6. Bultmann (1954), 99.

example, Käsemann judged that Jesus may have begun with the Baptist's imminent expectation, but then abandoned it entirely. The few words in the synoptic Gospels which speak of the temporal nearness of the kingdom of God would not stem from Jesus but would be a product of the post-Easter enthusiasm of the disciples, who awaited a speedy return of the risen one as judge over the world. Precisely as historian one must "speak of an incomparable mystery of Jesus."[7] The proclaimed nearness of the kingdom of God meant that Jesus was open to the God who was near and to the neighbor in the moment, open also even to accept his suffering."[8] Many others judged similarly. Thus Merklein thinks that the words about nearness in time (Mark 9:1; 13:30; Matt. 10:23) are to be attributed to the post-Easter community.[9] In other sayings about the imminent kingdom of God (Mark 1:15; Luke 10:9 and parallels) he thinks it is not nearness in time that is primary, but the proclamation of God's eschatological decision to a skeptical generation.[10] Schürmann makes a similar judgment in interpreting the nearness of God's reign in the sense of personal nearness and construing the "constant expectation" in the preaching of Jesus to be fundamental as a "fixed expectation of nearness."[11]

A. Strobel especially has delivered quite a sharp judgment from the exegetical standpoint on the many attempts to play down or even eliminate the temporal element in the imminent expectation. According to him, Jesus was in no way anti-apocalyptic, but was characterized by a powerful orientation to the end-time.[12] This orientation also took hold of his disciples no later than his last journey to Jerusalem. The hope of a great act of God became for him more and more related to his own person as the "Son" in relation to the "Father."

Von Balthasar largely followed Strobel's view. There are "some logia which doubtlessly attest a temporal eschatological expectation. They are neither demonstrably from the post-Easter community nor to be reinterpreted existentially (in the sense of a 'continual expectation')." Jesus on the contrary awaited the breaking out of the kingdom, and this on the one hand "with the composure of one who lives completely for his mission" and on the other hand expected it within his life, as he walked toward "the great hour which awaits him in Jerusalem."[13] According to Balthasar, the imminent expectation of Jesus was in no way related

7. Käsemann, "Zum Thema der urchristlichen Apokalyptik," in Käsemann (1960, 1964) 2:105–31.
8. Ibid., 119.
9. Merklein (1978), 150–54.
10. Ibid., 157.
11. Schürmann (1981), 60.
12. Strobel (1967), 88–100.
13. Balthasar (1973–83) 2/2:81, 83, 84.

to a cosmic event, but entirely to his hour of suffering and his Easter glorification.

This brief overview shows that we are dealing with a complex problem. The Old Testament background, where God is always believed in as one who acts within history, suggests to us not to skip too quickly over the temporal dimension in the message of the kingdom of God at hand. If Jesus spoke of the eschatological action of God, which is accepted by those who usually play down the temporal dimension, then we are led to suspect that he understood this action in a temporal way also, and not merely personally or existentially. If the basileia message has to do with God's eschatological decision, already made,[14] we must ask whether not only the proclamation but also the implementation of the decision necessarily demanded time. Balthasar, over against the existential interpretation, rightly emphasizes the dimension of time. But when he says that the expectation is directly related to the "hour" of the cross and the glorification, the question has to be put to him as to whether the basileia message does not have its own time. Should his view not be more closely aligned with positions which attempt to understand Jesus entirely from the viewpoint of the basileia message? *Does not all unilinear thinking fall short, and should not the action of God be seen more dramatically* — not in the sense of cosmic catastrophes, but in the sense of events which have their particular moment in time and which involve the interplay of free agents? The nearest available horizon of understanding, the Old Testament, shows how God made promises, met the resistance of his people, "repented" of his actions, acted in anger and overcame his own anger again by his mercy, and made possible new beginnings for his people. If Jesus announced a new act of God, a similar dramatic scenario should not be excluded a priori. On the contrary, it must form the first contextual framework in which his message and his destiny can be thought through. Superficial and unilinear models of thought are in any case problematic.

A dramatic point of view promises to provide an answer to the question which is occupying us here, namely, how the present and the future of the kingdom of God were related to one another in the proclamation of Jesus, without one dimension being underplayed at the expense of the other, as often happens. If we may distinguish different acts within God's total action, then the first can have already begun even when the others are not yet at hand. When such a thing happens, there are no spectators, no one who can survey the whole scene from the beginning, but only actors whose actions also help to determine how the drama develops. With such an understanding of the action of God, at the first

---

14. Merklein (1978), 157.

announcement the details of future events would not yet be fixed; rather, these would first emerge out of the response to the proclaimed message, so that it would hardly be possible to speak of an error on the part of the proclaimer. Whether such an interpretation is actually valid must be proved in the extent that it does justice to the total evidence of the synoptic Gospels. But before we take the problematic of present and future of the kingdom of God any further, we must once again dig deeper and ask about the really decisive element in it. What does it proclaim about God and God's action in relation to humankind?

God's Turning toward His Enemies

Jesus called for love of one's enemy and based this high demand on the observation that God even lets the sun rise over the good and evil and the rain fall on the just and the unjust (Matt. 5:43–47). Jesus' radical demand on people to love their adversaries arose out of his conviction that God himself treats his enemies — sinners — graciously. The theme, so important in the Old Testament, of God's anger and vengeance, was absent from his message from the start. Just as he himself had experienced Yahweh as Abba, so he proclaimed him as the gracious Father who forgives sinners.

A particularly characteristic feature of God's new action, as Jesus preached it, was seen in his own behavior. He turned toward sinners, tax-collectors, and prostitutes, and his conduct was so conspicuous that he drew the reproach: "Behold, a glutton and drunkard, a friend of tax collectors and sinners!" (Matt. 11:19). Since this reproach is so rough that we can be sure it was not made up by the community of the faithful, we have here a saying which directly divulges how Jesus' enemies saw him. They found it particularly offensive that he even shared in meal fellowship with sinners (see Mark 2:15–17; Luke 15:1ff.; 19:1–10). This was not simply a question of social convention. If for the common Eastern understanding, community around the table already meant a relationship of peace, trust, and forgiveness,[15] in Jesus' Jewish context it had an even deeper sense. "In the Jewish tradition community around the table means especially community in the eyes of God since it is established from the principle that by eating a piece of the broken bread, each participant in the meal receives a share in the blessing that the Father of the household speaks over the unbroken bread."[16] That was also the deciding reason why faithful Jews separated themselves, at least when eating, from the pagans and those who did not know the law. It follows that Jesus' sharing of meals with tax-collectors and

---

15. Jeremias (1971), 117.
16. Ibid.

sinners was connected with his new proclamation of God, and was an expression of his mission. This emerges not only from the general Jewish background, but also especially from his answer to the reproaches which were made against him. Against the charge that he even ate with sinners, he defended himself through parables which speak of God's actions (lost sheep, lost drachma, lost son [Luke 15:1–32]). His behavior toward sinners could by itself have been interpreted as a lax attitude toward the law, which, in view of the different tendencies in the Jewish world at that time, may well have been tolerated. Equally, the parables by themselves could have been interpreted as graphic language about the divine mercy, already familiar in the Old Testament (see Hos. 11; Jer. 31:20; Isa. 54:8). But both together, the deviant behavior and its interpretation through parables, resulted in a new proclamation. From the mercy of God Jesus drew conclusions which were different from those that Jewish teaching had drawn, for he claimed that God turns in a special way toward his enemies, sinners. In his parables Jesus gave expression to God's compassion for sinners and his joy in bringing them into fellowship with him; indeed, he "gave his hearers to understand that here and now, in this scandalous table fellowship, God was acting and that the joy of finding a treasure again invited their joy in response: a joy responding to God's joy and thus their yes to Jesus' table fellowship with the lost, with whom he celebrated God's joy."[17] While the Pharisees and John's disciples fasted, Jesus had himself invited as "bridegroom" to the fellowship of a meal by those who stood, from the viewpoint of the law, outside God's community.

Moreover, the Gospels report that Jesus, in addition to the indirect forgiveness of sins through the sharing of a meal, also imparted forgiveness to sinners directly (Mark 2:1–12 and parallels; Luke 7:48). Whether we have here before us original words and deeds of Jesus is very much disputed in historical-critical tradition. In the light of the message, as it speaks to us from the behavior and parables of Jesus, we might perhaps be more inclined to accept them as original, but this question is not of decisive importance. It is thinkable that the ecclesiastical tradition simply converted those two pericopes in which Jesus expressly laid claim to the power to forgive sins and reformulated and converted into "ecclesiastical language what historically took place in Jesus' association with sinners."[18]

In order fully to grasp the forgiveness of sins by means of the basileia message, a comparison with the temple cult is indispensable. Since the preaching of the prophets, particularly since the time of the exile,

---

17. Linnemann (1964), 78.
18. Schillebeeckx (1976), 186.

the Jews had an acute consciousness of sin and of the necessity for atonement. The latter was carried out in countless guilt and atonement sacrifices, but especially, as Leviticus 16:1–34 shows, in the celebration of the great Day of Atonement (Yom Kippur), when the high priest, the people, the temple, and the altar were purified by sacrifice and the rite of the scapegoat. In fact Jesus never attacked the prestige of the temple and he had a positive relationship to it as "house of prayer" (Mark 11:17). But there is nowhere any indication that he granted the sacrificial cult an importance for salvation. In his proclamation of the kingdom of God and his turning toward sinners he must therefore have claimed de facto those functions which up until then fell to the temple cult. Thus he extended reconciliation not only to those pious people who followed the many prescriptions of the law, but especially to those sinners who did not know or hardly knew the law.

Something similar can be seen in Jesus' position toward the law and the Sabbath command. The position that he consciously set aside the law and ignored or even eliminated the purity regulations must be viewed as an exaggeration, for the early Jewish-Christian community could not, as Bultmann remarked, "possibly have taken for granted the loyal adherence to the law and defended it against Paul, if Jesus had combatted the authority of the law."[19] It would be most accurate to say that he introduced a significant shift concerning the law. He emphasized the inner sense of the law to such an extent that the external letter of the law, for example on the purity prescriptions (Mark 7:15–23), could fade into the background and practically lose its importance. Thus it became possible to take the step across the sacred boundary toward sinners. Neither did Jesus demand any spiritual practice of the law before he extended God's mercy to sinners. In his basileia message, salvation and penance seem to have exchanged places. It is consequently not decisive for Jesus' attitude toward the law that we answer the disputed question whether and how he was able to disregard this or that regulation. His interpretation of the law must above all be seen in connection with his turning to those without the law and with his proclamation of God, which distinguished him from the exclusive rigorism of the Qumran sects and brought him as well into difficulties with the Pharisees.

In the parables of God's kingdom, in his dealings with the temple and the law, and in his relationship to sinners, Jesus gave expression to his heavenly Father as a God who turns in a new way toward sinners. Herein lay the deepest dimension of his message of the dawning

---

19. Bultmann (1926), 57; Eng. trans.: *Jesus and the Word*, trans. Louise Pettibone Smith and Erminie Huntress Lantero (New York: Charles Scribner's Sons, 1934, 1958), 62.

kingdom of God, and it is from that point that his further proclamation and his life's destiny should be interpreted. If this clear reference point is not seen and made productive for interpretation, contradictory interpretations necessarily result, and the door is left open to arbitrariness. In order to understand the full consequences of God's new turning to sinners, one further aspect of Jesus' message and mission has to be noted: the will, implicit in the divine forgiveness, to create a new community.

The Gathering of Israel

Israel understood herself as the people chosen by God, and from the time of exile onward described the new, hoped-for working out of salvation primarily as a "new gathering." As the symbolic action of the meal shows, Jesus' preaching also envisaged the creation of a new community. He wanted to give peace of heart to people who were "troubled" (see Matt. 11:28), who "were tired and exhausted like sheep without a shepherd" (Matt. 9:36; see also Mark 6:34), and to gather them together anew as the people of Israel (see Matt. 12:30; 23:37 and parallels). His sending out of the disciples is a witness to his will to reach the whole of Israel, but above all the constituting of the group of twelve was an action of prophetic symbolism, through which the new Israel (with its twelve tribes) was already initially realized. He did not want to renew a "holy remnant," but the whole of Israel, even if he only invited a portion to immediate discipleship. Even his healing of the sick had this meaning, for according to the messianic texts to which he appealed (see Matt. 11:5ff.; Luke 4:18ff.), it belongs to the new people that the blind see again, the lame walk, the deaf hear, and the dead rise up.

The prayer which Jesus taught his disciples includes in it the incipient existence of a renewed Israel — for "our Father" is not the Father of an individual but of a people — and at the same time it aims toward the further coming of God's kingdom. The petitions involving the sanctification of the name and the coming of the kingdom belong closely together, as is clear from Ezekiel, for God promised by this prophet that he would act anew not because of the sinful people, but for his name's sake, and that he would show himself as holy when he gathered Israel together again from its scattered state of exile (Ezek. 20:41, 44; 28:25; 36:22, 24). Although for Jesus the actual gathering of Israel from the banishment of exile could no longer play a role, he was in a position to take over the language of Ezekiel. Even for Ezekiel it was not only a matter of the return of the people from exile, but at the same time the turning of Israel to its God (36:25–32).[20] The request of the Our Father for sanctification of the name consequently pleads for that double event in which God is

---

20. G. Lohfink (1982), 27.

sanctified as Lord by his gathering together of the people and turning them toward himself. So we concur with what Jeremias says: "the *only* meaning of the total reality of Jesus is the gathering of eschatological people of God."[21]

The new Israel is no anonymous collective, but rather it involves the conversion of each individual. Jesus from the beginning linked the call to conversion with the proclamation of the kingdom of God: "The time is fulfilled, the kingdom of God is near. Repent and believe in the Gospel" (Mark 1:15). The announcement of the kingdom of God at hand led seamlessly into the demand for conversion. Not only the sowing of the seed but also the collection of the fruit belongs to the kingdom of God, as is evident from the parables of the sower (Mark 4:2–20 and parallels) and of the talents (Matt. 25:14–30). The basic form of conversion consists in the total turning to the God of the basileia, to the Father of Jesus. Through his own complete trust in Yahweh as Abba and through his human health and wholeness he awakened in many hearers the faith which made healings possible. Several narratives which report marvelous healings events end with the words: "Your faith has saved you" (Mark 5:34 and parallels; 10:52 and parallels; Luke 7:50; 17:19). Jesus attributed wonderful events not only to his authority, but related them to the faith of the sick people or of the bystanders. In his hometown where he found no faith, he was unable to work miracles (Mark 6:5), but it was the opposite when people pressed trustfully around him (see Mark 1:32–34). To the despairing request of a father — "But if you can, help us!" (Mark 9:22) — he gave not a protestation of his own powers, but a general answer which included the person he was addressing: "Whoever believes can do everything" (Mark 9:23; see also 11:20–25).

It is evident that intensive interaction took place in the healings between Jesus and the sick people. It required tremendous effort of him. When the father of the possessed child told him what his son was suffering from and that the disciples were unable to heal him, he heaved at first a deep sigh: "You faithless generation, how long must I be with you? How long am I to bear with you?" (Mark 9:19). Such a complaint presupposes that it was hard for Jesus to awaken faith and that he suffered from the unbelief of his hearers. But his complaint makes understandable the otherwise surprising interpretation of his healings in the light of the suffering servant (Isa. 53:4), which is given in Matthew 8:17: "He has taken our sufferings upon him and borne our illnesses." The post-Easter community related the song of the suffering servant of God especially to the suffering and death of Jesus. That a prophetic quo-

---

21. Jeremias (1971), 167.

tation from this song could find fulfillment earlier, in his healing activity, seems unfamiliar to Christian ears and indicates an original experience. When Jesus healed, he must have got so involved with the sick that he shared the burden of their lack of faith and their suffering in order to free them from their inner captivity. Moreover, a certain sort of contact with the sick would render the healer unclean.

His wonderful deeds were not isolated "tricks" to bring people to a state of astonishment. The dawning of God's kingdom in his free-ing and healing work was much more of an intensive, interpersonal event, in which the pure belief of Jesus touched the innermost hearts of his hearers and was affected by them in reciprocation. The wonder-ful healings were the expression of that communicative process, through which the kingdom of God was dawning and the new gathering of Israel beginning.

Even the interpretation of the law, as Jesus proposed it in the Sermon on the Mount with its antitheses in Matthew 5:21–48, introduced not merely a "radicalization" in the sense of an absolute orientation toward the God of the basileia. It was at the same time defined by the concern for the new gathering. The correct interpretation of the Sermon on the Mount is certainly difficult, and the discussion of it goes back a long way. It stretches from the traditional teaching concerning the command-ments and counsels and the Lutheran distinction between the Christian person and the secular person, across the ethical rigorism of the enthu-siasts and the ethics of conviction of liberal theology, to the modern proposals (interim ethics, contrast ethics, the ethics of love, eschatologi-cal and theological ethics, etc.). In fact careful distinctions are needed in framing the questions in ethics and pastoral theology. But prior to these there is a strictly theological question, and this concerns the connection between the kingdom of God, the new mode of human behavior, and the new gathering. If the basileia fully arrives among humankind only with the founding of the new people, if the new gathering of Israel is an essential constituent of Jesus' proclamation, then the Sermon on the Mount might describe exactly what is necessary for human behavior, so that the new people might be really different from the old, and all those evils which were never overcome in the history of Israel might finally be conquered. Before we ask how "realistic" the high demands are, we should notice that Jesus spoke to his hearers of the love of the heavenly Father and called them to a perfect trust, by means of which he hoped to create the new community. If people act as the Sermon on the Mount expects, then the new people becomes a reality. The high de-mands are not arbitrary commands but, objectively speaking, they prove to be absolutely necessary if the new life is really to begin.

The inner connection between the individual demands of the Sermon on the Mount becomes particularly clear if they are compared with the analysis of conflict as it has been elaborated by R. Girard from literature which is permeated by Christianity. According to this, people are fundamentally creatures of desire, and their aspirations are not autonomous but are determined, as if by osmosis,[22] by a desire which fastens on models so that they act out of imitation. Consequently, if the aspirations are instinctively directed toward something which another person's desire, mediated by a model, is already longing for, then two appetites are "unintentionally" aiming over and over again at the same object, which must awaken reinforced desire, rivalry, and finally aggression.

The indication that desire is imitated from others in a quasi-osmotic or nonconscious way may help to make sense of judgments in the Sermon on the Mount which otherwise leave us simply in a state of puzzlement. Why are getting angry and throwing out insults (idiot, fool) judged in the same way as murder (Matt. 5:21ff.), and why should a lecherous look be already adultery in the heart (Matt. 5:27)? If a desire can be picked up so spontaneously from others that one's own aspirations are determined thereby even before one is fully conscious of it and before one can explicitly react to it, then anger and the lustful look inevitably have an effect on a community. They set profoundly in motion an interwoven dynamic of desire, which exerts continual pressure and can easily lead to adultery and murder. Whether the result of desire is then an act of adultery or physical murder, the consequence of desire becomes no longer a matter of greater or lesser righteousness but almost entirely of external circumstances and stability of social regulations.

If the "old" behavior, which in its instinctive imitation inevitably produces evil, is really to be overcome, then the conversion must be very radical and must likewise start with inner desire (see Matt. 5:27–30). Spontaneous words of aggression and lecherous desires should be taken just as seriously as completed acts. The decisive thing is that the pattern of imitation should be broken, which is why precisely those demands in which Jesus turns against "an eye for an eye" and "a tooth for a tooth" (Matt. 5:38–42) are especially important. The entire ancient system of the sacred and revenge rests on the "wisdom" of this imitative, negative symmetry, which must be overcome by a gracious human goodness which mirrors a preceding divine mercy (Matt. 5:31ff., 38–42). Only then can the kingdom of God really commence on earth. Since this de-

---

22. Girard (1978), 89. Girard's theory helps not only better to see the inner connection between the individual norms of the Sermon on the Mount. In its light many subtle features of other specific pericopes appear more clearly. Girard (1988), 163–276, demonstrated this with the following texts: John 11:47–53 (Caiaphas speaking to the council); Mark 6:14–28 (beheading of John the Baptist); Mark 14:66–72 (denial of Peter); Mark 5:1–17 (healing of the demoniac of Gerasa); Matt. 12:23–28 (Satan casting out Satan).

siring imitation begins so instinctively and subtly that no one can fully control it in themselves or in others, nobody may judge another (Matt. 7:1–5) and all are in need of continual forgiveness and of constantly renewed reconciliation (Matt. 5:23–26; 6:14ff.). Such action is possible only if the fundamental desire is freed from its instinctive imitation. For this a prayer is needed which does not simply babble like the gentiles (Matt. 6:7, 16–18), but which expresses complete trust in the heavenly Father (Matt. 6:5–13) and thus frees a person from self-accusing thoughts and the cares that wear one down.

The regulations of the Sermon on the Mount consequently do not contain random demands of God; they only show what sort of conversion and what kind of new behavior are objectively necessary if people who come from a world of desire, rivalry, and the sacred vengeance system are to be really reconciled with one another in obedience to the will of God and to form a new community. What may at first appear as unrealistic is in truth nothing other than the model, contained within the dawning kingdom of God, of a new gathering and a new society which is different from all other societies. In these societies revenge, violence, or other retributional systems keep human passions under a certain external control, cover over deep unrest, and temporarily stabilize the societies, without being able to overcome the actual evil.

Through the experience of God as Abba such a deep communicative process was made possible between Jesus and his hearers that many were healed of their bodily afflictions and freed — like the possessed — from their psychic states. Was this communicative healing event able to reach even their innermost soul and their freedom? This was the question which decided whether Jesus' proclamation actually led to a perceivable dawning of the kingdom of God. The nearness of the kingdom was not fixed in advance, but partly depended on how far people allowed themselves to be touched in their innermost selves. The proclamation of the kingdom of God was an event which indeed rested initially on the new turning of God to sinners, but in second place it involved also the preparedness of the hearers. The event could consequently succeed or fail. The kind of nearness of God's kingdom was conditioned by this. Was Jesus able to touch people so deeply with his new experience of God that they also were overwhelmed by fatherly love and allowed themselves to be taken completely into the service of a new community life, or did their old desires remain the deepest ones and thus serve also the defense mechanisms against God and their neighbors?

Since the proclamation of Jesus involved a fundamental risk, we again ask the question about Jesus' role in this event. Did the success of his mission depend on the direct result he achieved with his hearers? Was he so identified with the service of the basileia that an initial failure would have meant that he himself had failed, or did the basileia depend ultimately so much on his own person that he could take it forward at the beginning all by himself in the case of an initial failure? Was the person conditioned by his message, and did God act only with a view to the kingdom, or did Jesus' proclamation result from the particular nature of his person, and did God act in a special way both on him and through him? The interpretation of his entire subsequent destiny depends on the answer to these questions.

Jesus' Claim and His Messianic Consciousness

At first Jesus proclaimed the kingdom of God, not himself. At the same time, however, he made a high claim for his own activity. In interpreting his turning to sinners by means of the parables of the kingdom of God, he acted neither like a prophet nor like a teacher of wisdom, but he dared, as E. Fuchs formulated it, "to act in God's place in that he drew sinners to himself who would have otherwise had to flee from God."[23] This may be the decisive point in Jesus' self-understanding. Indeed, he never methodically explained his relationship to the Father, but he did give witness to the certainty of God's gracious action through his preaching and ministry, "placing an inconceivable certainty in the ears of his hearers... including God's gracious acts toward the tax collectors."[24] He also gave expression to his "I" in a way which contrasted with the tradition of the prophets. While these presented their message as a "saying of the Lord," he introduced his with "Amen, I say to you." His "I" came out particularly clearly when he set it over against the tradition of the ancients and thereby claimed for himself an authority which went beyond that of a mere interpreter of the Torah.

Jesus never appeared in the role of a fundamental religious and political revolutionary. In everything he entered into the great tradition of Israel, and yet everywhere he carried out small but finally decisive shifts. It can always be disputed whether the countless individual points really make a break with the religious tradition of Israel. But together they add up to a new picture. Jesus did not serve the tradition; he used it rather to give expression to his new experience of the dawning of God's kingdom. Starting from the new action of God as it affected him, he dared to give a new interpretation of the whole faith history of Israel, changing little in individual details but at the same time putting everything into a quite different light.

From the tradition of Israel only one idea could allow for this innovation, namely, that of the Messiah. Thus it is suggested that Jesus

---

23. Fuchs (1960), 156; see also 154.
24. E. Schweizer (1976), 32; see also Linnemann (1964), 93; Mussner (1975), 97f.

understood himself as the Messiah. The synoptic Gospels testify to this in fact, even if in a very cautious way. According to Mark the possessed at first acknowledged him as such, but they were then ordered by Jesus to remain silent about it (Mark 1:23–26). After that Peter confessed the Messiahship of his master (Mark 8:27–30), but he too was forbidden to speak of it. Only before the Jewish council did Jesus himself confess his high dignity and was condemned for it (Mark 14:61–64). These utterances fit into the picture that we have produced so far, for in that picture Jesus is seen as both restrained and yet as clearly testifying to his claim. However it is strongly disputed in critical exegesis whether Jesus did in fact understand himself as Messiah. Since it is by this title (Messiah/Christ) that the New Testament writings classify Jesus in the covenant history of Israel and since the Messiah question plays an important role also in the understanding of his condemnation and execution, we must examine the historical-critical question rather more closely and thereby at the same time continue the discussion about the historical-critical method.

The Pre-Easter Jesus and Post-Easter Prophecy

During the last few decades, historical-critical exegesis has been strongly characterized by one principle, that the authenticity of specific texts must be demonstrated. As E. Käsemann has stated, "On the basis of form-critical work our interrogation has sharpened and widened, so that now we must prove and make credible not the possible inauthenticity, but precisely the authenticity of the specific textual material. What must be demonstrated now is not the validity of criticism, but its boundaries."[25] This principle arises from the form-critical method, as Käsemann himself mentions, a principle which "illumines the mutual relationship between style, form, and genre on the one hand and the life of the primitive Christian community on the other."[26]

From the stylistic form and the linguistic genre of an utterance, the questions posed refer back to the conditions of its origin and the nature of its original use by the community. Typical representatives of form criticism are thus of the opinion "that the tradition primarily gives information about the interests and needs of the community."[27] Form-historical work consequently, as a general rule, expects at first a post-Easter origin of the stories and utterances of the synoptic Gospels and only recognizes something as pre-Easter where it can be explicitly proved.

---

25. Käsemann, "Das Problem des historischen Jesus," in Käsemann (1960, 1964), 1:203.
26. Iber (1957–58), 308.
27. Iber (1959), 309.

But just as important for historical-critical exegesis as the question of method is the view of history which it attributes to the post-Easter community. According to this, Jesus' disciples lived during the first years after the death and appearances of their master in high expectations of his second coming. In this period they are supposed to have hardly worried about the past; rather there were prophets among them who in the name of their ascended master said things which were taken up by the faithful as possessing the highest authority. The community therefore "inattentively and foolishly combined their message with that of their Lord or even substituted it."[28] Concern for history arose only later when an attempt was made to ward off enthusiasm and docetism and to safeguard against the idea that salvation could be gained outside the visible church in history.[29] But at that time everything is thought to have already been combined in the early community's tradition.

Is this picture of the period after Easter really accurate, and is the hope which is placed in form criticism justified? That there were early Christian prophets is not disputed and is expressly confirmed by the Acts of the Apostles and the letters of the New Testament (Acts 13:1; 15:32; 21:10; 1 Cor. 12:28–29; 14:29; Eph. 2:20; 3:5; 4:11). However there are serious questions to put to the role ascribed to them above and the picture just sketched of the early Christian community. These are as follows.

1. If the words of the prophets, given as first-person sayings of the ascended one, had not been distinguished from the historical words of Jesus, the prophets would have to have had a dominant position in the early Christian community, since they would have been the most important authority mediating the words of the ascended Lord. But the New Testament letters show that it was not the prophets but the apostles who played the leading role, i.e., those who had themselves known the Lord during his life on earth, or at least had met the risen Lord. The clear distinction between apostles and prophets indicates that the words of the latter were hardly confused with Jesus' words.

2. The prophets were certainly — next to the apostles — highly respected in the early Christian community, but they were soon also under "suspicion," for the problem of "false prophets" arose, as earlier in Israel's tradition. That prophetic sayings were taken over quite

---

28. Käsemann, "Das Problem des historischen Jesus," in Käsemann (1960, 1964), 1:191; see also Bultmann (1964), who identifies particularly apologetics and polemics as the motive: 106, 135, 160, 176, 393.

29. See Käsemann, "Das Problem des historischen Jesus," 1:199–203; Käsemann, "Zum Thema der Nichtobjektivierbarkeit," in Käsemann (1960, 1964), 1:224–36, especially 233–36.

uncritically and simply combined with Jesus' words seems in this situation highly unlikely. It is rather the opposite assumption which imposes
itself, that post-Easter prophetic sayings were measured against the
Jesus-tradition.[30]

3. It is striking that we find no direct utterances and instructions in
the synoptic Gospels for the time between Easter and the parousia. This
fact would be, as Schweitzer has already argued, unintelligible if the
post-Easter community had unconcernedly placed its own utterances on
the same level with those of Jesus. "If the 'theology of the community'
had recast the tradition, as is always claimed, then it would have depicted Jesus giving indications to his intimates about what to do after
his death. The fact that we do not find any such suggestions is the best
proof that there can be no question of such a deeply interventionist
later reworking."[31] If on the other hand it is thought possible to prove
that the really central revelation scene after the baptism of Jesus had its
source in the much less vital discussion with John's disciples, how to explain, e.g., that the long and deeply rooted controversy between Jewish
and pagan Christians in the post-Easter communities led to no clear and
unambiguous narratives in the synoptic tradition? Why was, e.g., the vision in Joppa (Acts 10:9–16) handed down as a vision granted to Peter
and not fused with the tradition of Jesus?

With these questions we are not trying to put forward the view that in
the early Christian community there was no formative intervention into
the pre-Easter tradition. Our critique is aimed at a far too simple picture, which takes too little account of the diverse elements and ignores
decisive factors.

4. Through careful investigations J. Roloff was able to show that
concern for history did not first arise in a later phase of the early
church — after a break with the prophetic enthusiasm of the beginnings — but the tradition was determined from the beginning. Certainly
the community always pursued therein the interests of faith, but these
were also of a historical nature; among other things, it was a question
of understanding Jesus' way to the cross "on the basis of the presentation of his conflict with the Jewish tradition and its holy institutions."[32]
Similarly the community handed down the miracles of Jesus differently
from those that happened in their own lives. The latter were understood

---

30. "My objection to Bultmann stems from the observation that everywhere else in
the historical 'trajectory' of Judaeo-Christian prophecy authentic prophecy has been ac-
companied by false prophecy and prophetic communities have been strongly insistent on
the need to test putative inspiration" (Dunn [1978], 197). On the problem of "true and
false prophets" of that time see Berger (1974).

31. A. Schweitzer (1933), 408; see also 410.

32. Roloff (1970), 109.

as comforting signs for believers and were handed down as such. Hence they had no significance for outsiders. But Jesus' miracles were related precisely with the point of inviting and calling people to faith. The very detailed investigations of R. Pesch on the pre-Marcan history of the passion indicate further that in the post-Easter community the interest in the earthly destiny of Jesus must have been greater than form criticism has usually assumed.[33]

5. The sobering results of form criticism warn us to exercise caution, since no one has yet even approximately succeeded in bringing clearly definable literary forms into unambiguous relationship with precise needs and activities of the post-Easter community. The consensus among scholars over words which are definitely attributable to Jesus is even greater than the consensus over words and narratives which certainly have a post-Easter origin. Even if form criticism is still valid it must "give a better answer to the historical question."[34]

6. An important development within form criticism itself resulted from the question about the first bearers of the Jesus tradition. H. Schürmann among others was able to show with a high degree of probability that there is no reason to take the tradition as starting only after Easter.[35] Already the pre-Easter disciples — as a "sociological fact" — can be considered for such a role in the tradition, for Jesus had sent out his chosen ones for proclamation and had consequently communicated to them what they had to proclaim.

7. In order to make the theological connection between the message of the kingdom of God at hand and the form-historical problematic more comprehensible, E. Jüngel proposed an important further step,[36] which has been up until now hardly noticed or taken up. If, in the name of the dawning kingdom of God, Jesus called people to decision and gathered together disciples, then his group must have been determined by his words and precisely as this group must have had a vital interest in his words, since it owed to them its very existence and its cohesion. The eschatological event of the kingdom of God consequently created for itself, through the new gathering which Jesus set in motion, the place in society where it could be passed on as language and word. We can go further: because the circle of disciples was specifically characterized as

---

33. Pesch (1976, 1977) 2:1–27; Pesch, "Das Evangelium in Jerusalem: Mark 14,12–26 als ältestes Überlieferungsgut der Urgemeinde," in Stuhlmacher (1983), 113–55.

34. Hahn (1985), 468. A well-balanced picture of the process of transmission in the post-Easter congregations is sketched by Polag (1977), 187–97. He succeeds also in drawing out clear consequences for the pre-Easter tradition.

35. Schürmann (1968), 39–65; E. E. Ellis, "New Directions in Form Criticism," in Strecker (1975), 299–315; Riesner (1981); Gerhardsson (1986).

36. Jüngel, Excursus II of "Eschatologie und Formgeschichte (Eine methodologische Besinnung)," in Jüngel (1964), 290–300.

eschatological community, specific linguistic forms must have stemmed from it which were not derivable from a more general style. Thus the priority of linguistic form in the form-historical method cedes its place in favor of content. "The sociological formulation of questions proper to the form-historical method is thus corrected or even hermeneutically surpassed within the framework of the form-historical method by the eschatological formulation of questions."[37]

8. Despite the weighty and well-known reasons mentioned so far, there is a sizeable number among the historical-critical exegetes who have not moved away from the methodological assumption that the post-Easter "sociological" framework of reference must initially occupy the foreground and that any suspicion of the inauthenticity of a synoptic Jesus-saying or narrative should be taken more seriously than the opposite. With this firm stance in critical priorities, there is one reason which up until now we have not considered and which might play an important role. Bultmann in discussion with his pupils, who wanted again to attach a theological significance to the historical question, formulated the point clearly: "The greatest embarrassment in trying to establish a picture of Jesus' character is that we cannot know how Jesus understood his end, his death."[38] If we really do not know Jesus' attitude toward his own death, then the historical perspectives and the post-Easter faith perspectives, according to which the cross and resurrection are the actual saving events, are poles apart on the most decisive point. Continuity in the eschatological message and in the tradition of the circle of the disciples refers then only to questions of secondary importance and increases the theological problematic rather than solving it. In this case the dilemma inevitably arises, as we have already seen in the introduction: Is salvation granted to us through the message of the kingdom of God at hand or through faith in the expiatory death of one who represents us? Or indeed are both promises problematic, because they stand in no inner agreement with one another? In order to escape this contradiction, Bultmann, precisely in the interest of Christian faith, completely dissociated and separated the kerygma of the early community at a theological level from the historical question about the pre-Easter Jesus. The question raised in the introductory section about the relationship between eschatological and crucifixion doctrines of salvation proves consequently to be not only an important individual problem of content. The whole problematic of exegetical method depends, to a large extent, on the answer to it.

---

37. Ibid., 295.
38. Bultmann, "Das Verhältnis der urchristlichen Botschaft zum historischen Jesus," in Bultmann (1967), 452.

9. The problematic concerning the understanding of Jesus' death is finally even linked, as Bultmann in the above-mentioned discussion also powerfully formulated it, with the problematic of critical research in general. According to him, historical research can never reach and uncover a truth which is capable of speaking to people through their conscience.[39] Historical research deals with an objectifying way of seeing which rules out precisely that illumination by which Jesus' objective historicity is given a kerygmatic significance. Behind this opposition of Bultmann's lie conceptions from the philosophy of history of the nineteenth century, according to which the purely objective facts have to be distinguished from the interpretation of the facts and kept separate from them. Interpretation is always a more or less subjective light shone on the facts, but not itself coming from them. More recent historical-critical exegesis has to some extent moved away from these ideas from the philosophy of history of the last century, without fundamentally coming to grips with them.[40] We must therefore briefly go into this question.

The Kingdom of God and Scholarly Methods

If a first encounter with the message of Jesus leads to the conclusion that he spoke of a new action of God in history, then the question arises directly whether such an unusual claim can be true. All reflections on method must be put to serve this central question, and there is no appropriate exegetical method which can be carried through independently of this question. The answer we find will determine the manner of further research into his person and his work. For if we consider his claim not to be worthy of belief, then he has to be classified as one in that series of cases of extreme religious conviction which we come across in other figures from the history of religion. In this case, research must make use of those methods which are applied in other disciplines of the human sciences. It can give its full attention to finding out how such an experience could arise, what personal, cultural, social, and political factors were at work, and how to explain that this experience was able to provoke so great a historical effect. When the questions are formulated this way, the value of the explanation for scholars lies in offering as coherent a picture as possible of the interplay of the factors mentioned, and one which is in overall agreement with other similar experiences.

But things are very different if Jesus' claim is taken as worthy of belief. In this case the intention of research must primarily be to search out and present the inner coherence in what was proclaimed by Jesus as

---

39. Ibid., 454–69; see also Robinson (1967), 102–12, 135–46.
40. The systematic work of W. Pannenberg represents an important attempt at a solution. We will probe this attempt later.

the action of God. Absolutely no predominant role should be accorded to the remaining historical, cultural, social, and political factors. The message of Jesus consequently faces scholarly research with a dilemma toward which it must adopt a clear stance if it does not wish to let the answer be dominated by hidden presuppositions. For if the usual historical methods are followed with regard to his claim, then already, at least indirectly, a negative judgment about it has almost been made, because research has tried to achieve coherence of explanation from the interplay of the psychological and sociological factors mentioned and must categorize the talk of "God's action" as like any other religious idea. If one trusts Jesus' claim, however, then "God's action" is not just some human idea, but the central event determining everything, on the basis of which the destiny of Jesus is to be interpreted. Between a real "action of God" and a divine action understood as merely a religious idea there is a profound difference. If one accepts a real action, then it is important above all to notice the reaction of those spoken to and to ask how the action develops in view of their reply. If one takes it, on the other hand, as a general religious idea, then it is necessary to investigate how this idea is related to other similar or antithetical ideas and what extra-ideational factors were at work so that this or that idea found acceptance. Thus the question of which investigative method is to be used comes down to a prior decision concerning "God's action."

In view of the unavoidable decision, we choose a similar procedure to the one Anselm of Canterbury tried out in his doctrine of redemption, although based on different assumptions. He started out from the insight that the objective formulation of the question — if not also the emotional one — in the step from unbelief to belief is finally the same as in the step from a belief which is geared toward (biblical) pictures to a belief based on understanding. In both cases there are crises to go through — Anselm speaks of a method of despair — in which familiar opinions, habits of thought, and action are subjected to criticism. Starting from this assumption, the bishop of Canterbury was able, at the level of direct argumentation, to put in parentheses the truths of faith which concerned his theme — *remoto Christo*, "apart from Christ" — and allow himself to be led only indirectly by the broader context of the biblical problematic.

My method may appear initially to be contrary to Anselm's; but it is finally similar. From the beginning we shall take Jesus' claim as hypothetically true. From this presupposition we will ask whether and what sort of coherence is manifested in what Jesus spoke of as the action of God. Only in connection with the Easter reports will the question about truth be put directly rather than hypothetically. It can be better answered from the standpoint of the end (Easter), for in the meanwhile it will have been shown more clearly what the "action of God" actually means in the destiny of Jesus.

Given this way of proceeding, we cannot stay entirely with any established method and therefore have to advance very carefully. We must keep looking out for those pointers established by the historical-critical methods, since at least behind these there already lies a long history of self-criticism, and in this fashion the decisive problems will not be passed over. At the same time we may hope that our dramatic model, strongly inspired by the dramatic history of the Old Testament, may to some extent do justice to what Jesus spoke of as "God's action."

The problem of Jesus' messianic self-consciousness, from which our excursion into methodological reflection started out, directly lines up with this cautious preliminary probing. The problem shows that one should not approach the historical and theological question with fixed ideas. Messianic representations in the Jewish tradition at the time of Jesus were so various and open that it is absolutely impossible to compare him adequately with *one* of these possible "pictures." Even less should one assume a priori that his message and his self-understanding remained in all points unaltered during his ministry. If he was really determined by what was to happen in the dawning kingdom of God and knew himself for certain to be sent by the Father, then the deepest and most inaccessible point of his identity must lie in his current, new experience of God, and not in some images conditioned by the history of religion. E. Fuchs has explicated by means of the parables that Jesus lived completely in the present and was borne along by the conviction that "everything has its time."[41] If this is relevant, then it must also be taken into account that he was not constrained to do, to relinquish, and to proclaim the same thing on each occasion of his ministry.

---

41. Fuchs (1960), 339. In this "defusing" of the future sayings what matters is "neither their existential reinterpretation...nor the question of a 'between-time' spoken of by Jesus between his resurrection and his return..., but the determination that both belong at the same time to his entire work and conduct: the expectation of the One coming without fail and the peace of the One who without haste realizes his mission in each day that is given (see Luke 13:32f.)" (Balthasar [1973–83] 2/2:83).

Second Act:
The Rejection of the Kingdom of God and Judgment

Jesus spoke of God's coming as a coming of goodness, and yet in his proclamation we find harsh words of judgment. The connection between these two apparently opposing messages constitutes the big, unsettling problem in all theological outlines of the doctrine of redemption. But the judgment sayings raise questions which have an effect beyond the theological realm, and they have led to the quite frequent reproach that Jesus — despite his message of love for our enemies — showed an attitude of intolerance, and even serious faults of character. Thus, e.g., W. Hirsch thought it necessary to make the following judgment: "No one is more intolerant toward his opponents than he. He wants to see not only his 'enemies,' but each person who refuses to believe in all his eccentricities, punished by 'eternal damnation,' and he wants to throw them into the water with a millstone around their neck."[1] Also the well-known English philosopher B. Russell thought that Jesus had a serious fault of character because he believed in hell and repeatedly showed a vengeful rage against those people who did not wish to listen to his preaching.[2] There is consequently a pressing problematic around the judgment and hell sayings of Jesus; but this is for the most part not taken sufficiently seriously in modern exegesis. Often the corresponding Gospel utterances are passed over without further commentary, or they are attributed, with more or less justification, to the post-Easter community, without explicitly saying what this achieves from the theological point of view. If one is working on a predominantly post-Easter origin of the judgment sayings, it should at least be said what authority is given to them in this case. Are they optional, because they don't come from Jesus, or do they all have the same binding force? If one accepts the latter, then the tension with the message of God's goodness remains.

The judgment and hell sayings are an inevitable touchstone of whether what we have gathered together up to this point about the proclamation of Jesus is coherent and conclusive, or whether the result achieved so far is only the product of a one-sided selection of texts. Through the confrontation of the basileia message with the judgment sayings it must once again be shown how the proclamation of God as Abba is really to be understood. Has this proclamation despite everything a dark, terrifying "hidden face," which cannot be harmonized with the message of goodness? What would be the theological

---

1. Hirsch, *Religion und Civilisation vom Standpunkt des Psychiaters* (1910), 133; cited in Strube (1972), 116.
2. Russell (1969), 30f.

consequences of having to work with this possibility and thus with a Janus-headed countenance of God?

The Situation of Rejection

> If the Gospels, especially Matthew, clearly fall into two halves —
> into a first half with the proclamation of the kingdom of God,
> and a second with the apocalyptic announcements and the Pas-
> sion — then it is because between these two parts there lies the
> negative event, heavy with consequences. This negative event is
> that those to whom the proclamation is directly addressed behave
> indifferently or contemptuously, so that it is immediately stifled.[3]

This judgment of René Girard, reached from a systematic perspective, can be formulated more precisely by means of detailed historical-critical work. A careful analysis of those logia of Jesus which were handed down in common between Matthew and Luke (source Q) leads A. Polag to the following division and distinction:

> The pattern according to which the different utterances can be or-
> ganized is not the thought-model for a state of affairs, nor even
> for the description of a personality, but a process, the course of an
> event: the bringing of a message and a decision provoked by the
> messenger on the part of the one addressed. This event considered
> as a whole contains a shift. For in the collection of the sayings two
> levels of utterance can be distinguished in relation to the situation
> of the speaker. On the one side there is the situation of the public
> proclamation of the message of salvation with promise and ex-
> pectation; on the other it must be assumed that the overwhelming
> majority of those addressed rejected the message and the speaker
> therefore stands in a situation of rejection.[4]

From this distinction, which takes account of a second event, of a negative type, beside the event of the dawning kingdom of God, the conviction grows that the salvation and judgment sayings should not be considered on the same level. The suggestion is that the former are to be interpreted as the unconditional and unambiguous command of God, while the latter express the unavoidable consequences of negative human decisions.

Polag's distinction has not met with universal agreement. Thus, e.g., L. Oberlinner thinks that "such a periodization" is "neither meaning-ful in itself" nor does it "account for the facts which are historically somewhat in need of verification," and consequent further investigation

---

3. Girard (1983), 211.
4. Polag (1977), 118.

would show "far-reaching consequences for the proclamation of Jesus itself."[5] The last remark is certainly to the point, but perhaps it is just in this way that problems which are otherwise overlooked or which remain open are brought to a solution. Oberlinner tries to justify the argument that Polag's distinction is not in itself meaningful in the following way:

> One can only meaningfully compare, as similar and comparable, a period or length of time which is characterized or qualified by relationship to the person who acts — in this case the time of the "offer" — with another length of time, equally determined by this person and his effect. The period of the offer can therefore only be meaningfully replaced by the ending and/or refusal of the offer. In the same way "acceptance" is the only appropriate preceding period to "rejection."[6]

What at first strikes one in this line of argument is that it tacitly absolutizes a unilinear thought model. If one starts, on the contrary, with a dramatic model, then no difficulties arise against the assumption that the first period of time is characterized by the action of one protagonist, and the following one especially by the reaction of others. But even this is not the decisive point. What is more striking is that Oberlinner overlooks the moment in Polag's model where the decision is made, takes insufficient note of its explicit talk of two "levels,"[7] and transforms the problematic into that of two successive periods of time. Certainly, the decision model can in some circumstances be associated with the two times, but this is not at all necessary since the situation or the level of open proclamation can also exist simultaneously with the situation or level of rejection.

Though Oberlinner thinks that Polag's distinction does not make sense, the reverse can be shown, that it is actually necessary if one wants to hold on to what historical-critical exegesis has developed with a reasonable consensus in the last three decades concerning the peculiar nature of the basileia message. The peculiarity of this message is that Jesus broke with the religious thinking of Israel to the extent that with him salvation and repentance exchanged places,[8] and he offered the sinner God's forgiveness, irrespective of whether the sinner was willing to repent or unprepared to do so.[9] But this new content of the message necessarily allocates a new place to the decision and the judgment sayings. Whereas the preaching of the prophets contains an alternative

---

5. Oberlinner (1980), 93.
6. Ibid., 93f.
7. Polag (1977), 118–22.
8. See Bornkamm (1968), 76.
9. See Merklein (1978), 204.

("if you repent, you will find grace; if not, the judgment will be upon you"), the message of Jesus initially disregards the readiness to repent or the hardheartedness of the sinner and consequently *at this level* excludes the alternative "of rejection for not repenting." Preceding, and at first independent of, the actual human decision, it offers to oppressed humankind the pure mercy of God. If, nevertheless, it is a call to decision, as is always emphasized even in critical exegesis, then the pure offer of grace must be clearly distinguished from an arbitrary offer. It does not presuppose conversion, but wants to awaken it, and where the offer of pure grace is rejected a person falls prey to all the consequences of his or her own decision. With Jesus, grace and judgment are not two alternative possibilities within one single appeal; the predominance of grace is shown by the fact that the offer of grace takes place in advance of human choice. The problematic of judgment, on the contrary, emerges from the other side, from the human decision actually made. *In the framework of the message of Jesus, the judgment sayings can therefore be taken completely seriously — without any weakening of the salvation sayings — only if they are related to a second situation of proclamation, which is distinguished from the first by the human rejection of the offer of salvation that is given without prerequisites.* The two situations are, contrary to what Oberlinner thinks, opposed to each other not as offer and refusal of the offer, but as offer and demonstration of the consequences of rejection of the offer. The transition to the second situation is not made by Jesus, but it results from the reaction of his hearers. Jesus only makes clear the theological consequences of their decision.

The question about the moment of rejection, which, historically speaking, can hardly be answered with any precision and which theologically is of no decisive importance, can remain open. Mussner's thesis about the "Galilean crisis" expresses one of the possible answers.[10] But it is also equally possible that Jesus held on to the proclamation of salvation right up to the end, and at the same time, in the face of the first expressions of rejection, revealed its inner consequences through the judgment sayings. Finally, the assumption which best fits the evidence of the synoptic Gospels should not be a priori brushed aside as historically and psychologically impossible, namely, that Jesus came upon strong resistance very early on from the Pharisees, but, despite this, continued at first with his unconditional proclamation of salvation while at the same time beginning to talk of judgment. In this case it would have to be assumed that Jesus quickly saw just how his proclamation of salvation met with an unyielding reception. But this idea does not, as we will see,

---

10. Mussner (1973), 238–52.

contradict the basileia message; it is thoroughly anchored in the synoptic Gospels and closely bound up with the language of parable (see Mark 4:10–12 and parallels), so that one cannot on principle deny Jesus this insight. The tendency to attribute to the post-Easter community all sayings which speak of a clear rejection purely for that reason betrays in any case an unbalanced judgment.

The synoptic Gospels report clear judgment sayings on the towns of Galilee (Chorazin, Bethsaida, Capharnaum) in which Jesus was particularly active (Luke 10:13–15). A harsher judgment was spoken against these towns than against the pagan towns of Tyre and Sidon. In a different judgment saying, the generation of Jesus' time is compared with the Queen of the South, who had come to listen to Solomon, and contrasted with the inhabitants of Nineveh, who were converted at the preaching of Jonah. One who was greater than Jonah and Solomon spoke to them, but even so they did not bear the same fruit (Luke 11:29–32). In connection with these direct sayings of judgment on Jesus' audience, other logia and parables should be noticed which interpret in more detail the consequences of rejection of the basileia message.

"O Jerusalem, Jerusalem, killing the prophets and stoning those who are sent to you! How often would I have gathered your children about me as a hen gathers her chicks under her wing, but you would not!" (Matt. 23:37) In this saying, Jesus expresses in retrospect very clearly that from the beginning his whole activity was directed toward the gathering of Israel. Rejection was therefore not merely a private matter of individuals, affecting only their personal salvation; it went directly against his task of proclamation, his will to bring about the gathering. If God really acted in a new way in the ministry of Jesus, then what was at stake for his hearers was not merely their individual salvation. The generation which he targeted with his proclamation was given a *role in the history of salvation*. Even the parable of the wicked winegrowers sets out that the hostile reaction against the son was aimed at possession of the vineyard, by which, it is clear from Isaiah 5:1–7, is meant the chosen people of God. The interest of this story consequently lay not merely in the individual fate of the wicked winegrowers but equally in the son's lot and in the question of for whom the vineyard bears fruit. The winegrowers speak: "This is the heir; come, let us kill him, and the inheritance will be ours" (Mark 12:7 and parallels). What is involved is, in the first place, the success or failure of the mission of the son and only then the question of human wickedness and violence.

Many exegetes object that Jesus would have had difficulty in establishing a *definitive* rejection, and for that reason the clear judgment sayings should rather be associated with the post-Easter community. Against this, however, it should be said that even in the first years after

Easter there had not yet occurred any definitive separation from the Jewish community. If this line of argument were to be followed, one would have to postpone the origin of the judgment sayings till a later time — roughly after the destruction of Jerusalem — which would throw up completely new anomalies in another direction. But, above all, the objection is formulated against a horizon of understanding which does not match up with what we have seen so far as the specific nature of the basileia message.

Here is a concrete instance of what we spoke about in the excursion into methodological reflection under the heading "God's actions." If Jesus had only announced a general idea or doctrine about God, it would obviously not have been easy for him to establish whether and how far this idea was accepted by his hearers. But if his proclamation was essentially an event, an action of God, which had its kairos, its moment of fulfillment, then things are quite different. One can often discern quickly whether an event succeeds or not. Now, we have seen how in his healing activity Jesus trusted in the communicative power of his mountain-moving faith. He must consequently have been able quickly to discover whether "the spark of faith" jumped across and reached people's inner being or whether it was only accepted insofar as it corresponded to their immediate interests. Even in his attempt at the gathering of Israel, he hardly needed very long to establish whether a new dawning was taking place or whether the old forces, which had defeated the prophets, were essentially still at work. One result of the new type of proclamation was that it must have quickly become clear whether people would let themselves be moved from their former world or whether after a superficial reaction nothing would finally change. The fact of rejection is therefore largely independent of the question of how decidedly, hesitantly, or noncommittally the individual hearers of Jesus acted. Because Jesus' task was thwarted, for whatever reasons, rejection actually took place.

The judgment sayings, which speak of resistance to Jesus' mission, disclose the actual consequences of open or more indifferent rejection. *If the kingdom of God was dawning in his activity and his proclamation, then any human will which opposed Jesus' will for a new gathering blocked the fate of the basileia itself.* The kingdom was caught up in a dramatic situation, since it was on the one hand unconditionally promised by God and yet on the other hand it was turned down by those whom it would have embraced and who should have contributed to its complete arrival. As God's action was oriented toward including people's actions, rejection raised not only an ethical problem. It put in question what "God's action" can mean at all with these presuppositions. It was the aim of the kingdom of God to unite wills, the will of

God with the will of people, and people among themselves as brothers and sisters of Jesus (Mark 3:31–35 and parallels). But in fact initially the exact opposite occurred. The will of people stood clearly against the will of Jesus: "how often *would I have*..., but *you would not*" (Matt. 23:37).

Diagnosis of the Opposing Will: Lying and Violence

In that saying where Jesus so explicitly spoke of the wishes of those who opposed his task of assembly, he also gave a precise description of the forces hostile to him. "Jerusalem, Jerusalem, you kill the prophets and stone those who are sent to you. How often would I have..." (Matt. 23:37). Jerusalem, the holy and chosen city, in which the "holy people" and the "redeemed of the LORD" (Isa. 62:1–12) were meant to come together and which was destined to be a place of peace for the nations (see Isa. 60:1–22; Zech. 9:9–11), was experienced by Jesus in a very different way, namely, as a city of murderers of the prophets. The contrast between the promise and the judgment which he delivered could hardly be greater. This opposition invites us to look for a deeper interpretation of Jesus' words of judgment. Before asking how Jesus came to his judgment, we must take note of other utterances which point in a similar direction.

In the parable of the wicked winegrowers, Israel's leaders are addressed as those who systematically persecute and kill the master's servants and finally even the last messenger, the beloved son (Mark 12:1–12 and parallels). In this parable, rejection with violence appears as the recurring denominator in the wicked actions of the winegrowers (leaders of Israel), and from this point of view a continuity is suggested between the fate of the prophets and that of Jesus. The problem of violence thereby holds a structural importance for the understanding of the entire Scriptures.

In a further saying of Jesus, the problem of violence is shown as central: "Therefore also the Wisdom of God[11] said, 'I will send them prophets and apostles, some of whom they will kill and persecute,' that the blood of all the prophets, shed from the foundation of the world, may be required of this generation — from the blood of Abel to the blood of Zechariah, who perished between the altar and the sanctuary. Yes, I tell you, it will be requited to this generation" (Luke 11:49–51). The mention of Wisdom in Jesus' saying makes visible a connection with tradition. The prophets of Israel reproached leaders and people over and

---

11. In Matthew this statement is not introduced as a wisdom saying, but is spoken directly by Jesus (Matt. 23:34–36). See Christ (1970), 120–35, on the question as to whether the version in Luke or Matthew is more original, whether it concerns a Jewish wisdom saying, and whether Jesus or the primitive community first formulated it.

over again most harshly, not just for idolatry but also on account of oppression, violence, and the spilling of blood,[12] and for that reason they
were often themselves persecuted. Hence in the Deuteronomic view of
history, the theme of the violent fate of the prophets was developed and
used to bring out the systematic obstinacy of Israel toward the messengers of God,[13] and this theme joined up with the Jewish tradition
of Wisdom already in pre–New Testament times.[14] In these texts, violent action is described as the recurring denominator in humankind's
behavior toward those sent by God. The saying of Jesus takes up this
tradition and adds to it two further decisive elements. A comprehensive
view of the past goes back to the beginning of the world and sees how
the history of violence already began before Israel, with Cain. In the
problematic of judgment a similar broadening of horizon occurs, taking
in all individual groups or nations, and placing the origin of violence
where the history of humankind — after paradise — had its beginning.
Over this whole history, and this is the second element, a judgment is
pronounced which is imminent, since it stands over the present generation, to whom, in consideration of this, a special role is consequently
given in salvation history. On this generation "all the righteous blood
shed on earth... " (Matt. 23:35) is "avenged." The imminent expectation in the basileia message thus corresponds — and this is surprising
at first — to an *imminent expectation of judgment,* which draws in the
whole of past history.

A saying of Jesus about the scribes and Pharisees offers us a further
look at the question of judgment:

> "Woe to you, scribes and Pharisees, hypocrites, for you build the
> prophets tombs and adorn the monuments of the righteous, saying,
> 'If we had lived in the days of the fathers, we would not have taken
> part with them in shedding the blood of the prophets.' So you wit-
> ness against yourselves that you are sons of those who murdered
> the prophets. Fill up, then, the measure of your fathers! You ser-
> pents, you brood of vipers! How are you to escape being sentenced
> to Gehenna?" (Matt. 23:29–33)

Besides the decisiveness of the reproach, what is striking in this saying
is the way in which it links up with a Jewish custom,[15] but nevertheless seems to have no parallels in Jewish literature. Its particular style

---

12. For example: "For as often as I speak I cry out 'Violence and destruction!' " (Jer. 20:8). See Schwager (1978), 58–63, 100–17.
13. See Steck (1967).
14. Ibid., 164, 208.
15. On the historical question of the prophets' graves see Jeremias (1958).

of argumentation (turning back the opponents' actions against themselves) suggests that it is from Jesus himself.[16] This saying is also of great importance since it uncovers a mechanism of exculpation, by which true self-knowledge is prevented. Precisely those central historical events which should have enlightened Israel about itself and which should have brought home the necessity for conversion were used to camouflage them. With the erection of monuments and with the affirmation that they would have acted differently from their fathers, the Pharisees denied any solidarity between themselves and their fathers and put themselves — by their words — on the side of the prophets, yet without being able to give a credible explanation as to why they were better than their fathers. As all Israel's writings show how the people failed again and again, one could conclude from them only the fundamental necessity for conversion and the awareness of a deeply rooted human tendency to self-deception. If the Pharisees distanced themselves from the long history of their own people, then (like most critics of the past) they thought themselves fundamentally superior to their fathers and claimed to be qualitatively better. If they were not at the same time able to show in a convincing and credible way why they were free from that self-deception which they established so clearly in their fathers, then their position became more than questionable. However, as they were now themselves about to persecute a preacher who spoke of the necessity for conversion, thus doing exactly the same as their fathers did, their claim to be fundamentally different from them became thoroughly groundless and ambiguous. They made the victims of violence, who unambiguously revealed the nation's failures, into an object of veneration and thereby neutralized the question about their own behavior. They put themselves arrogantly above their fathers and assumed without verifiable reason that they would have acted differently from them, although they were about to do exactly the same thing. It was in their claim, which arose from a totally false judgment about themselves, that there lay the deepest cause of the hypocrisy for which Jesus reproached them (Matt. 23:13, 15, 23, 25, 29), for he certainly did not primarily mean individual, conscious lies and distortions. His pronouncements of woe are about something more fundamental, about the instinctive self-deception from which many individual wrong judgments necessarily arise.

The saying about the tombs and monuments for prophets and the just is aimed particularly at a definite way of handling Scripture. It criticizes a type of exegesis which makes the failure of others a cause for self-glorification. It thereby also puts in question later Christian exegesis which — from the time of the fathers of the church onward — could not

---

16. See Matt. 12:11, 27; 21:24f.

do enough to condemn the Pharisees (and the synagogue) and yet did not notice that it was falling into exactly the same mechanism which Jesus had uncovered in them.[17] But it also stands critically against the sort of contemporary exegesis which wants rather to rehabilitate the Pharisees and for that reason accuses the early community (or Jesus). With all these interpretations, the same mechanism of exculpation is at work, evading the problem of violence in their own actions. This mechanism, as we have already seen briefly in the first part, plays a dominant role in history, and it should for that reason be used to put an important self-critical question to the historical-critical method. Does this method only have the tools to criticize others, or is it able to turn criticism back onto its own way of proceeding?

Besides the judgment sayings and the pronouncements of woe, the problematic of violence is found especially in the so-called apocalyptic texts. Since J. Weiss and A. Schweitzer, many have seen in them impressive evidence that Jesus was trapped in very time-bound and unrealistic ideas. Thus they thought it necessary to demythologize his sayings in this vein from the higher standpoint of modern knowledge and to reinterpret them. But are the apocalyptic texts in fact so mythological? They speak of a shaking of the forces of heaven and a coming of the Son of Man on the clouds (Mark 13:24–27 and parallels). Apart from these brief but ultimately austere words, there are only descriptions of things that happen on this earth. There is talk of leading astray and poverty, of wars, rebellions, and famine, of strife in families and above all of persecutions (Mark 13:3–20 and parallels).[18]

Does the content of this part of the apocalyptic texts, which, compared with the description of the (cosmic) end-events, is much more comprehensive and also clearly distinguished from those in the Gospels,[19] not largely coincide with what has continually happened in the history of Israel? Do the apocalyptic texts contain in essentials anything different from a description of those forces which — in contrast to the new community in the kingdom of God — actually dominate history? If it has often been thought that the apocalyptic speeches would betray a mythological worldview, one can also turn this suspicion around and ask those who judge in this way whether they are not continuing to hold on to marginal elements and losing sight of the crucial utterances. Does not the way in which apocalyptic texts have been treated over the last decades, which have been full of war and other forms of violence, betray

---

17. See Girard (1983), 168–72.

18. "The definitive point of view is that the Gospels do not ascribe to God the apocalyptic violence predicted by them" (Girard [1983], 192).

19. See Conzelmann (1959b), 215.

something of that exegesis which Jesus criticized in the saying about the tombs of the prophets?

Even if post-Easter influences are to be assumed in the description of the end-time, what emerges is absolutely no justification for ascribing everything to the theology of the early community. The essential elements fit coherently into the situation of rejection and the judgment sayings of Jesus. They make clear the important opposition between the laws of the world (see Matt. 20:25) and of God's kingdom, and they highlight, in agreement with the prophetic proclamation, the situation of judgment upon the world. Without this very realistic view of history, the call to decision and the message of judgment risk being too quickly spiritualized and thus finally dissipated.

Doubling of Sin and Hell

According to the great faith-tradition of Israel, the rejection of a message from God does not leave people just as they were before. Rather, the negative decision has an effect on the one who makes it and, with repetition, leads to obduracy. The Egyptian pharaoh fell prey to it in the face of the repeated requests and demands of Moses (Exod. 5–11). The proclamation of Isaiah, as was explicitly noted, had the same effect (Isa. 6:8–13), and Jeremiah also met increasing, obstinate resistance. Must not rejection of the message of God's kingdom have resulted in a similar or an even more definite hardening?

The idea of an intensification of sin is frequently found in the synoptic Gospels, even if it is presented by means of a whole range of images, which may be an important indication that we are dealing with a broad tradition. There is the word-picture of an impure spirit, which leaves a person, but because it cannot find a place it returns to its original "house," which has in the meantime been cleaned up, and brings with it seven other spirits, who are even worse than itself. From this comes the conclusion: "Thus in the end it will be worse for that person than at the first. So it shall be likewise with this evil generation" (Matt. 12:45). If the verbal image makes a direct reference at the end to the present "wicked generation," then it is at least being emphasized by the evangelists that the proclamation and impact of Jesus upon "this generation" has led to an intensification of their disastrous situation. He began with driving out demons and cleaning up like new many a devastated "house." The rejection of his message may have been connected with relapse and may have effected a worsening of the previous condition.

The parable is introduced in Matthew on the grounds that it is not given to all to understand the mystery of the kingdom of God. To this surprising utterance is immediately added a reason which to our ears is not only just as surprising, but downright repugnant: "For to whoever has will more be given, and that in abundance; but from whoever does not have, even that will be taken away" (Matt. 13:12). Does not this measuring with a double measure, which is elevated to a principle of conduct, directly contradict the behavior of Jesus, who devoted himself to sinners and outcasts and who took on precisely those who have nothing in the eyes of God? Before we venture to a judgment, we must first of all take note that the saying that is repugnant for us turns up in two other places with almost the same wording. The double measure is found on the one hand in the parable of the money entrusted by the master, where the one who has only one talent has even this taken away from him and given to the first one who already has ten talents (Matt. 25:14–30; see also Luke 19:11–27); on the other hand it is mentioned in Mark in connection with a warning of Jesus about human judgment. Precisely this connection may offer the best help for a deeper understanding. The warning runs: "Take heed what you hear! By the measure you give it will be measured to you, and more will be added. For to whoever has will more be given, and from whoever has not, even that will be taken away" (Mark 4:24–25). Jesus begins his appeal with the warning to listen carefully to what is to come. So it seems to be about something that one can easily miss. He than stresses that it is people themselves who set up the measure by which it is allotted to them. Being judged does not involve an arbitrary laying down of punishments by a higher authority, but rather the measure which individuals use for themselves determines what is bestowed on them, and how. The saying of Jesus is valid in the positive and negative sense, as becomes clear above all through his further warnings against judging: "Judge not that you be not judged! For as you judge, so will you be judged, and the measure you give will be the measure you get" (Matt. 7:1–2). Judging is a dangerous thing, in which one can easily get caught, for those who condemn another lay down the measure which will be applied to them. So it is always individuals who determine the measure according to which something happens to them, whether it be for good or for evil.

This image is found also in the parable of the money entrusted by the master. In this, the first two servants are praised by their master because they acted in a way appropriate to the gifts which they had received. The entrusted money did not remain with them unfruitfully, but it led to a doubling. The third certainly did nothing wrong, but he buried the talent that he had received. In rendering his account, he justifies his strange action by using what he thinks he knows of his master: "Master, I knew you to be a harsh man; you reap where you did not sow and gather where you did not winnow. So I was afraid, and I went and hid your money in the ground" (Matt. 25:24–25). The master in his judgment does not correct the picture that the servant has drawn of him, but he uses it precisely as a norm by which he judges the behavior of his servant: "You knew that I reap where I did not sow and gather where I did not winnow? Then you ought to have invested my money with the bankers, so when I returned I could have received what was my own with interest" (Matt. 25:26–27). The master judges his servant only according to that picture which the servant himself has made of him. In the slightly altered version of Luke, the master actually says explicitly: *"I will condemn you out of your own mouth"* (Luke 19:22). The first two servants acted in accordance with the experience that they had of the master. They received from him and were led to increase what they had received. But the third had his fixed picture of the master, which could no longer be altered even despite the fact that he received a talent. Thus he acted according to the norm and the picture that he already carried within himself, i.e., according to the picture of a strict master, who had to be feared. Because he did not let go of this picture — despite the talent he had received — he was judged according to it. In his defense before the master he laid down the measure by which he was measured and by means of which he lost again what he previously received. The whole incident with the three servants is finally summed up by the master in the words: "For everyone who has, to him will be given and he will have in abundance; but whoever has not, even what he has will be taken away" (Matt. 25:29). The context shows with unusual clarity that by the double allocation no arbitrary arrangement from outside, favoring the rich over against the poor, is meant. Those who have are those who see that they have received and who by this grateful recognition become capable of receiving yet more. Those who do not have are those who refuse to recognize what they have received as such, who make for themselves a harsh picture of the giver and trap themselves in the role of self-defense. They become thereby less and less capable of receiving and fall into a mechanism of obduracy.

The understanding which we have achieved concerning the haves and the have-nots leads us back to Jesus' speech about parables which is introduced and justified by the saying in question (Matt. 13:12 and parallels; see also Mark 4:25). The parables therefore set in motion a double process. Whoever sees becomes through them even more seeing; and whoever is blind becomes obdurate through them. The parables attempt to open up a new vision of those everyday things which are in themselves recognizable by everyone, but which not all see. Jesus made his new teaching clear from everyday experience also in other connections. He justified the demand for love of one's enemy from an experience which is accessible to everyone, but from which normally no lessons are drawn, or quite different ones: "for he [the heavenly Father] makes his sun rise on the evil and on the good, and he sends rain on the just and on the unjust" (Matt. 5:45). Looking at the sun and the rain could teach people something crucial, as also looking at the birds of the sky, which do not sow, and at the lilies of the field, which do not work (Matt. 6:26, 28). From the experience of how God cares for them, people ought to learn to let go of their own cares and trust the heavenly Father. Similarly with the experience of the sower, the weeds among the wheat, the mustard seed, the leaven, the buried treasure, the pearl of great value, and the fish net thrown out into the sea (Matt. 13:1–53). All these experiences of everyday life can, when they are read correctly, give witness to the kindly Father, his proximate coming and dealings with people. Even if the new community in the kingdom of God contrasts completely with the old laws of the human world, it is however not something unrealistic. It only needs a new look to see signs of it everywhere in our everyday world. If people defend themselves against this new vision of reality, if they remain in their old positions of fear and self-defense, then they necessarily defend themselves also against what Jesus brings. Thus they lock themselves even more into their old world and give themselves up to a process of judgment, which runs according to self-chosen and stubbornly defended norms. Hence the parables lead those who hear them, and yet do not hear, into a process of self-induced hardening of heart (Mark 4:10–12 and parallels).

The connection sketched out between the goodness of God in his dawning kingdom and the harsh words of judgment is confirmed in an impressive manner by the parable of the unforgiving servant. The master in this parable sets at the outset no condition for his servant, to whom he remits a gigantic debt without any return deed, and links with his action only the expectation that the fortunate man in turn treat his fellow servants in accordance with the experience that was granted to him. But this expectation is not fulfilled, and the servant, who had to pay nothing back, clings slavishly in his dealings with his fellow servant to the old norm of payment and repayment, so he is called back and made to explain himself: "and should not you have had mercy on your fellow servant, as I had mercy on you?" (Matt. 18:33). The debt already remitted to him is now counted against him again. The master, who at the beginning was pure goodness, behaves after the servant's refusal precisely according to the norm which the servant — despite his experience of generosity — applied in his treatment of his fellow servant. As the servant had his fellow servant thrown into prison, "till he should pay the debt," so the master gives him over to the torturers "till he should pay all his debt" (Matt. 18:30, 34) Jesus concludes the parable with the clear application: "So also my heavenly Father will do to each one of you, if you do not forgive your brother from your heart" (Matt. 18:35).

A similar teaching is found also in Luke directly following Jesus' warning: "Be merciful, even as your Father is merciful!" (Luke 6:36). Certainly, the positive precedent is emphasized here, but precisely in this way it becomes clear that the dramatic process of doubling and intensification comes from the picture of God and the experience of God: "give, and it will be given unto you . . . " (Luke 6:38). Giving sets off an overflowing positive dynamic, while condemnation and ingratitude result in the opposite dynamic, which leads to complete self-absorption. This is why people should not fear judgment, despite their weakness, as long as they take notice of this one thing: "Judge not, and you will not be judged; condemn not, and you will not be condemned; release one another from debt, and your debt will also be forgiven" (Luke 6:37).

Wherever people are ready to forgive and to receive there they will be given more, and they will become ever more able to give themselves. Wherever they are not ready to receive, and remain trapped in the norms of payment and repayment, there they will lose again even what they have received, and they hand themselves over to a process of judgment, based on repayment and payment down to the last penny. As each of us is a debtor, no one can endure this process; the demand for repayment becomes ever greater and the end of this escalating process can only be hell. Thus the unmerciful creditor ends up with the "torturers" (Matt. 18:34), and in the parable of the money entrusted by the master the third servant is thrown out into "outer darkness."

The sayings of judgment and hell, insofar as they are related to a new situation in the proclamation of Jesus, are not in opposition to the message of the dawning of the kingdom of God, and there is no regression because of them into the old norms of retribution, but rather they show how radical the basileia's call to conversion is. Only with the judgment sayings does it become clear what decision people are faced with and how disastrous the old and apparently proven "wisdom" of retribution finally is. Jesus' call to conversion is consequently not first of all about better obedience to one or the other commandment, but about the choice between two visions of the whole of reality and between two basic ways of behaving. Does a person accept the invitation to the king's wedding feast, and thereby take over God's new standard (the wedding garment), or does the person persist in former activities and ways of behaving, which necessarily set off a process of self-judgment? If someone becomes involved with that God proclaimed by Jesus and made available to experience through his parables, his healing, his driving out of demons, and his treatment of sinners, then there opens up for that person a world with new "rules of the game." However, the empty formula of a declaration of belief in the words of Jesus is not sufficient for this step (see Luke 6:46);[20] what is decisive is whether the new standard of God's action also determines one's own actions toward one's neighbors.

The negative dynamic of judgment can also be made clear from the dispute that Jesus had with his opponents over the driving out of demons. The Pharisees could not dispute the fact that he drove them out, but they tried to put Jesus' deeds in a completely different light: "Only by Beelzebul, the prince of demons, does he cast out demons" (Matt. 12:24). If Jesus had claimed to act only by the power of his heavenly Father, his adversaries wanted to uncover a very different force at work behind him, a satanic one. The accusation demonstrates how two completely opposite visions of reality confronted each other. Although Jesus had appealed for an end of condemnations, this process still continued against him. The accusation of conspiring with the highest of the devils betrays the fact that in the judgments and charges of his enemies a satanic dimension was involved (for in their view Satan had still not fallen from heaven). The Old Testament proclamation of violent judgment has consequently become radicalized through the basileia message of Jesus and transformed into the New Testament drama of the satanic and of hell.

What we have discovered so far can again be substantiated by a control test. K. Erlemann attempts in a comprehensive study to present the picture of God which emerges from the synoptic parables.[21] In so doing, he neither distinguishes between the parables of the kingdom of God and the parables of judgment, nor does he pick up the clear utterances where Jesus speaks in the synoptic Gospels of self-judgment. Hence he comes to the following conclusion:

> The picture of God in the parables is stamped with unresolved tensions owing to antithetical ideas: reward according to work versus reward out of kindness; wrath versus compassion; universalism versus particularism; invitation versus exclusion, (partial) generosity versus unrighteousness, fulfillment versus "crisis," marriage festival versus judgment, adhering to Israel versus surrender of prerogatives to others. Now one aspect, now the other is emphasized, depending on the question posed and the situation.[22]

If these tensions, correctly noted by Erlemann, really remain unresolved, as he himself says, and if it cannot be clearly defined in what situations one or the other aspect stands out, then the systematic theologian, the

---

20. See Bultmann (1964), 163.

21. "As far as I know, no comprehensive exegetical work on the picture of God in the Gospels has yet been produced — apart from the contribution of R. A. Hoffmann" (Erlemann [1988], 24).

22. Ibid., 279.

preacher, and even the reader are finally at the mercy of arbitrariness. It seems to depend purely on themselves which trait in the picture of God to bring out or what alternation between the different pictures to choose. The doctrine of God thereby loses its inner coherence. In the trinitarian and christological problematic, theologians and the ecclesiastical profession have not resigned themselves simply to leaving "unresolved tensions" as they are. Why should things be different for questions of justice, judgment and anger, and also necessarily for the question of redemption? The consequences would in every case be very great. Reference to the work of Erlemann is therefore very helpful in order to make clear that the choice of the dramatic model does not derive from some arbitrary fashion. The central question which is at stake is rather whether one wants to resign oneself to an unresolved tension of opposing aspects in the picture of God, or whether a dramatic scheme, and with it a solution to the logical contradictions, can be successful. Whether this is possible will be answered only from the viewpoint of the end of the drama. But before we pass on to the next act, we still have to consider an important interim question, which is crucial above all for the problematic of the connection between the person of Jesus and the judgment on sins. This problematic comes together in the phrase "Son of Man," by which Jesus characterized himself according to the manner of speaking of the evangelists.

The Son of Man

There is hardly a question in historical-critical exegesis so disputed as that of the Son of Man. The dispute is an old one and has produced an immense literature over more than a hundred years, which has however led to no generally recognized results.[23]

---

23. Kümmel (1984), 5: " 'The question belongs to one of the most complicated, indeed, muddled, of the entirety of New Testament theology. The literature on this topic is as impossible to review completely as the tangles of opinions are thick and impenetrable.' So wrote the Strassbourg New Testament scholar H. J. Holtzmann in 1897 at the beginning of the section on the Son of Man in his exposition of the 'proclamation of Jesus' in his *Lehrbuch der Neutestamentlichen Theologie,* which encompassed the research of the nineteenth century (note 1: Holtzmann, 246). And eighty-five years later, in 1982, the Oslo New Testament scholar R. Leivestadt explains in his contribution to the anthology *Aufstieg und Niedergang der römischen Welt,* entitled 'Jesus-Messiah-Son of Man': 'In no area of New Testament research does so great a confusion reign as in the area of the concept of the Son of Man.... Among the many proposed solutions one could very well be right. Unfortunately, for the time being it is only possible to demonstrate that most of them are false' (note 2: Leivestadt, "Jesus," 232). Whoever surveys this theme a little from the last twenty years... will scarcely be able to contradict these judgments; he will even be inclined to ask, with a new article, 'Is the Son of Man Problem Insoluble?' (note 3: A. J. Higgins in *Neotestamentica et Semitica,* FS M. Black [Edinburgh, 1969], 70–87)."

The Problematic and the Need for a Preliminary Decision

The debate turns on the one hand on the meaning of the Aramaic words which lay behind the phrase unknown in secular Greek: *ho hyios tou anthropou*. Did they denote a messianic-apocalyptic title, or did they describe man (people) in general, or did they serve as a formula to refer to 'I' or 'me'?

On the other hand it is debated whether Jesus spoke of himself as "Son of Man" or whether this title was first attributed to him by the post-Easter community. According to the three possible meanings of Son of Man, this second question has a different meaning. Hence it comes about that, since Bultmann, three different types of Son of Man saying are distinguished: sayings which relate to his earthly ministry, others which speak of his coming sufferings, and finally those which describe him as heavenly judge. Countless variants arise from this: Jesus may or may not have spoken this or that saying with this or that meaning. Bultmann, e.g., takes it as probable that the sayings about the Son of Man as heavenly judge go back to Jesus himself, but that he was not speaking of himself but giving notice of a figure, distinct from himself, who would appear at the end of time. Consequently the issue is extremely complex.

From the linguistic evidence it is striking that the Son of Man sayings appear very frequently in the Gospels, but almost only — with the exception of Acts 7:56 — in the mouth of Jesus. This fact can only be satisfactorily explained, in the opinion of many scholars, by the assumption that Jesus did indeed speak of himself as Son of Man. In fact it would be incomprehensible why the Greek-speaking post-Easter community should have adopted an expression which was at first meaningless for them, if they had not been obliged to do so by a tradition. The New Testament letters and the early Christian literature show further that the expression Son of Man played absolutely no further role in the later theology of the community. In consequence, the assumption would have to be made that the title arose after Easter, dominated everything for a short while so that it was able to penetrate into every layer of the Gospels, and then immediately disappeared from the theology of the community. But even this highly unlikely assumption would not be enough to explain why the expression always arises only in the mouth of Jesus and never in narratives and sayings about him, if the community is supposed to have naively combined its own representations with his message. It would equally remain incomprehensible why such an indirect self-description was attributed to him.

Despite these strong arguments, there is, as mentioned, no unanimity among exegetes. An important counter-argument runs: "It is impossible from the strict concept of the kingdom of God that Jesus awaited the coming Son of Man or identified himself with him."[24] Why is this impossible? The categorical way in which Vielhauer formulates things might betray where the problem lies. Is it possible to make of the kingdom of God, proclaimed by Jesus, a "strict concept," without determining with one's own fixed ideas what Jesus must have meant? Can the basileia message after all be captured in a single concept? By his judgment, Vielhauer clearly betrays that it is not the different verdicts about historical and linguistic details which make the decisive contribution to the diversity of opinions on the Son of Man question, but above all the "concept" that one forms of Jesus' message and his destiny. M. Müller also points to this basic problematic at the end of his investigations: "Here we inevitably run up against the difficulty that the criteria of the individual exegetes even on this point are very closely tied up with the question of what, in their opinion, the earthly Jesus believed about himself and what, in their opinion, the community is responsible for, as it attempted after the first Easter to understand and to interpret from its holy writings Jesus' fate and meaning for salvation."[25] Thus since the decisive question is whether the Son of Man sayings of the Gospels are to be made "intelligible in the framework of Jesus' life on earth"[26] or not, we can spend a little more time on this question, without allowing ourselves to be crippled by the many contradictory verdicts of the experts on points of detail.

The Son of Man Coming in Judgment

"The resolution of the question whether, and in what sense, the historical Jesus spoke of the Son of Man depends on the evaluation of the logion Mark 8:38 and parallels, in addition to which a corresponding parallel can be found in the Q-tradition: Matthew 10:32ff. and Luke 12:8ff."[27] The important saying runs thus: "For whoever is ashamed of me and my words, of that one will the Son of Man be ashamed when he comes in the glory of his Father with his holy angels" (Mark 8:38; see also Luke 9:26). Matthew and Luke have this logion in a second version, namely, as a double saying, in which a promise precedes the threat: "And I tell you: everyone who acknowledges me before men the Son of Man will also acknowledge before the angels of God; but whoever denies me before men will also be denied before the angels of God" (Luke 12:8ff.). In the parallel passage, Matt. 10:32ff., the logion is found in slightly altered form, as Jesus is speaking here not of the Son of Man, but both times, including the postscript, in the first person. The double

---

24. Vielhauer (1965), 88.
25. M. Müller (1984), 258.
26. Ibid.
27. Lohse (1974), 47.

version shows first of all that we are dealing with a broad tradition, which tends to vouch for its age. Above all the content of the double saying should be noted. The specific peculiarity of Jesus' proclamation lay, as we have seen, in the fact that he spoke of the coming of the kingdom of God as definitive and that he brought it into an inseparable relationship with his own ministry. He understood his own activity as a new call to gathering, demanding conversion and leading in the case of a negative response to a final judgment (self-judgment). The double saying about acknowledging and being ashamed is really saying nothing essentially new, but only confirms in a striking way what we have already established. His person and salvation in the kingdom of God cannot be separated. Neither the "yes" to his message and his call to assembly nor the "no" to himself are something provisional, but both are decisive for the final judgment.

If we can start from the basis that Jesus spoke of himself as the coming Son of Man, then it remains to be explained what he may have had in mind when he said this. In the New Testament writings we find, it is true, few quotations from the book of Daniel, but there are countless allusions to this prophetic-apocalyptic text.[28] This should be a clear sign that the corresponding ideas were very widely known in Jesus' time and that of the early community. But what was meant by the vision in Daniel 7:13ff. of the Son of Man who comes "with the clouds of heaven" and to whom is given "an everlasting dominion" over "all peoples, nations and languages"? In the attempt to give a more precise meaning to this vision within the context of the entire prophetic body of writings, different layers of tradition are normally distinguished, which is why there is even talk of a whole Daniel cycle.[29] It can be shown that the representation of the Son of Man in the whole cycle remains "very closely within the bounds of a specific belief in angels."[30] More important, however, than the exact modern interpretation of Daniel is the question of how the symbol of the Son of Man was or could be understood at the time of Jesus. The pictorial accounts of the Ethiopian Book of Enoch and of 4 Ezra give an insight which is relevant to this question. In the pictorial accounts there is clearly talk of an "elected one" who is identical with the Messiah, hidden at first by God, and who is also spoken of as Son of Man.[31] We are not dealing here with the introduction of a new figure, nor is any new function attributed to the preexisting Messiah, but it is

28. See *The Greek New Testament,* ed. K. Aland et al. 3d ed. (Stuttgart, 1984), 898f., 909.

29. See K. Müller, "Der Menschensohn im Danielzyklus," in Pesch and Schnackenburg (1975), 37–80.

30. Ibid., 80.

31. See Enoch 46:1–4; 48:2; 62:5–14; 63:11; 69:26–29; 70:1; 71:14–17.

only the book of Daniel's symbolic expression which is applied to him, and he is probably to be identified with Enoch.[32] The situation is similar with 4 Ezra, which also has a Messiah appearing at several points. At the beginning of the sixth vision there is a description of one like a man climbing up out of the sea in the course of a tempest, flying with the clouds of heaven and starting a war with great armies of men. The act of climbing out of the sea is interpreted in the same vision as the expression of the preexistence of the Messiah-redeemer (4 Ezra 13:25ff.). Even here there is no description of a Son of Man different from the Messiah, but only the symbol which is used by Daniel for the Messiah, as 4 Ezra sees him. The vision of the Son of Man from the book of Daniel served subsequently in apocalyptic circles to express the conviction of the preexistence of the Messiah.

If Jesus spoke of himself in a manner which was bound to recall Daniel's Son of Man, this shows that he had a concept of the Messiah which was broader than that of the earthly national son of David. But he cannot have taken over for himself everything which could at that time be associated with the symbol of the Son of Man. In Jesus we find practically nothing of the colorful visions of the apocalypticists, so that in this respect the distance between him and the apocalyptic groups must have been very great. From that overflowing world of images he took hold only of the one idea of judgment at hand, and at the same time he understood this judgment in a quite different way. Whereas the judgment according to the visions of the apocalypticists takes place in the struggle against the enemies of God, Jesus proclaimed his Father as a God of love for one's enemies and interpreted the judgment as a self-condemnation of those who shut themselves away from this love. From his experience of God as Abba he thoroughly transformed the few allusions which he took over from the world of Daniel.

What would have emerged if Jesus or the early post-Easter community had become completely involved in apocalyptic thought is shown to some extent by the Revelation of John, who at certain points only superficially Christianized the representations which he took over, and above all by the apocryphal Christian Apocalypses. There is not a trace of the many sights, visions, revelations, and word-pictures about everything under the sun which are found in the apocalyptic writings either in the Gospels or in the Acts of the Apostles, despite the imminent expectation which they share with apocalyptic writings. From this comparison there again emerges a good reason against the assumption that the community lived after Easter unreflectively in a state of apocalyptic enthusiasm and no longer distinguished between prophetic sayings from its midst and

---

32. See Hooker (1967), 33–48; M. Müller (1984), 67–80.

the sayings of the Lord. If this had been the case, a far more colorful world of images would have emerged.

The Son of Man Who Is Handed Over

Besides the coming judge, we should take note of those Son of Man sayings which speak of his earthly ministry and his suffering. From the viewpoint of investigations into the history of religions, K. Müller judges that these sayings would have "a considerably better claim to originality if anywhere among the christological sovereignty-utterances it can be deduced from the synoptic sayings about the earthly Son of Man that they are constituent parts of Jesus' proclamation."[33] R. Pesch also comes to the conclusion, after careful research into the logia of the suffering Son of Man, that Jesus should be "trusted" when he makes a prediction of his suffering.[34] Such a view has been on the whole rejected in historical-critical research since Bultmann,[35] as critics have seen in the announcements of suffering only subsequently fabricated prophecies (*vaticinia ex eventu*). However this is to leave an important point of view almost unconsidered, for the question should be asked not just about Jesus but also about his disciples.

It should be beyond all doubt that in a world which was already shaken up by the preaching of the Baptist about the judgment at hand, the message of the kingdom of God at hand was bound to awaken further messianic expectations, even a state of excitement. His disciples could not remain uninfluenced by this, and the questions became particularly relevant for them when the reactions of rejection manifested themselves clearly and confrontation intensified. There were already in existence two important imaginative models from the prophetic and apocalyptic traditions, of which one shows how the Messiah will act toward his enemies, and the other announces what may happen to prophets and the just before his victorious coming:

1. Numerous prophetic-apocalyptic texts of the Old Testament announce that God will destroy his enemies at the coming of the Messiah (Mic. 4:11–5:5; Isa. 61; 63:1–6; Zech. 9:1–14; Ps. 2; 110). In noncanonical literature the notion consequently received a widespread currency that the Messiah himself will wage a great war against the godless. In the Syrian Apocalypse of Baruch he destroys all the nations which have ever oppressed Israel, and he subdues the others (72:1–6).

---

33. K. Müller (1973), 66.

34. Pesch (1975), 195.

35. "I will not linger however with the prophecies of suffering and resurrection, which have been long recognized as secondary constructions by the church" (Bultmann [1964], 163).

In the Slavonic Book of Enoch there appears an "elected one" (Messiah/ Son of Man) whose mere speech kills all sinners and destroys all the unjust (62:2; 69:26ff.). Similarly there flows from the mouth of the Son of Man, as he is described in 4 Ezra, a stream of fire and breath of flame which burns to death a countless army of enemies (sixth vision 1–11). Such images could, as the example of the Zealots shows, be bound up with the conviction that one had to urge on the destructive action of God's judgment by oneself attacking the enemies.[36]

2. Alongside this image of the victorious and violent Messiah there was in the faith of Israel the completely different tradition, according to which those sent by God must before the final event suffer violence from their enemies.[37] The fate of the just was very frequently experienced in the time before Jesus as one of humiliation and persecution. Already in the psalms of complaint, the one who prays calls again and again for Yahweh to help him from his enemies and free him from out of the deep "well" (Ps. 69:15), out of the "horrible pit" (Ps. 40:2) and the "gates of death" (Ps. 9:13).[38] In the last two centuries before Christ, at the latest, the hope became alive among the devout people of Israel that God would even rescue from death the just who have been persecuted and killed and give them heavenly glory. There is talk of a just man in the book of Wisdom who calls God his father and for that reason is persecuted by the evil-doers. They want to examine him scornfully, to find out if he is really "Son of God," and to see if God snatches him from their hands (Wisd. 2:18). At the judgment these evil-doers discover to their horror that he whom they have persecuted is counted among the "sons of God" (Wisd. 5:5). While they themselves pass away "like the smoke which the storm dispels," the just receive the "kingdom of splendor" (Wisd. 5:14, 16).

Also in the Testament of Job, the suffering just man instructs his opponents: "My throne stands in the world above and its magnificence and splendor is on the right hand of the father" (33:3). Beyond these summary indications, L. Ruppert has demonstrated how the theme of the persecuted just man was developed from the individual "enemy psalms" both through a wisdom line and also through an eschatological (Qumran and the teacher of righteousness) and apocalyptic line.[39] If it was at first a scandal for the faith of Israel that the just man should suffer, with time there was a complete reversal of this reaction, and after the second destruction of Jerusalem (70 C.E.), it became a sort of dogma that

---

36. See Hengel (1961), 277–96.
37. See Steck (1967).
38. See also Ps. 30:4; 49:16; 56:14; 68:21; 71:20; 86:13; 116:8.
39. Ruppert (1972).

the just man will be persecuted.[40] Further concerning this conclusion, K. Berger has been able to show that in the late Jewish and early Christian period the idea of the persecuted just man and of the violent fate of the prophets was extended even to God's last messengers, to the last prophets. In connection with the interpretation of Daniel 7, the theme had been developed especially in the Enoch and Elijah tradition: "God's last messenger will be killed, but God will rescue him from death, i.e., he will show his power in raising the messenger up and thus end all conflict about the true worship of God. This is the 'last act' before the judgment."[41] The only true just men, returning before the end, Enoch and Elijah, are killed by their opponents, but are raised up by God — even before the parousia and the judgment. The important distinction between resurrection and parousia emerged with reference to the fate of the prophets of the end-time, a distinction which did not have to be derived first from the fate of Jesus, but was already existing at least in an initial form.

Against the background of the two great traditions informing the faith of Israel, and in view of the growing resistance, the question must necessarily have nagged at Jesus' disciples as to how their master, and how God, would react to the enemies. Should they hope for a powerful attack which would destroy their enemies, or were they expected to see him and themselves under the sign of the precursors, the persecuted just men and the murdered prophets? To ask the question clearly like this is already to give the answer. Because their master was not for them just some precursor, they must have been very far from imagining a possible violent death. The very opposite possibility stirred them. Simply because a village in Samaria was not hospitable, James and John wanted to destroy it with heavenly power: "Lord, do you want us to bid fire from heaven to fall and consume them?" (Luke 9:54). As Jesus gave the two of them the name "sons of thunder" (Mark 3:17), they cannot have reacted in this way just in this one situation, and there are no indications that the other disciples were different from them in this respect. When Jesus was arrested, one of his companions, Peter, attempted a direct act of resistance with a sword (John 18:10).

In view of the explosive situation it is unthinkable that Jesus abandoned his disciples to their own imaginings and dreams without a single word of clarification. Against the background of the dilemma facing the pre-Easter group of disciples a double scene obtrudes, as we find in Mark 8:27–33 (acknowledgment of the Messiah/announcement of sufferings), which is to be seen as the "compositional center of Mark's

---

40. Ibid., 157–80, 188.
41. Berger (1976), 142.

Gospel."[42] After this, Jesus drew a conclusion from Peter's acknowledgment of him as the Messiah, which Peter certainly did not think of. He established a new connection between the popular representation of the Messiah, which Peter himself may have shared, and the theme of the violent fate of the prophets and applied both of them to himself by means of the symbolic saying of the Son of Man. The resistance that Peter put up against such ideas reveals how unusual they were for the disciples. Equally informative is the reaction of Jesus to the defensive attitude of Peter: "Get behind me, Satan! For you are not on God's side but do what men want" (Mark 8:33). These harsh words show that Jesus in no way abandoned his disciples without comment to their own messianic dreams, and equally he did not allow them to lay down the law on how to act. In the post-Easter community there is no imaginable situation in which a narrative like Mark 8:31–33 could have arisen, but it is clear that a conflict such as described here must necessarily have happened before Easter. The widespread messianic expectations with their pictures of violent victory were not in harmony with the way of Jesus, who taught nonviolence. There was therefore a "sociological necessity" to speak with the group of disciples about the question of being persecuted and killed. It is never a simple matter to hold together a heterogeneous group, let alone in a situation of great crisis. If Jesus did not want to become the victim of the anxieties of his followers, he had to make it quite clear what way he intended to walk along and where he wanted under no circumstances to let himself be drawn to. The defense, "Get behind me Satan," gives an answer at exactly that point where clarification was already needed for reasons of group sociology. Such a clarification was even more urgent if Jesus did not want to leave his disciples in complete ignorance about his way.

Even the initially surprising phenomenon of the number of times in the synoptic Gospels that Elijah is the subject in the conversation between Jesus and his disciples (Mark 6:15; 8:28; 9:4, 11–13) can be easily explained from the pre-Easter situation. J. Jeremias[43] and K. Berger have demonstrated convincingly how strongly held was the image of the return of Elijah in connection with messianic expectations.[44] Even the suggestion that Elijah must suffer "as it is written of him" (Mark 9:13), which was not sufficiently comprehensible from

---

42. Pesch (1976, 1977), 2:44. Pesch places the double scene in the pre-Marcan Passion story (time or origin perhaps even before 37 C.E.). For the linguistic analysis of Mark 8:27–33 and the messianic secret motif, see ibid., 27–56.

43. See article "Elias," *Theologisches Wörterbuch zum Neuen Testament* 2:930–43.

44. "How anxious the expectation was is shown in the reports that people reckoned John the Baptist could be the Elijah who would appear again (John 1:21, 25) and that there were circles who were convinced Elijah had reappeared in Jesus (Mark 6:15 parallel Luke 9:8; Mark 8:28 parallel Matt. 16:24; Luke 9:19)" (ibid., 938).

1 Kings 19:10 alone — as the prophet was only persecuted and not killed at the time of King Ahab, and afterward carried away to heaven — is made understandable by the noncanonical literature, which speaks of the murder of the prophet and raising him from the dead. In the death which befell the resurrected and returning Elijah, as people expected at that time, Jesus was able — in connection with the murder of the Baptist — to see his own fate prefigured, even if the step toward the image of a Messiah who was persecuted and killed remained a big one. This will be shown more clearly later.

No fundamental historical difficulties can be raised against the utterances in the synoptic Gospels, according to which Jesus announced the handing over and the suffering of the Son of Man, even if much may remain open in detail. But from this the question arises as to what could have caused Jesus to use the indirect symbolic expression "Son of Man" for his role in the coming judgment, as well as his anticipated suffering and even his claim concerning himself?

The Sense of the Indirect-Symbolic Figure of Speech

Psychological reflections concerning the person of Jesus are nowadays more or less taboo, but all the same they should not be pushed altogether aside and may even be legitimate insofar as one remains aware of their limits. If Jesus in his proclamation and in his ministry made a claim which went beyond that of the Old Testament prophets, and if at the same time he was a person who knew periods of exhaustion and for whom the crush of people was troublesome (see Mark 3:9; 9:19), then he inevitably faced the heavy task of integrating these elements of extreme tension in his experience and in his consciousness. But even in the case of much smaller tensions it often happens that the individuals concerned feel in certain circumstances distant from themselves and see themselves as third parties. Above all, when it comes to saying the most personal things and matters which are the hardest to understand for the everyday awareness of most people, then indirect speech readily suggests itself. Paul gives us a notable example of this, when on one occasion he writes of a "person" who — whether in the body or out of the body — was taken up to the third heaven and there heard things that cannot be told (2 Cor. 12:2–4). Although it is quite clear that the apostle meant by "person" himself, yet the unusual experience, in which he did not know exactly what had happened to him, caused him to speak as if of a third party. The tension in the consciousness of Jesus must have been even greater than that of the apostle. On the one hand he lived completely for his Father, and on the other he had to adapt himself to the modest horizons of his disciples. If in conversation he put himself on their level and perceived things by means of their mental and spiritual framework, then his own innermost experience must have appeared to him as that of someone quite distinct from himself. The assumption consequently imposes itself that it was the unusual character of his claim which caused him to speak of himself and his mission in an indirect way.

The psychological explanation for the use of the term "Son of Man" is necessary, but in itself it is insufficient. We must look also for a theological meaning. In the Sermon on the Mount, Jesus clearly removed himself from the principle of "an eye for an eye and a tooth for a tooth" and challenged people to offer no resistance to those who do evil to them (Matt. 5:38ff.). He certainly did not mean by this that one should give in to evil as such. What was crucial for him was the insight that direct resistance at the same level (an eye for an eye) leads only to imitation of the evil which an adversary wants to do to one, so that the vicious circle is not broken but only continued. Immediate and direct confrontation with evil has the result that one adapts to it and sooner or later becomes the mirror image, or *Doppelgänger,* of the adversary.[45] A clear example of this danger is given by those apocalyptic texts in which the act of judgment of the Messiah is frequently described in a way which hardly distinguishes it from the activity of a monstrous doer of violence and a demonic being. If the Messiah does not wish to be confused with the one (antichrist) who makes himself his *Doppelgänger,* the manner of his arguments with the enemies of God becomes crucial. In the disputations it is striking the way Jesus mostly chose an indirect strategy (turning back the actions of the adversaries against themselves, counter-questions, shifting the discussion to a different level, etc.). The Son of Man sayings fit into this style of discussion. If in confrontation with his adversaries he spoke of his function as a judge; if, face to face with his disciples, he expounded to them a path which they did not want to take; and if in other critical situations he made his claim for himself, then, by using the Son of Man terminology, he was not directly setting up his own "I" against another "I," but he was referring to someone who at first appeared to be a third person. Immediate confrontation in the sense of blow and counter-blow, argument and counter-argument, was thus avoided, and a future was opened up in which his claim could be established and prove its truth. From the standpoint of this analysis, it is quite right to say that the Son of Man terminology is to be "subordinated in essentials to the prediction of a judgment."[46] We are concerned here "not with the authority of Jesus in general, but with the rejection of this authority which results in judgment."[47]

---

45. See Girard (1983), 22–31.
46. Polag (1977), 113.
47. Ibid., 114.

Jesus' indirect but yet precise way of proceeding is shown also in his interpretation of the Holy Scriptures. Faced with burning messianic expectations, he raised what was apparently a side issue: "What do you think of the Christ? Whose son is he?" (Matt. 22:42) When the answer came that he was the son of David, he needed just one further question to leave the Pharisees completely at a loss. By merely referring to Psalm 110:1 "The Lord spoke to my lord," he succeeded in bringing into the open a fundamental problem in the interpretation of the Old Testament writings, which his adversaries — and not only they — always glossed over. The Messiah is supposed to be on the one hand son of David, and on the other hand he was addressed by David himself — according to the exegesis of the time — as lord. Behind this linguistic problem there lies also one of substance. As son of David the Messiah is supposed to stand squarely in the tradition which comes down from the great king of Israel, but at the same time he is to bring rescue from a history which was always one of failure. How can the two coexist? Jesus must have felt the problem very intensely and precisely to have been able to express it through one single question and thereby to touch on a fundamental theme of the Old Testament. Since the problematic of the Son of Man sayings, with their utterances about heavenly and earthly manifestations, belongs to the same theme, the question arises as to whether Jesus' indirect self-designation did not subtly suggest more than many exegetes credit him with. By a choice of words, which allowed allusions to the different Son of Man representations in Ezekiel, Daniel, and Jewish apocalyptic, he could have been preparing an answer to that great question before which the Pharisees were completely at a loss. In the parable of the wicked winegrowers, which, at least in its original form, as we have seen, may go back to Jesus himself, the master's "son" is clearly separated from all the "servants" sent by him, and as "heir" he is placed by the side of the master. The "son" and the "Son of Man" thus stand in an inner connection with one another, and both these indirect self-designations of Jesus are in accord with his high claim in the basileia message. Thus there emerges a picture which has inner coherence and which carries in itself its own credibility.

Problematic of the Judgment Sayings

The fundamental tension between the announcement of God's kingdom at hand and the threat of judgment, which at first appeared as an unbridgeable opposition, was softened by the discovery that the different utterances corresponded to two different linguistic levels. At the same time it became clear that, even at the level of content, the judgment sayings do not detract from the promise of salvation of the basileia message, but only set out unambiguously its unconditional, decisive character.

God is always in himself the kind father who meets sinners with anticipatory love; only if the sinners, despite the experience of grace, cling to their own criteria of judgment do they imprison themselves in them. The judgment sayings are not a sign that God has a double face, but they bring out with great seriousness that people possess no power to save themselves and God carries out against them no "violence to compel love."

Despite all this, the problematic is not resolved. Does not the Old Testament show how much people cling to their old world and its norms? Is there not visible in the history of Israel a fundamental anxiety in the face of life, which at the same time necessarily leads even the members of the chosen people to make themselves secure and to defend themselves? In view of this heaviness of the human heart, was not Jesus' message — despite its great beauty — a hopelessly impossible demand? In fact it effected a sharpening of the situation and a hardening of the heart. But does it make a difference whether an angry God damns people or whether a "kind" God looks on as his creatures damn themselves almost of necessity? The result is the same. So the pressing question faces us: is Jesus' message of salvation after all really a message of salvation? "Is not Israel itself rejected precisely because of the rejection of the last messenger, who proclaimed God's unconditional will to save? Does the eschatological mediator of salvation become in historical fact the mediator of damnation?"[48]

This difficult question can even be directed against Jesus himself. He demanded of people that they should not judge, but he himself was very harsh in his judgment on his opponents. In doing this, did he not set up a standard by which he must himself be measured? Did he not imprison himself in his own judgments? Was not everything that he reproached his opponents for bound to turn against him? This question arises necessarily, but it can take on two entirely different meanings. Jesus' claim could turn against him in the sense that it manifested its absurdity. The evil which he uncovered and judged may also fall back on him just as it is suggested in the sayings of the handing over of the Son of Man. Every way of speaking becomes ambiguous here. The question about God's goodness and anger, his justice and his judgment, proves to be so unfathomable, that even the meaning of the questions that are asked in this context can be turned unendingly this way and that. The judgment becomes a judgment about all sayings. The critically questioning consciousness is placed before the alternative of instinctively withdrawing to its own position or of surrendering itself up to a process which offers no clear view of where it is leading.

---

48. Pesch (1978), 105.

Third Act:
The Bringer of Salvation Brought to Judgment

In his *Kirchliche Dogmatik,* K. Barth asks what should be expected to happen after the rejection of Jesus and his judgment sayings, and he answers: "That a legal process be instituted against that world of men which so humiliatingly rejected Jesus of Nazareth, a trial which should have included Israel and even the community of disciples — that one would have to expect. One might almost postulate that the destruction of Jerusalem and the temple must *now* happen and its exposition should form the continuation and fitting counterpart to that first phase."[1] But what could have been expected did not appear. It is true that we are told the story of a judgment, but not one that seems in any way to fit in with Jesus' proclamation. For he who announced the judgment is himself brought to judgment. This astonishing event caused Barth to deal with a central section of his doctrine of redemption under the provocative heading: "The Judge as the One Who Is Judged in Our Place."[2]

What so challenged Barth's thinking was seen by historical-critical exegesis as hardly a problem. Quite wrongly! One could have expected from the time-scheme and from the theological freedom which is usually ascribed to the post-Easter community that Jesus only spoke of his return and of the judgment on the world after his resurrection. But nowhere is such a narrative order to be found. If, conversely, one understood the Gospels only as historical documents, one could satisfactorily explain the position of the judgment sayings by the suggestion that Jesus spoke of this theme even before his suffering. But since this is not the understanding of historical-critical exegesis, and since this exegesis attaches little importance to the usual time-scheme, it is necessary from this point of view to ascribe an eschatological and theological significance to the outline of the Gospels. Such a dimension results in fact from the connection between Jesus' ministry and the kingdom of God. Since his person cannot be separated from God's new work, what happens to him must be of interest not only historically but also theologically. The narrative sequence of the Gospels must accordingly be theologically relevant, and the strange fact that the one who announces judgment later stands before judgment himself deserves the greatest attention.

As the synoptic Gospels do not consciously reflect on the dramatic structure of their narrative, it may be that they did not make this one up themselves, but only mirrored what was acted out in the fate of Jesus. Certainly, all this is not easy to sort out, and it poses a big challenge for research. The historical judgment depends, as we have established

---

1. Barth (1932–67) 4/1:248.
2. Ibid., 231–311.

several times already, to a high degree on the overall picture that one has of Jesus' ministry and his fate. This picture becomes particularly full of tension, even bewildering, when it involves a judge who is himself judged. Jewish tradition transmitted the idea of the suffering just man sharing, after his death and elevation, in God's judgment over sinners. But if the dramatic narrative sequence of the Gospels is theologically relevant, then it also follows that the judgment was already being acted out in the persecution of Jesus. The connection between judgment and suffering hinted at by the symbolic title "Son of Man" finally becomes visible with all its consequences. All of this is hard to understand from the viewpoint of the usual historical assumptions, and for this reason it is not surprising that the discussion is particularly controversial when we come to the question of how Jesus saw and understood his death. At this point the final twist is given to the problematic of whether it is possible to combine a historical and a theological point of view. Hence we must look very carefully to see whether and how theological reflections have an influence on historical judgment, as well as whether and how historical facts are relevant to theological judgment.

The Process of Judgment against Jesus

It is undisputed that Jesus was arrested and executed by the Romans. The guilt for this event has been laid in Christian tradition primarily, if not exclusively, at the door of the Jews. Nowadays there is a strong tendency in the opposite direction; according to this, the guilt lay almost entirely with the Romans, who were taken in by a political misunderstanding. That the political issue was relevant in one way or another is witnessed by the inscription on the cross, "The King of the Jews" (Mark 15:26), and is beyond question in scholarly research. But what role did the religious claim of Jesus play and what was the immediate occasion for the campaign against him to be set in motion?

A few days before his arrest, Jesus undertook a campaign in the Temple (Mark 11:15–19 and parallels) which led to controversy (Mark 11:27–33). He took action against the dealers, merchants, and money-changers, and got in the way of their activities. As this trade was necessary for the sacrificial cult, there was an official concession for it, and it took place in the great forecourt (approximately 412 x 275 yards), which even the gentiles were allowed to enter. So Jesus' prophetic act took place in the "gentiles' forecourt," which already suggests that it was not aimed directly against the sacrificial cult. The saying which was handed down in this connection also speaks of the gentiles. It contains, besides an allusion to Jeremiah 7:11, a quotation from Isaiah 56:7 in which the Temple is described as a "house of prayer for all nations" (Mark 11:17). The sense of this saying becomes even clearer if it is considered in its immediate context of Isaiah 56:6–8. There we find mention at first of "foreigners, who have joined themselves to the Lord," and then it is said about them: "these I will bring to my holy mountain and make them joyful in my house of prayer...." Thus the context makes clear that the description of the Temple as house of prayer is not primarily an attack on the cult, as the gentile converts themselves offer sacrifice there. At the center stands rather the great promise of assembly, which refers not merely to Israel, but includes also the many nations. With the highlighting of "house of prayer for all nations," the accent is placed entirely on the assembly of the nations. Since yet another saying of Jesus is handed down, which equally speaks of the assembly of the nations (Matt. 8:11ff. and parallels), this sense may have been central in his Temple saying and thereby also in his symbolic action in the "gentiles' forecourt." The assembly of Israel which he had begun would have been continued with the assembly of gentiles, so that the Temple would have become a house of prayer for all nations. This continuation was already rendered impossible as Israel had already rejected the kingdom of God which was to have begun with her. For this reason Jesus was no longer able realistically to set about the second step in the task of his mission, but could only indicate it by means of a prophetic symbolic act.

In the saying about the house of prayer for all nations, which was at first in no way critical of the cult, there lurked, however, because of the allusion to Jeremiah 7:11 ("den of robbers"), a pointed comment on the actual business transactions of the Temple. A further saying belongs in this context, which is handed down both in the framework of the interrogation of Jesus and also (in John) together with the action in the Temple: "Destroy this temple, and in three days I will raise it up" (John 2:19). Here also the criticism of the cult remained in all probability indirect ("Destroy this temple..." and not: "I will destroy...."), and hence Jesus' lofty claim stands out all the more: "In three days I will raise it up" (John 2:19). The new Temple — not made by human hands (Mark 14:58) — can only be the new people of God assembled by the Messiah.

Thus the prophetic action in the Temple fits in extremely well with what we have seen up until now about the ministry of Jesus. By means of this action he brought to a conclusion the first task of his mission, the assembly of the new people of God, which because of Israel's resistance was no longer realistically possible, *on a symbolic level*. In this way the cult of sacrifice was not directly attacked; but as Jesus unambiguously shifted the emphasis, this emphasis on prayer involved an indirect criticism of the cult since his symbolic act took place in full view of the leaders in Israel, for whom the legal sacrificial cult was the most important thing. His action in the Temple, which could have become a high point of his mission, thus became just the reverse, the immediate cause of his arrest. With the end of his first task, he began to give himself over to the kingdom of God in a new manner.

The Judgment by the Jewish Authorities

Even those who dispute that the High Council pronounced an actual death sentence against Jesus assume that Jewish authorities were involved in the action of the Roman authorities against the preacher from Galilee. The much discussed and disputed question of whether the Jewish High Council at the time of Jesus had the authority to carry out a sentence of death, whether it made a judgment on him in the formal, juridical sense at all or only established that he had committed a crime worthy of death, can be left open in the framework of our particular line of questions. In any case it should be a firmly established matter that the Jewish and Roman authorities cooperated — even if from very different motives — in his condemnation and that there was a hearing before the Jewish authorities with a final resolution against Jesus.

According to Mark, Jesus was confronted before the High Council at first with accusations concerning his Temple sayings. Some of those in historical-critical research hold, for linguistic reasons, that precisely this part of the hearing should be excluded from the original tradition. Seen in connection with Jesus' prophetic action in the Temple, which sparked off special controversies, this seems unlikely. But we can pass over this question in our context, as the examination of witnesses in any case did not produce any result which could have satisfied Jesus' opponents. The outcome was that no crime worthy of death was found, which is understandable in view of the "indirect behavior" of Jesus, as it often appears in the Gospels. The accusation consequently had to try to lead him to make a compromising utterance about himself. According to Mark, in answer to the direct question of the high priest, Jesus professed himself unambiguously to be the Messiah and spoke of his coming as "Son of Man at the right hand of power" on the "clouds of heaven" (Mark 14:62). In Matthew and Luke, the profession of the Messiahship ("Son of the Blessed") is explained by the term "Son of God" (Matt. 26:63ff. and parallel Luke 22:70), and in all three synoptics the profession of Jesus is followed by the judgment of his opponents: blasphemy.

To the question as to what could appear blasphemous in Jesus' answer, there are two main opinions (apart from the writers who, following H. Lietzmann, see the whole scene of the hearing as the product of later redactional work). One opinion assumes that Jesus was condemned on account of his claim to be the Messiah and the eschatological judge, the Son of Man. But because it is not easy to see how the profession of Messiahship could be considered by his opponents as blasphemy,[3] the second tendency holds "that Jesus' claim to be Son of God must have played an important role in the hearing before the Sanhedrin."[4] But as this second view is strongly bound up with the literary-critical thesis that Luke made use of his own special tradition besides Mark (and Q), we must leave open the decision between the two opinions. It is unlikely to be of systematic significance, for the question here is not only exactly what Jesus could have said in his self-profession, but also, and above all, what his opponents were able to understand. We have already seen that he saw the relationship with his father as one which went beyond Jewish messianic expectations. Just as clearly, it has been shown that he formulated his claim in a predominantly indirect style. His utterances could therefore be understood in different ways. As the scene of the hearing clearly communicates the impression that for Jesus' opponents the verdict was already decided from the beginning and that for that reason they made no effort to understand him more deeply, it can hardly be assumed that they fully understood him and his claim. But how could they then condemn him as a "blasphemer"?

The realization that other claimants to be the Messiah were not rejected in the same way is not enough by itself to provide an answer. Rather, the crucial point is how these fitted into the framework of Jewish expectations. Under the influence of apocalyptic expectations there was a lively doctrine of false prophets coming at the end-time, who would mislead the people and fight with the true prophets (Enoch and Elijah), and these latter would at first even be overcome (killed). God would however raise up his true prophets,[5] and they would subsequently convict their opponents at the judgment: "The struggle over whom God acknowledges will be decided by the fate of the witnesses."[6]

The question as to who in truth can call upon God was also decisive in the dispute about Jesus. As he had not only made a high claim, but also stood in opposition to the religious authorities, what was at stake at the hearing before the High Council was not only the question of the Messiah, but equally whether he or his opponents (high priests) possessed the true Spirit. Already during his public ministry, the reproach had been levelled at him that he was possessed and was in league with Beelzebub (Mark 3:22–30 and parallels). As the question of who was of the divine spirit and who of the demonic was already an acute one

---

3. "None of the numerous pretenders to Messiahship in Jewish history was ever accused of blasphemy" (Mantel [1961], 275).

4. Mussner (1979), 300; (1988); see also Catchpole (1971), 141–48; 153–203; 271; Lamarche (1962); for the older, particularly Catholic authors who hold this view, see Blinzler (1969).

5. See Berger (1976), 9–149.

6. Ibid., 126.

beforehand, it was bound to be asked also at the hearing in one way or another. In view of the conflict reigning between them, the question concerned not only the accused but also the accusers. If Jesus refused to play a subordinate role to theirs and put forward a messianic claim against them, then he thereby condemned them indirectly as false leaders, as "sons of lies," who are ruled by the spirit of darkness. If, as Mark handed down, he made, along with his own profession, the announcement: "And you will see the Son of Man sitting at the right hand of Power and coming with the clouds of heaven" (Mark 14:62), then he strengthened all the more his claim that not they but he would be, before God, the true judge. Since, according to Deut. 17:12, to show contempt for an ordinary judgment of a Levite priest counted as a crime worthy of death, all the more must his threatened judgment on the high priests and the High Council have been considered a deed which deserved death. According to the witness of Paul, it seems that there was at that time the idea that the adversary of the end-time exalts himself and even "proclaims himself to be God" (2 Thess. 2:4).[7] If Jesus' opponents saw in him a figure who was in league with Beelzebub and ruled by the spirit of lies, then it was not hard to understand his claim in connection with the adversary of the end-time, and to interpret it as blasphemy.

The central point of the discussion may consequently have lain in the question of who possesses the true spirit of God and can convict his adversaries in the final judgment. As Jesus had already made the claim during his ministry that the verdict in God's judgment depended on the attitude taken to him on earth, his proclamation must have been even more offensive to that human court which dared to pass a judgment over him. If he did not withdraw his message as a prisoner before human judges, then he stood before them with the provocative assertion that, because of their verdict against him, they showed themselves to be enemies of God and deceivers of the nation.

What role did the law play in the judgment against Jesus? W. Pannenberg thinks: "The Jew faithful to the law was unavoidably inclined toward rejecting Jesus insofar as he was not ready to distinguish between the authority of the law and that of the God of Israel.... Jesus finally came to destruction not because of some inadequate individuals, but on the Jewish law itself, whose transmitted authority was placed in question by his style of public ministry."[8] This view starts from the presupposition that the Jewish law was of an unambiguous scope and Jesus consciously set himself against it. But both assumptions are wide of the mark. We have already seen that Jesus had clearly perceived ten-

---

7. See Gundry (1987).
8. Pannenberg (1964), 259f.

sions within Israel's Holy Scriptures (see Mark 12:35–37) and had also seen the contradictions in the interpretation of the law by his opponents (Mark 2:23–28 and parallels; 7:1–13 and parallels). He argued from the context of Scripture (Mark 12:18–27) and even asked about the most important of the many commandments. For him, the law was not of a fixed scope; he nowhere directly attacked it, but neither did he ever rely casuistically on the letter, nor did he ever begin an explanation like that of the later Mishna with its 4187 propositions. In view of countless prophetic utterances which condemn a cultist-legalistic piety and instead demand justice and love, an interpretation of the law which was entirely determined by the occurrence of the kingdom of God at hand was in no way in contradiction with Scripture. If we look at all the holy books of Israel which were acknowledged at the time, his interpretation was in fact easier to defend than his opponents' casuistry. To that extent, it is not correct to say that Jesus failed because of Jewish law — unless one understands by the law that interpretation which was gaining ground in Jesus' time precisely among the devout and which later came to dominate entirely. In order to avoid the coming judgment, people tried to be as just as possible, and therefore held on as faithfully as possible to the many individual laws. They failed to notice that in this way the basic questions of justice and love in practice lost their central place. To that extent the reason for Jesus' failure was not "a few inadequate individuals" but a particular legal tradition, which, however, was not identical with the law as such, as it is presented in the whole framework of the books of Moses, the writings of the prophets, the historical books, the psalms, and wisdom literature.

From Jesus' interpretation of the law it followed necessarily that people have to give up passing judgment on one another, as, in view of the demands of true living, no one may count themselves among the just. Jesus expected this renunciation of judging not only of individuals but also of the new people which he wanted to assemble, and thereby of its leaders and of the High Council. But this "expectation" was too high, and they stuck by their "well-tried" practice, so that in fact they served as a clear negative model for what was set out in Jesus' proclamation of judgment. The high priest and councillors — giving full expression to salvation history — played the part of those who judge, pronounce their victim guilty of death as a blasphemer, and thereby bring judgment on themselves.

The Process of Expulsion

The condemnation of Jesus becomes fully understandable only if it is seen in the framework of a more comprehensive process. In the theological tradition of the Christian churches, there have been long and detailed discussions as to whether Jesus bore our sins (Luther, Barth) or whether he underwent that punishment which we deserved (Athanasius, Maximus the Confessor, Grotius, Storr), or whether he carried out an atoning deed (Anselm of Canterbury) in place of the punishment which was deserved. In Jesus' understanding of his death, which we will have to go into explicitly later on, there are no precise indications to be found by which we could judge later theories of redemption. But rather the judgment against him was part of a comprehensive dramatic process which has to be examined very precisely in order to understand in terms accessible to experience the background of what was to lead later on to intricate theological theories.

It is already evident that the concerted action of the Jewish authorities was possible only because groups which otherwise were at variance with one another found themselves for once together in a common action. "That Jesus turned all sections of the Jewish leadership against him must have been a decisive factor in their cooperation. At the same time it is self-evident that in the capital the initiative against Jesus was taken by the high priestly group, while in Galilee it was the Pharisees who appeared as the principal opponents."[9] After the first hearing, things seem to have developed into a scene dominated by the rabble, in which the servants gave rein to their cruel fun (see Mark 14:65 and parallels). But for the execution the cooperation of the great adversary, the Roman occupying power, became crucial. How the events were played out in detail, how far the Romans themselves seized the initiative and how far they were pushed, can no longer be accurately established. The Messiah question in any case brought together Jewish and Roman fears or interests against Jesus, and thus the emphasis of the accusation could easily be shifted from the religious to the purely political level, without the need for any conscious two-facedness, since, according to the Jewish understanding of the Messiah, the two aspects could not be separated. The assumption that the accusation before Pilate was just a deliberate and deceitful slander is unlikely for the added reason that such a varied group as the Sadducees and the Pharisees would hardly have worked together at the level of pure lies, especially as the Pharisees were people with high moral claims. They no doubt had their own interests and convictions, on the basis of which they considered a momentary collaboration with the Romans both appropriate and necessary. Even groups from among the people played a part in their own way, as the Barabbas story suggests (Mark 15:6–15). Luke is able to report a tradition according to which Pilate brought Herod into the affair of Jesus, and thereby made a friend in him, even though they had

---

9. Pesch (1976, 1977) 2:412.

been enemies before (Luke 23:6–12). Finally, Jesus became the victim of the Roman soldiery, who not only did their "duty" but gave way to their coarse mockery (Mark 15:16–20). All these groups each had its own motives; they each acted out of conviction or opportunism or simply got into the affair by accident. In any case they played their greater or smaller parts in that process by which Jews and gentiles, those with responsibility, servants, and the people joined hands for a moment against Jesus.

From the viewpoint of the message proclaimed by Jesus, the behavior of his own disciples took on a particular significance, since the kingdom of God had found its first realization in their gathering. Consequently, whether this beginning was genuine must be seen in them; whether it proved itself even in the face of great resistance showed that the coming God of Jesus had completely won their hearts and wills. But at the critical moment this proof was not forthcoming and in fact the opposite occurred. According to Mark, Jesus ended the great judgment speeches with the challenge "Watch!" (Mark 13:37), and shortly afterward the Gospel reports how the disciples were the very opposite of wakeful and instead they slept, while their master prayed alone to God in his anxiety and his need (Mark 14:32–42). The threefold warning of Jesus and the threefold sleeping of the disciples in the garden of Gethsemane depict graphically how the disciples failed fundamentally in their task. Even if the narration of Jesus' struggle with death is shaped by later linguistic formulation, it should nevertheless give a clear picture of how the disciples, even before the arrest of their master, failed at the decisive moment.

The drama of this failure reached its climax in the assertion of Peter that he would never fall away from his master (Mark 14:26–31 and parallels) and in the threefold denial which followed shortly after (Mark 14:66–72). This drama touched its final depths of mystery in that it was one of the innermost circle of the chosen who betrayed his master to the Jewish authorities (Mark 14:10–11, 43–45) and thus immediately set into motion the action against him. That the other disciples, who are not specifically named, had a part in this failure, is shown in their flight at the arrest of their master (Mark 14:50 and parallels).

In the disciples we not only have before us examples of human weakness. More important than the moral question is the theological one, and in particular the question about the destiny of the kingdom of God. As this had its actual beginning among the disciples, it was again radically put in question by their failure. It was consequently shown that the message about the goodness of the heavenly Father, even for those who were at first won over, was not able to transform their deep anxieties and their instinctive will toward recognition and self-assurance into trust and hope. The shepherd was struck down and the sheep ran away (Mark 14:27 and parallels). Even more: through their betrayal — even if in completely different ways — Judas and Peter cooperated with Jesus' opponents, and the others were drawn along in their wake. From the perspective of the proclaimed kingdom of God it is consequently shown that the intended gathering of God's people completely changed into its exact opposite. Because of the anxieties in people's hearts and because of the hardness of that will which opposed the will of Jesus (see Matt. 23:37 and parallels), the result de facto was an assembly against him. Everyone worked together at the different levels of possible human failure in that process which led to his expulsion and execution. What happened was not merely one of those accidental concentrations of human weaknesses which have often come about in history. As Jesus in his ministry proclaimed the coming of God, the result of the apparently accidental working together against him was a fundamental exclusion of the kingdom of God from this world.

In the judgment sayings Jesus diagnosed the forces lined up against the kingdom of God as lies and violence, and he disclosed in his opponents a will to self-assertion which must lead finally to hell and which is of satanic nature. *Exactly these forces which he had laid bare now confronted him.* He was found guilty of blasphemy, condemned by lies, and brought violently to his death. By lies are meant in the first place not individual, conscious untruths, but that great coalition of habit and lethargy, of human fear and opportunism, and finally of the hardened heart and arrogant condemnation of others, which has the effect that individuals act within a web of deceptive representations which become so familiar that they are for the most part unable any longer to see the lies that they contain. This lie Jesus uncovered, and it confronted him by means of violence, which is bound up with it as a twin sister.

So, has humankind unloaded its own guilt onto Jesus? Was he made into a scapegoat? In order to avoid misunderstandings concerning this question, it should be noted exactly what is meant by the image of scapegoat. In the framework of the great Jewish Day of Atonement (Yom Kippur), there was a rite in which the high priest transferred the sins of the whole people onto the head of a he-goat which was subsequently driven out into the wilderness, carrying away the sins of all (Deut. 16:8–10, 20–22). In the sense of this rite, Jesus was certainly not a scapegoat, since the high priest at the hearing certainly did not want — in his conscious intentions — to place the sins of others upon him, but to condemn him for his own offenses. But the word "scapegoat" has acquired another meaning in modern usage, a meaning expressing a deep change of consciousness over against ancient societies. This change is probably a long-term cultural consequence of the message of the cru-

cified one.[10] The modern sense of the word speaks of a process which
takes place on two levels. Those acting think (more or less honestly)
that they have to reproach someone for something. The victim or third
parties however are of the opinion that an injustice is being done to
the accused and that the accusers only want to shift their own problems and faults onto him. In this modern sense, Jesus really was made
a scapegoat, although at the same time he differed fundamentally from
other scapegoats. By his exclusion the society in and around Jerusalem,
suffering as it was from many tensions, did not find genuine peace, for
Jesus differed from other victims in that the violence which struck him
was not accidental. Through his message of the basileia he himself had
awakened the forces which concentrated against him, and he lured them
out of their hiding-place by his judgment speeches. He was no accidental
scapegoat, as is usually the case. By his claim expressed in the message
of the basileia and by his relentless judgment sayings, he himself set in
motion that process which was bound to turn against him.

Not only did the dark forces which he disclosed strike back at him,
but also the goodness which he had given to people was given back
to him in perverted form. "Others he has helped, but himself he cannot help" (Mark 15:31 and parallels), was held against him jeeringly
as he hung on the cross. The helping deed did not find its corresponding
answer, but it was mocked at as weakness by a world in which only self-
assertive power counts. Even the great task of his mission, the assembly
of a new people in the image of the new Temple, was turned back on
him jeeringly in words which distorted his innermost task (Mark 15:29
and parallels). And the future itself was spoiled by his opponents and
rendered no longer able to surprise, for they immunized themselves in
advance beneath the cross against the possibility of conversion by means
of a provocative readiness to believe, which was put on for show: "Let
the Christ, the king of Israel, come down from the cross so that we may
see and believe" (Mark 15:32). Where the idea of a possible future conversion is made into a means of mockery, one closes oneself off precisely
from this possibility.

In his proclamation, Jesus had interpreted the judgment in a new way.
He transformed the picture of a threatening God step by step into the
message of the equally threatening danger of self-judgment. There is an
impressive demonstration of how this closing off of self works in the
scenes of mockery at the crucifixion. Here we have an account not only
of the lethargy of the human heart, but there is sketched in miniature the
functioning of that mechanism by which the world around Jesus drags
down the demands made of it to its own level, distorts them, and uses

10. See Girard (1983), 135–38.

them in this form against itself. The appeal to enter into a new community with God ossifies in the world's hands into a means by which to protect oneself all the better against such a demand. The Son of Man was thus himself confronted by that process of self-judgment which his message triggered off. Jesus warned against judging, and yet himself uttered relentless judgment sayings. In view of this tension, we put this question at the end of the Second Act: Was he not bound to find himself caught up in that mechanism which he diagnosed in others? At that time, the question remained ambiguous. It could be directed against his claim or point to a new, unexpected happening. Now it can be seen that by his judgment sayings he actually triggered off a process which struck back at him and hit him: he became the victim of the sins of others, a scapegoat. But this was a judgment process of a completely new type. The usual assumptions which we have in connection with the word "judgment" are in no way adequate to describe this event. The deciding factor should be how Jesus himself reacted to the evil which confronted him and struck back at him. Did he just become a victim, or did he manage in a new way to stand firm before the destructive power and to conquer it?

Jesus Encountering the Hostile World

Because of the expulsion of Jesus by every group and milieu in the world around him, the question of the kingdom of God was thrown back at him. Since even its initial realization with the group of disciples was shattered again through their failure, its destiny had to be played out at the crucial moment by him alone. Insofar as his claim really stemmed from God, he had to show in his own behavior how God is able to come into a world which is ruled by quite different forces. For this reason we must enquire more closely how he behaved face to face with his enemies, what sense he saw in the death which was threatening him, and what new experience his suffering brought him.

Jesus' Conduct toward His Enemies

In the series of appeals which makes up the Sermon on the Mount, Jesus demanded of his hearers that they love their enemies and not offer resistance to evil. Because of the rejection and the hostile reaction given to him, he was challenged to put his words into practice. But it was not just a case of the coherence between his proclamation and his own actions, for the threatened fate of a violent death posed a question which had not been addressed in so many words in the Sermon on the Mount. Within the framework of the basileia message, the willing love of those who heard it was intended to invite any opponents to conversion. This is why in the Sermon on the Mount, the blow on the cheek, being cheated of a shirt, and being coerced to walk a mile with another, are mentioned (Matt. 5:38–41). The question of a death threat remained at this level unconsidered, as this issue would not have arisen in the case of a successful kingdom of God because enemies would have been converted by the willing love they encountered. But because of its rejection, the situation which Jesus had not at first addressed became pressing. He had to give an answer which would lead toward a resolution, and he gave it by going in his own behavior beyond what he himself had demanded. In view of the evil which confronted him, he did not fall back on the old mechanisms of retribution. He answered the redoubling of evil by taking his love to the point of a readiness to accept without any resistance the death with which he was threatened.

Over and above the high ethical example which Jesus hereby gave, we should look particularly at the implicit theological message which was expressed in his new way of acting. Since his whole public ministry took place within the framework of the dawning kingdom of God, after its rejection the question arose as to how God would react to those enemies who were not won over by the offer of unconditional forgiveness. In the parable of the unmerciful creditor, the master calls back the servant who does not pass on to his fellow servant the kindness that he has received, and he allows the harsh punishment to be carried out on him to the full. Because of the rejection of his message, it could also have been Jesus' task to give a foretaste of the coming, threatening judgment in his own actions. But he did not do so, at least not in the hitherto known form of judgment, but by his behavior he doubled his already gracious message of love of one's enemy and thereby indicated that the mercy of God goes even beyond that spoken of in the parable of the unmerciful creditor. His action consequently points to a dimension of God's love for his enemies whose depths are still to be plumbed.

Jesus' behavior is all the more striking in that it not only conflicted with the purely political picture of the Messiah, but also equally clearly diverged from the expectations which the picture of a more spiritual Messiah awakened, as found for example in the extracanonical Psalm of Solomon 17. Similarly to the parable of the wicked winegrowers or to Jesus' saying about the murder of prophets, the history of Israel is depicted in this psalm as an unbroken series of disloyalties and sins. Because from the king down to the people all have transgressed in a similar way, judgment rightly intervened in the (first) destruction of the holy city and of the throne of David. But as things did not go any better afterward and the few just people were harshly persecuted, the psalmist asks that God might raise up for these persecuted people a new son of David. The awaited one will be no ordinary political leader, for he trusts neither in kingdom nor in steed, rider, bow, or the mass of soldiers

(17:37). Rather, God himself will be king and his anointed will be strong in trust in God alone (17:38), by means of which he will assemble the holy people in Jerusalem (17:28–31).

So far the picture of the coming son of David is easily harmonized with what Jesus proclaimed and did. But already within this picture there can be seen an important difference. Before the Messiah builds up again the tribes of Israel as the people consecrated to the Lord, he strikes the wicked leaders with the "word of his mouth" (17:39) as with a "rod of iron" (17:26) and purifies Jerusalem from all pagans and all criminals. The pagan nations will from then on be under his yoke, and people will come from the ends of the earth to marvel at the splendor in Jerusalem. We can see that neither in the royal kingdom of God nor in the trust in God, neither in the assessment of past history nor in the messianic expectation, neither in the hope of a new establishment of the tribes of Israel as a holy people nor in the broadening of view to include the pagan nations, are there structural differences between the proclamation of Jesus and the great picture of Psalm of Solomon 17. The only, though fundamental, difference lies in the question as to how God deals with his enemies. That the Messiah might share a meal with sinners is hard to imagine from the point of view of Psalm of Solomon 17; but in this context it would be simply outlandish to think that the Messiah could permit himself to be at the mercy of the criminals in Israel and the pagans. That is precisely why he is expected: so that he can finally put an end to the persecution of the just. As the Messiah acts entirely from trust in God, his way of behaving does not directly witness to a higher or lower moral ideal, but it is entirely concerned with the question of God. Jesus' decision to hand himself over to the violence of his enemies is therefore charged with the highest theological significance. When this central aspect is overlooked, the heart of his message and of his mission is ignored.

Because the question of God is crucial and because a clear difference can be seen here, the question about trust in God arises again retrospectively. Does the trust which Jesus lived out match up with the picture in Psalm of Solomon 17? There it is said: "Also he is never weak in his God; God makes him strong in the Holy Spirit. . . . In deeds so mighty, in fear of God so strong, he guards the Lord's flock faithfully and properly, and in the pasture he doesn't allow one of them to become sickly" (17:42–45).[11] That God never abandons the one who completely trusts in him, is also the message of Psalm 91, which is explicitly referred to in the narrative of Jesus' temptations (Matt. 4:6 and parallels). In that psalm, it is said of him who dwells in the protection of the Most

---

11. Translation of the German rendering in Riessler (1966), 900.

High that nothing will happen to him even if thousands fall at his side and ten thousand at his right side: "For he [God] commands his angels to keep you in all your ways" (Ps. 91:11). Jesus appears to have consciously concerned himself with this psalm, for he pointed to it when at his arrest he ordered Peter to put his sword in his sheath, as reported by Matthew: "Or don't you believe my Father would send me more than twelve legions of angels if I requested them?" (Matt. 26:53). Jesus would have been able to find enough passages in Scripture which allowed him — like the anointed one/Messiah in Psalm of Solomon 17 — to ask God for powerful help against his enemies. That he took from Scripture a different task and prayed not against but for his enemies (Luke 23:34) shows that he read the holy texts in a different way than Jewish tradition did, which is of crucial importance above all in view of his understanding of death. Unlike the Messiah in Psalm of Solomon 17, his total trust in God did not mean that he had to be always "strong" and "powerful" in him. The way of weakness is not in contradiction to his messianic trust.

Jesus' Understanding of His Death

The renunciation of divine help toward the destruction of his enemies implies that Jesus was able to accept from within himself the violent death which threatened him. But how exactly did he understand it? This is to throw open the much discussed question, whether he took it on as a saving death or even in the specific sense of atoning for many, as witnessed by his words at the Last Supper. In broad sectors of historical-critical research, there was for a time something like a consensus that at least the words about giving himself for the many and about the blood of the covenant are additions of the post-Easter community. However, some important works of research have opened up again the area of discussion and influenced things in the opposite direction.

On the State of the Question. H. Schürmann starts from an understanding of Jesus as acting on behalf of sinners [German *Pro-Existenz für*] and asks: "Did Jesus have the confidence that the Father would accept the offer of his life given on behalf of sinners and make it an eschatological vehicle of salvation?"[12] As Schürmann, along with the overwhelming majority of scholars, is of the view that the precise formulation of the words at the Last Supper can no longer be established because of the different traditions, he attempts to answer this question of his against a broader context. He starts from the premise, confirmed by our own account of things so far, that Jesus understood himself to be the

---

12. Schürmann (1983), 198.

final bringer of salvation, and he draws from this the following conclusions: If the bringer of salvation actively held on in death to his action on behalf of sinners, then "this death must be described — quite openly — as an offer of salvation and in that way as significant for salvation."[13] In view of the rejection, Jesus could now hold firm to his offer "only with a final effort; loyalty to his task of presenting the salvation of the basileia swept through his body: interceding and offering his own person, he gave himself up to the judgment event."[14] The saying of the coming kingdom of God, which Jesus certainly spoke at the Last Supper (Mark 14:25 and parallels) further proves that he awaited his "being raised up into the position of eschatological bringer of salvation,"[15] and as a result his self-giving death in fact becomes a saving death. The symbolic sharing of bread and offering of the cup at the Last Supper prove finally his "servant-like giving," which was a giving of the final bringer of salvation to his death. Eschatological soteriology must therefore — according to Schürmann — have implications for our understanding of the cross.

R. Pesch comes to a similar conclusion by a different route. Linguistic analyses show him that the tradition in Mark's Gospel is the most original one.[16] In distinction to Paul's report (1 Cor. 11:23b–25), which is to be understood as "aetiology of worship,"[17] we are dealing here with a text which "does not tell of the establishment of the eucharistic celebration, but has as its theme Jesus' interpretation of his death given at the paschal meal."[18] It belongs to the pre-Markan passion story and should, as "the oldest piece in the tradition of the early community,"[19] capture precisely the words of Jesus at the Last Supper.[20]

Even before the two above-mentioned authors, H. Patsch submitted a detailed study in which, in distinction to Pesch, he believes he can show that it is impossible to reach a (Greek) original form of the account of the Last Supper.[21] But he does not stop at this negative conclusion, but takes it precisely as the starting point for his further argument. If, in spite of the fact that the texts cannot be derived from each other, essentially the same elements are found in all of them, then these must have been contained in the original (Semitic) Last Supper tradition. In a fur-

---

13. Ibid., 207.
14. Ibid., 209; see also Schürmann (1975), 85–90.
15. Schürmann (1983), 212.
16. Pesch (1978), 21–53.
17. Ibid., 34–66.
18. Ibid., 89.
19. See Pesch (1983), 113–55.
20. Since the entire argumentation is made on form- and redaction-critical grounds and strongly contradicts a provisional result (the prior stage of Mark) of the approach of other researchers, we cannot here take a position on it.
21. Patsch (1972), 69–89.

ther step, Patsch argues that the idea of universal vicarious atonement was alive in the Palestinian Jewish tradition at the time of Jesus, and that — with the exception of the Last Supper sayings and Mark 10:45 — one cannot prove any influence of Isaiah 53 on the early Christian profession of Jesus as the Christ.[22] After the "underivability from post-Easter theology has been proved,"[23] Patsch sets out how the pre-Easter Jesus' representation of the atonement can be made understandable.

Schürmann, Pesch, and Patsch come — by partly different ways — to an essentially similar result. The cogency of their efforts certainly suffers from the fact that the opposing judgments about the originality and meaning of the pre-Markan tradition — especially between Pesch and Patsch — strike at least one central nerve of their respective arguments. All the same, these three scholars, relying to some extent on the important work of J. Jeremias,[24] between them bring together so many individual elements that one could well think that historical-critical exegesis would have to follow this direction, unless another, more comprehensive, counter-proposal were put forward that went into all the many individual points and at the same time showed concretely how the representations of atonement could have developed in the post-Easter period. No such proposal has been put forward, and yet there are recognized, prudent scholars for whom it is quite clear, even despite the above-mentioned works, that the idea of atonement in the Last Supper sayings cannot come from Jesus. Thus, for example, P. Fiedler, who in an article directly discusses Pesch and Schürmann and in passing Patsch as well,[25] continues firmly to reject their views. First of all he brings out the contradictions in the evaluation of the different Last Supper traditions in order then to deal with the problematic itself. Thus for example he points to the "Jewish horror of consuming blood"[26] and to the problem of how the understanding of atonement in Isaiah 53 can have become comprehensible for Jesus within the history of tradition.[27] His real difficulties become visible when he asks about the "possibility of uniting the basileia message of Jesus with the expectation of a death which mediates salvation"[28] and tries out three possible answers, those of Pesch, Schürmann and Vögtle. Pesch, and Schürmann are finally criticized with similar arguments, and the choice falls on Vögtle, according to whom the elements needing interpretation in the Last Sup-

---

22. Ibid., 151–82.
23. Ibid., 179.
24. See Jeremias (1967).
25. Fiedler (1982).
26. Ibid., 199–201.
27. Ibid., 201–4.
28. Ibid., 205–15.

per tradition (new covenant, vicarious atonement) presuppose the Easter faith. In criticism of Pesch and Schürmann he proposes a brief sketch of Jesus' ministry, according to which Jesus in Jerusalem did not think of death at all, but intended to return to Galilee after the feast days. Fiedler himself has to note: "It hardly needs to be emphasized that the evaluation of Jesus' situation sketched here cannot be harmonized with the view that would see his basileia proclamation as rejected by Israel before the paschal death."[29] He starts, then, from a presupposition which is in contradiction to the conclusions we have thus far reached. In order to make clear the consequences of his own view, he would also have had to say clearly which of Jesus' sayings in the synoptic Gospels he attributes to the post-Easter community, to explain how he intends to consider the way they arose in detail, and to evaluate the theological worth of the post-Easter judgment sayings. As long as no unambiguous answers are given to such important questions, his line of argument cannot in the final analysis become sufficiently clear. Behind the historical sketch and in the criticism of Pesch and Schürmann, however, there can be discerned in Fiedler's writing important elements of a theological conception. He thinks that the representation of Jesus' atoning death involves fundamentally a "massive backward step"[30] even from the Old Testament picture of God, and that atonement would not help Israel any further, as the people, despite this "substitute performance" of Jesus, would stand in danger of final rejection. Fiedler raises the same theological objection against Schürmann's statement that Jesus left it to the Father as to how the latter wished to grant salvation to the world, whether through a proclamation or through his death.

> If this alternative, which is here very pointed — not to say macabre — had been formulated before Good Friday, it would not only have brought with it a turning away from the proclamation of Jesus among the public. The expectation that salvation would be granted "through his death" (as the means) would also have meant — here we see the same objection as against Pesch's construction — a massive backward step from the knowledge which lay behind this very proclamation as also behind early Jewish thought and the Hebrew Bible about the sovereign, saving actions of God, whose forgiveness is not allocated on the basis of a death, not even that of the "representative" of his basileia.[31]

Fiedler's line of argument relies at the decisive point on the question of the picture of God, and here he articulates those objections which

29. Ibid., 205.
30. Ibid., 206.
31. Ibid., 210f.

liberal theology has already put forward in the name of the basileia message against the church dogma of the death of the redeemer. Thus, for example, H. J. Holtzmann in his *Textbook of New Testament Theology* argued from the point of view of the kingdom of God against the doctrine of redemption in the following way:

> For the moment the fact of assured forgiveness remains firm, without any reservation being made concerning a satisfaction-bearing, atoning passion, which only appears subsequently as an objective *causa meritoria remissionis peccatorum* (meritorious cause of the remission of sins), just as there is talk in Matt. 6:12=Luke 11:4; 15:20–24; 18:13, 14; Matt. 18:22 of forgiveness coming to the person who admits sinfulness and repentantly seeks pardon. The very simple rule is spelled out in Luke 6:37, "Judge not, and you will not be judged." The promise corresponding to this command directly links to the penitent and trusting prayer for forgiveness this forgiveness itself...; as in those prophetic passages which in many other ways offer strategic insights into Jesus' proclamation (Hos. 6:6; Mic. 6:6–8; Jer. 3:12–14; 1 Sam. 15:22), forgiveness likewise appears linked not to sacrificial deeds but to the single condition of moral conversion, purification of the heart, and works of obedience.[32]

According to this judgment, the God of the basileia message and of many prophetic utterances is directly played off against the doctrine of atoning death. A choice has to be made between the two. Thus A. Jülicher even thought that Jesus would have been "guilty of seriously misleading his listeners"[33] if he had taught the necessity of atoning death in his proclamation.

This problematic, stemming from liberal theology, poses a genuine question, which many opponents of this theology have not seen clearly enough. This can be made clear by a statement of H. Patsch, whose remarks on the Last Supper we can follow in essentials, but whose interpretation of the atoning death raises very difficult problems: "Satisfaction is made to the divine order of retribution, which was valid in Israel and over the entire world; the judgment of God is fulfilled vicariously upon the one who in God's place grants forgiving communion with him to the lawless."[34] According to this judgment, the proclamation of Jesus left the idea of a vengeful God, which Patsch — as distinct from Holtzmann, Jülicher, Fiedler, etc. — considers as central for the Old Testament

---

32. Holtzmann (1911), 1:254f.
33. See also Jülicher (1899), 364f.; Vögtle (1976), 51–113.
34. Patsch (1972), 224; see also the corresponding interpretation of atonement in the Old Testament: Gese (1983), 85–106.

representation of God, quite unaltered. The goodness of God, which Jesus proclaimed in the basileia message, would only have meant that retribution no longer affected sinners directly, because it was poured out onto the one pure of sin, who was condemned vicariously for others.

In discussing the Last Supper sayings we have consequently arrived at that problematic which we mentioned in the introduction concerning the relationship between God's goodness and anger (justice). The historical answer with respect to the Last Supper sayings depends entirely on the answer to the systematic problem. A step toward clarifying things should be possible only if one avoids setting out from fixed representations, either concerning atonement or concerning the kingdom of God. We have seen so far that Jesus operated entirely within the framework of Israel's holy Scriptures, but by means of many small shifts he finally proclaimed a new overall picture of God, which contrasts in important points with the Old Testament one. The idea of judgment was not weakened, but it certainly appeared in quite a new light. From this transformation in the representation of judgment, the question necessarily arises whether the image of atonement had to change within the drama of Jesus' destiny and whether the apparently unreconcilable contradictions between the basileia message and atoning death do not stem from the fact that the starting point is a preconceived idea of atonement and that the statements made against it in fact contradict this. The central role of the picture of God allows us in any case to pursue further the problematic of the Last Supper in the framework of our reflections, even if we are unable to go into many individual points.

The Answer of the Kingdom of God to Rejection. In the following we intend first of all to bring together some of the results of historical-critical research, which seem to some extent established, in spite of great differences of opinion. After that we turn to the decisive question, whether from our findings up until now an answer can be found to the question concerning Jesus' understanding of his death which will do justice both to those arguments which support the originality of the Last Supper tradition and to those considerations which, since the liberal theologians, have been voiced against the notions of atonement, in the name of the proclamation of God's kingdom.

1. Because of their Semitic (Aramaic/Hebraic) choice of words (semitisms) — even in the Greek partially recognizable — the Last Supper sayings point to an origin in the Palestinian community.[35] Paul, too, explicitly says that he himself received from the Lord what he handed

---

35. Jeremias (1967), 165–81; Patsch (1972), 69–105; Pesch (1978), 69–76; Green (1988), 207–9.

down to the Corinthians (1 Cor. 11:23). So he was convinced that his tradition went back not only to the Palestinian community but to Jesus himself. However, as he was in Antioch at the latest in the early 40s C.E., probably in the late 30s, the corresponding Last Supper tradition must already have been in circulation there and have been considered as coming from Christ. Also creedal formulas like 1 Cor. 15:3b–5, which, according to his own witness, Paul himself received, point back to the Palestinian community. We are coming fairly close to the events themselves.

2. Although Isaiah 53 was never followed up in the canonical writings of the Old Testament and "remained uncomprehended like an erratic block"[36] in the realms of early Jewish thought there thrived, alongside the traditional representation of death as atonement for one's own sins, also the concept of *vicarious* atonement, as E. Lohse was able to show by unambiguous documentary proofs in *Martyrs and the Servant of God*. But Isaiah 53 was hardly decisive in this. "For it must give food for thought that almost no reference is made to Isaiah 53 as the scriptural basis for atoning death."[37] K. Wengst was able to throw light on this strange fact by showing that the documentary evidence collected by Lohse practically all stems from the Hellenistic Jewish world.[38] Here on the one hand the traditional Jewish barriers against the representation of vicarious atonement were less effective, and on the other the Greek representation of the hero's death for a friend or for the fatherland could be combined with the traditional Jewish idea of atonement for one's own sins.[39]

However there is one important point where this conclusion is in need of clarification. Jewish-Hellenistic representations of atonement differ from Isaiah 53 and the New Testament in that for Judaeo-Hellenism vicarious atonement has only a temporary effect and that is only for the benefit of Israel and never of the "many nations." "Atoning death attracts a temporary merit, which God can apply to Israel, which keeps Israel alive, but it effects no final forgiveness, it has no positive significance for the world of the nations. 'For the nations there is no ransom' was a saying of the Rabbis."[40] Atonement in the early Jewish sense is valid for this life,[41] and it benefits only Israel.

From these preliminary ideas based on the history of religions there

---

36. Koch (1966), 237.

37. Lohse (1963), 105. "But that means that Judaism developed its atonement understanding in all its domains without reference to Isaiah 53!" (Patsch [1972], 157).

38. Wengst (1972), 62–71; see also Patsch (1972), 155–58; Fiedler (1982), 202–4.

39. Ibid., 67–70

40. Patsch (1972), 152.

41. Jeremias (1966), 219, 222.

arises an important consequence for the question about the ideas of
atonement in the early post-Easter community. Since both the Last Supper tradition and the profession of faith that Jesus died for our sins
(1 Cor. 15:3–5) were already available to Paul, as he himself expressly
admits, both must have been known to the Palestinian community. But
as corresponding representations of atonement were not current in the
Palestinian Jewish world of the time, the young Christian community
cannot have taken them over from there.[42] Nor was there any compelling necessity for them to make up for themselves such a theology,
since they were able, as proved by old, comprehensive formulations of
faith, equally to be found in the Pauline writings (see Phil. 2:6–9; 1 Tim.
3:16), to express their faith from the first without a direct profession
of the atoning death. The result of this is to leave only one possible
historical explanation for the post-Easter representations of atonement,
namely, to trace them back to Jesus himself.

The same conclusion is forced on us from a second direction. The
understanding that the one presiding over the meal should give himself in symbolic form to the participants at the meal to eat was totally
alien to Jewish custom[43] and only in the Hellenized Jewish world are
certain indications in this direction to be found.[44] Even further from
Jewish belief was the representation of drinking blood (see Lev. 7:26ff.;
17:1–14; Deut. 12:23–25). Now, if both, i.e., the presider over the meal
giving himself to eat and drink and the "blood" being drunk, are found
early on in that Palestinian community which was still entirely Jewish-
Christian, then this praxis can only derive from him who in fact brought
something new and to whom the community knew itself bound.

3. If the post-Easter tradition points us clearly back to Jesus himself, then the further question arises as to whether the new element,
which the acts and words of the Last Supper certainly contain, is understandable in the framework of his proclamation. In order to answer this
question, we can start with something which Schürmann strongly emphasized, Jesus' existence on behalf of sinners and his having been sent
on account of the basileia. If his message was inseparable from his person, as is widely recognized in historical-critical research, then not only
what he did, but everything that he suffered, concerned the kingdom
of God itself. If this is granted, then it is no longer possible to see his
driving out of demons and his meal-communities as eschatological signs

---

42. Fiedler himself assumes (1982, 202–4) that the atonement concept was not alive
in Palestinian Judaism in Jesus' time. On the other hand, he is aware of Paul's statements,
yet he assigns the origin of the idea of atonement to the post-Easter community as though
there is no problem. He does not make clear how these three facts can exist side by side.

43. See Klauck (1982), 55–67; 86–91.

44. Ibid., 166–205.

touching on the kingdom of God itself and to suddenly ignore this dimension in his sufferings. Why should his condemnation and his violent death have been only his private affair and have had at the most the character of a moral example for his disciples? If one wishes to hold this view, one must at the very least also show when Jesus dissociated his person and his fate from the kingdom of God. But it is precisely the eschatological prediction in the framework of the Last Supper tradition ("I will no longer drink of the fruit of the vine until..." [Mark 14:25]), attributed by scholars with unusual unanimity to Jesus himself, which clearly indicates that, even when faced with his certainly imminent death, he saw his fate and the matter of the kingdom of God together. *Therefore his behavior toward his enemies was at the same time the answer of the kingdom of God to those who rejected it.*

4. The question of the forgiveness of sins played an important role in the faith of Israel since the time of exile. Through regular sacrifices, but above all through the celebration of the great day of reconciliation (Yom Kippur), the high priests, the Temple, and the people were supposed to be purified annually from their offenses (Lev. 16). How far the problem of forgiveness of sins remained acute and was at the time of Jesus associated in the Palestinian Jewish world with the Messiah, is, however, proved by Targum Isaiah 53. The fourth song of the suffering servant is here interpreted in an unambiguously messianic sense, but vicarious suffering becomes a plea of the Messiah for sinners: "Surely then he has borne our sicknesses and carried our sorrows.... But he was wounded for our transgressions, he was bruised for our iniquities" (Isa. 53:4, 5). From these utterances just quoted and from the broader context of the translation, in which there is further talk of forgiveness, K. Koch concludes: "Of all the acts of the Messiah, his ministry of *forgiveness of sins* is the most emphasized.... The Messiah frees his people from the burden of sin by interceding with God."[45] Prayer consequently took on a very great importance in the Jewish life of faith.

In complete harmony with the faith of Israel, forgiveness of sins also played a central role in the basileia message of Jesus. Through the preaching of God as Abba, sin was not trivialized, as the consequent judgment sayings made especially clear, but preparedness for forgiveness was stressed. As Jesus did not refer to the atoning sacrifice of the Temple, he must have allotted to his own ministry a dimension of forgiveness of sins. Through the rejection of his message, the question of forgiveness became more urgent, insofar as Jesus did not want to abandon people to a final judgment. There arose therefore — in analogy with Yom Kippur — the renewed question of a great act of atonement. For

---

45. K. Koch (1972c), 147f.

this reason, Blank can rightly maintain that the question of atonement in the fate of Jesus is to be looked at not only from the point of view of Isaiah 53, but also from that of the great day of reconciliation,[46] and that from this perspective his conflict with the Temple must be examined afresh. From the moment that Jesus began "to preach the great reconciliation of God with people independently of the Temple,"[47] the ground was prepared for a fundamental conflict, which had as its consequence violent death.

> The problem with which many authors wrestle, if they attempt to set the pre-Easter ministry of Jesus, the "eschatological soteriology" of the basileia and the post-Easter understanding of Jesus' death as a "death of vicarious atonement" in relation to each other... is precisely that they do not take seriously enough the radicality of the earthly Jesus' basileia-soteriology and do not situate it precisely enough in a historical sense as "the end of the cultic atonement ritual," as the behavior of Jesus in fact determined things.[48]

This dimension, which Blank so decisively brings out, is worthy of careful consideration. However it is not enough by itself, for the Qumran community also broke with the Temple cult in Jerusalem without finding a satisfactory substitute. But the deciding difference between the sect and Jesus was that they cut themselves off from the world and only expected salvation for those pious people who held by the law, whereas he proclaimed salvation precisely for sinners and outlaws. In Qumran they awaited a liberation from sin through a stricter practice of the law, while Jesus showed how even the apparently just are still completely entangled in sin.

5. From Targum Isaiah 53, in which the Messiah is described as intercessor for the sins of the people, and in view of Jesus' distance from the Temple, the further question arises whether he understood his task in the service of the kingdom of God which he announced as that of an intercessor. He himself challenged people to pray for their enemies: "Love your enemies and pray for those who persecute you" (Matt. 5:44), and

---

46. "In this connection there is a connection of historical motif between Isaiah 53 and Leviticus 16, specifically in the idea of the 'guilt sacrifice' or the 'scapegoat motif,' which is found in both texts" (Blank, "Weisst du, was Versöhnung heisst?" in Blank and Webick, eds. [1986], 78).

47. Ibid., 82.

48. Ibid. So we can agree with the facts of the matter as indicated by Patsch: "One will not go amiss with the assumption that initially the Jewish war, with the destruction of the Temple and the loss of Jerusalem and so the end of the cultic institution of atonement, could have prepared the ground for this concept of atonement..." (Patsch [1972], 156).

it is reported of him that he in fact spoke up for them with his heavenly Father when there was persecution (Luke 23:34). One more theme could point in this direction. Berger has referred to the early Jewish tradition of the "son of David" and called attention, for the correct grasp of this tradition, to an apparently regular pattern, whereby an eschatological figure (e.g., son of David) always corresponds to a historical figure (e.g., David):

> Now the validity of the following rule can easily be observed: The eschatological correspondent to a historical figure will be not so much endowed with features or names from the figure itself, as named after the figure's son or successor. Thus the eschatological antitype to David is called "son of David" — and he is provided with characteristics of the late Jewish picture of Solomon.... It must therefore be asked in principle what significance the late Jewish picture of Solomon has for the portrayal of the son of David in the New Testament.[49]

If one follows this suggestion, then it can be seen how already in 1 Kings 3:2–15 Solomon is presented as the king who begs not for private advantage but for the wisdom to govern the nation and is for that reason abundantly answered by God. Also in the Greek book of Wisdom, Solomon appears as the one who asks for wisdom (Wisd. 8:19–9:19) and looks back in the context of this prayer on the whole working out of divine wisdom from Adam to the exodus from Egypt (Wisd. 10:1–19:22). Furthermore, the most central prayers of Israel were the psalms. As most of them were attributed to David, so the messianic Psalm 72 and the equally messianic extracanonical Psalms of Solomon were attributed to the "son of David," so that the latter followed explicitly in the line of his father, the great maker of prayers. In several places,[50] especially in the Testament of Solomon, the son of David is portrayed finally as lord over the demons, who received this power from God after he "prayed day and night with his whole soul."[51] "In one of the texts which tells of people tormented by demons, an appeal is directed to Solomon: *basileu Solomon, hyios David, eleeson me,*[52] 'O King Solomon, son of David, have mercy on me.' "[53] The great maker of prayers, Solomon, was — as "son of David" — implored for help in a way similar to the way sick and

---

49. Berger (1974), 4.
50. See Flavius Josephus, *Antiquities* VIII 44–49; *Old Testament Pseudepigrapha* (1983, 1985) 1:944–51.
51. Test. Sol. I, 5.
52. Test. Sol. XX, 1.
53. Berger (1974), 7.

plague-ridden people frequently called on Jesus: "Son of David, have mercy on me/us" (Matt. 9:27; 15:22; 20:30ff.).

In view of these parallels to the synoptic Gospels, the question arises whether the picture of Solomon, the son of David, the wise sayer of prayers and the lord over demons, does not offer an appropriate background against which a convincing image can be sketched of how Jesus may have understood his task in the face of his enemies. Is there perhaps a way to interpret the idea of atonement from the viewpoint of the idea of powerful intercessory prayer so that everything that people find disturbing in the idea and that seems to stand in contradiction to the message of the basileia is discarded? The tradition of Jesus' prayer is so well rooted and the connection between love of one's enemy and intercessory prayer so central for the Sermon on the Mount and for Jesus' own behavior, that this aspect cannot be overlooked and should be continually kept in mind as a way into the problematic of atonement.

However, it is very questionable whether everything about Jesus' understanding of his death will be explained by means of intercessory prayer. If one reads, e.g., the whole Testament of Solomon, it very soon becomes evident that one is — despite some parallels to Jesus' proclamation — in a very different world from his. Prayer and magic are here too interwoven to allow one to make fully convincing parallels to the New Testament. Even the comparison with Targum Isaiah 53, from which we set out first of all cannot help us further in every respect. Even if the central link between Messiah and intercessory maker of prayers can be found here, the request made is very limited in scope. It extends only to members of the chosen people.[54] It is true that together with the prayer there is linked a certain idea of atonement. The sins of the chosen people must, in spite of the plea made, be borne by someone, but they don't fall on the intercessor. He stands for something quite different: The many nations must "atone" for Israel; the Messiah lets the guilt of the chosen people fall back on them and hands them over to hell.[55] In the relationship of the Messiah to the enemies of God (enemies of the elected people) the decisive difference can be seen once again between Jesus and the preceding tradition. In Targum Isaiah 53, the idea of atonement is certainly there beside the prayer of intercession, but it takes on quite a

---

54. In the background of Targum Isaiah 53 stands also Exod. 17:12, where Israel is stronger than its enemy Amalek as long as Moses stands on the mountain praying with his arm uplifted.

55. "When he [the Messiah] prays, he receives an answer, and before he opens his mouth he is heard. The mighty men of the nations he will offer as a lamb to the slaughter and as a mother sheep dumb before her shearers; and no one will open his mouth before him or say a word. For he will cause the glory of the nations to leave the land of Israel; he will strike them with the injuries committed against my people. And he will devote the godless to hell" (Haag [1985], 28f.).

different form than in Isaiah 53 and in the tradition of the Last Supper. The guilt of Israel (and of the nations) does not affect the suffering servant of God, but it must be borne by the nations themselves and be "atoned" through their condemnation to hell.[56] Targum Isaiah 53 consequently gives no cause to play off the idea of intercession against that of atonement, but rather it shows what ideas can be bound up with the concept of atonement. One must tread very warily with it, if one is not to fall short of the picture of God proclaimed by Jesus. The care taken by liberal theology and by many contemporary theologians in this respect should be taken seriously.

6. The theme of intercessory prayer has led us back to the question about the fate of the enemies of God and to the problematic of hell. Since judgment and hell sayings also play a part in Jesus' proclamation, we must once again bring to mind what we have established concerning this theme. Because the meaning of both retribution and atonement depends on their context, all the other decisive elements in the way that judgment is seen must be determined. Jesus in his preaching about judgment did not teach that the goodness of God comes to an end at a particular point and is transformed into its opposite, since he offered only boundless forgiveness as the measure for the new life. However he made clear that all those who do not open themselves to the *rule of God* remain under the law of the *rule of retribution*. From the viewpoint of this understanding of judgment, atonement can never mean that the divine order of retribution must still be complied with, as Patsch formulated it.[57] Such an understanding remains under the spell of that picture of God which Jesus set out to overcome with his message of the basileia. But, in view of the reality of how quickly and almost instinctively people closed themselves up against goodness, the urgent question arose whether those also who have taken the path of self-sufficiency and self-condemnation can be helped. Is there still help for the sinners who harden themselves or must they because of a deeply rooted anxiety, because of an instinctive seeking for self-security and the ensuing tendency toward lies and violence, almost "necessarily" founder on the goodness of God? Jesus saw himself confronted with this question in view of the rejection of his message, and the problematic of atonement must be tackled in the light of it.

7. Objections have been made (Vögtle, Fiedler, Oberlinner, among others), as we have already briefly seen, to this way of putting the problem, stating that it is quite impossible to speak of a definitive rejection by Israel of the kingdom of God, and that therefore one has to distin-

---

56. See Jeremias (1966), 222–24.
57. Patsch (1972), 224.

guish clearly between a *readiness* for death, which certainly ought to be attributed to Jesus, and a *certainty* of death, which is not demonstrable.[58] Consequently there are no historical grounds for the assumption that he understood his death as an atoning death and interpreted it that way to his disciples at the Last Supper. This view involves several historical judgments of detail which we have already considered and about which we came to rather different conclusions. But as the problematic of atonement is decisive for the way we understand the death of Jesus, we will have to turn to it again.

If God is imagined as an eternal, unaltering sun, which shines on humankind, unmoved, with constant goodness, then it might really be difficult to speak of a definitive rejection. With such a view, there goes a corresponding understanding of time, according to which there are no outstanding moments (or at most that of one's own death). Each hour is equally full of meaning or empty of meaning and therefore one can never say before the last moment of life that someone has definitively decided. At the most, there is a slow ripening toward goodness or a step by step falling away into evil. In line with this representation of time, one can even assume — with a corresponding doctrine of the soul — that the soul's processes continue after bodily death and never become definitive, as Origen may have assumed. In this case, the person and message of Jesus are seen entirely in terms of general ideas.

However, things are different if one thinks not merely of the general idea "Action of God," but of an actual action. Time appears in this case not as a continuous line, but it contains outstanding moments. With such an understanding, the kairos, the moment of fulfillment or opportunity, can be used or squandered. Now we have seen — in agreement with most critical exegetes — that Jesus announced the kingdom of God as an event, which could succeed or fail. It depended on his effectiveness — in teaching, healing, and bringing together — whether the spark actually passed from him to his hearers and whether the new assembly became an event. Jesus lived in a pressured time[59] (expectation of the imminent kingdom), and this should have become a time of celebration [German *Hoch-Zeit; Hochzeit* is the common word for "wedding"]; in fact, even before the public rejection, it became for him — because of people's lack of faith — a heavy burden, which subjectively made the time stretch out again: "O you unbelieving generation! How long will I yet be with you? How long must I yet bear with you?" (Mark 9:19ff. and parallels). So we can understand how it could weigh on him that

---

58. Vögtle (1976), 58; Oberlinner (1980), 23–167; Fiedler (1982), 204f.
59. To the drama of his life belongs the "compression" of time: F. Kienecker, "Theater–Tribunal der Zeit," in *Theater* (1969), 11–37.

these dark events provoked by his proclamation might soon come about: "I have come to cast fire upon the earth; and would that it were already burning. I must be baptized with a baptism, and how I am constrained until it is accomplished" (Luke 12:49ff.). These sayings are not easy to interpret. It is possible that fire meant in the first place the kingdom of God, which Jesus hoped would spread like a fire across the earth. But by baptism he certainly referred to something else. The disputed question, whether he was alluding to a coming baptism of judgment or whether he was more generally predicting an eschatological test, can remain open, as the sayings about baptism are enough to show that he was not proclaiming any general ideas, for which there was always a time. He found himself in a pressured train of events, and was pressed to bring things to an end himself.

Since the kingdom of God as the "time of grace" (Luke 19:44) was at the same time a time of decision, the answer was bound automatically to come out negative if the spark did not fly and the fire did not begin to burn. It was not a question of whether Israel consciously and expressly rejected Jesus by a numerical majority or whether one considers that later on many people would have given their approval. Since the event, which had its particular "time," did not materialize, and the "fire" did not begin to spread, a negative decision had de facto occurred. Before the outward resolution to kill Jesus there lay the inner decision, and he must have picked this up keenly, as his whole effort was being expended in summoning people away from the laws of their everyday behavior. Between the inner decision, which is essentially to be understood as a nondecision in the face of the summons given out, and which perhaps occurred very early on, and the outward reaction of his direct opponents, some time may well have elapsed, in which Jesus on the one hand continued his proclamation of the basileia — even if under a heavy burden — and on the other began immediately to make clear the consequences of rejection through the judgment sayings. It is important not to set up false oppositions here.

If the proclamation of Jesus was a salvation history event, then his hearers took on a role in salvation history. From the concept of role,[60] we can understand more precisely what is meant by definitive rejection. If one thinks of this as a final subjective refusal of God, then very serious difficulties result. On the one hand, in this case redemption would be won by means of the hell of those who rejected Jesus; on the other hand everyone would stand under the same threat even after Easter, as it is hard to see why the grace of redemption should be easier to accept than the grace of the basileia message. Everyone would stand in

---

60. So once more the significance of a dramatic view is shown.

danger of the final destruction, without a convincing reason for hope. But from the viewpoint of a thorough going dramatic understanding of Jesus' fate, such an interpretation of the definitive rejection is excluded. Since Jesus' hearers acted in a salvation history role, rejection was part of their action as *role players*. They made their decision, in view of the new life and the new divine standard which Jesus proclaimed, by remaining caught in the laws and forces of this world. *Definitive rejection* means in this case: it has been *definitively* shown that the forces and powers by which human history is ruled stand in *fundamental opposition* to that message and that life brought by Jesus. In this context, the question of individual salvation remained at first open.

One further problem can be explained by means of the idea of a dramatic role in salvation history. In the investigation up until now, the rejection of Jesus appeared in one way as something monstrous. How hard-hearted must Jesus' hearers have been if they did not open themselves to the message of pure forgiveness and unlimited goodness? In another way the rejection showed itself as something quite natural. Have not people always behaved the same way in history, and was not Jesus' demand concerning faith and love of one's enemy far too much for them, a utopian expectation? The idea of role allows these opposite aspects to be articulated together without contradiction. In the fate of Jesus a monstrous conflict between the kingdom of God and the laws of this world was in fact played out. But at the same time it became clear that the "players" are so ruled by strange forces that from their point of view no other decision could have been expected. Their actions were monstrous and totally banal at the same time.

The problems which are thrown up by the distinction mentioned above between readiness for death and certainty of death should consequently resolve themselves if the kingdom of God is understood as an event and seen in the context of the drama of salvation history. The question before which Jesus stood at the last meal with his disciples was not whether, after the rejection of the willing forgiveness of his Father, he should proclaim another opportunity for salvation, a "salvation on the basis of a substitute performance." The dramatic question was rather how the goodness of his Father can reach human hearts, after it has been definitively shown what opposition existed in the forces of this world and how far people were subject to them. The surprising answer of Jesus appears in allowing himself to be handed over to the dark powers (lies, violence, diabolical self-certainty) and to be struck by them.

8. Before we come directly to the Last Supper sayings, we intend to review briefly the steps taken so far. Paul with his witness referred us to the early post-Easter community. There was no starting point to be found in that community which would make the atonement sayings

comprehensible, which is why we are forced back to Jesus himself. Since his proclamation could not be separated from his person, even his death had to be seen from the event of the dawning kingdom of God. Comparison with the Temple's institution of atonement, from which Jesus distanced himself, suggests that the question of forgiveness of sins acquired a particular significance. The idea of the Messiah's intercession for sinners was shown to be equally important, but by itself insufficient, because the fate of the lawless and the pagans, but also of the alleged "righteous" in view of their hidden sins, cannot be clarified. Neither does the opposite attempt, to tone down the rejection of Jesus' message, lead any further, because it does not do justice to the kingdom of God as an event or to the dramatic atmosphere of the judgment sayings. Thus the only remaining explanation is that Jesus must have expressly asked himself the question as to how the salvation that he proclaimed as unconditional with the kingdom of God at hand can become a reality despite the resistance of those who should have given themselves freely to it.

The actions and words at the Last Supper give an answer which, although it was prepared by Israel's great tradition, was in the last analysis new. Jesus was able to look back on the violent fate of the prophets and see himself in their line; even the tradition of the suffering just man who is raised up to splendor and to a judicial position (Wisd. 5:16; Job 33:3, 9) stood at his disposal and could be without great difficulty linked with messianic notions. There existed a direct messianic interpretation of Isaiah 53 which, however, excluded the idea of atonement by the Messiah and transferred it to the nations. Finally there was the text of Isaiah 53 itself, which had been handed down as a hitherto uncomprehended utterance.

In the proclamation of the basileia, Jesus to a large extent continued the faith tradition of his people and simultaneously, through countless small shifts in meaning, drew a new picture of God. His judgment sayings were just as much in the tradition, and yet they were drawn into a process of reinterpretation. In his own behavior toward his enemies, Jesus allowed the nonviolence of the servant of God (Isa. 50:4–9) to find complete expression in reality. So it should not be a cause for surprise that he was able for the first time to give full meaning to the "erratic block" of Isaiah 53,[61] which diverged from the interpretations hitherto current. The nonviolence of the servant of God (Isa. 50:4–9) and his vicarious suffering (Isa. 53) belong together as much as Jesus' nonviolence, his love of enemies, and his readiness, shown in the Last Supper sayings, for the vicarious offering up of his life. His own behav-

---

61. See Koch (1966), 237.

ior shows how he saw and understood anew the texts which had been handed down.

9. After these preliminary summary reflections, we can now attempt to interpret the actions and sayings of Jesus himself. Although he proclaimed God's basileia and not directly himself, his person played an outstanding role in the event he announced. Through his "But I say to you" he also distanced himself clearly from the prophetic style of proclamation, in which message and person ultimately remained always separable. When his proclamation came up against rejection, his person stepped even more clearly into the foreground, as the question was now explicitly asked about him, what spirit was working in him (Mark 3:22–30) and with what authority he was acting (Mark 11:27–33 and parallels). With the Son of Man sayings, there began his indirect self-proclamation, and before his death he took the step in the circle of his trusted ones (Last Supper) and before the world (trial) toward direct self-proclamation.

He identified the gifts of the meal (bread and wine) with his person and his fate, but the question as to how this identification is to be understood still remains open. The decisive thing at first was that *the kingdom of God was now to be understood entirely from the perspective of his person and his fate and no longer, as before, the other way around.*

As there is no gift which can be so completely appropriated by the receivers as that which is offered to them to eat and drink, Jesus gave himself to his disciples through identification with bread and wine, so that he would be one with them — as food which is consumed becomes one with the eater. The kingdom of God was consequently from this moment on no longer present merely in the form of outward sayings or symbolic actions, but it assumed a form in which it could enter into people themselves and thus infiltrate their defensive wills.

The identification of Jesus with the gifts of bread and wine became possible only in connection with a second "giving," namely, with the nonviolent offering up of his own life in the confrontation with the enemies of God's kingdom. The two forms of giving mesh together and mutually clarify one another. On the one hand, the body that was given to eat emphasizes that the offering up to a violent death was far more than a noble ethical example. The fate of the kingdom of God was at stake. On the other hand, the body which was given up to death makes clear that the gift of God's kingdom in the situation of rejection was only possible thanks to a love of one's enemies which answered the violent rejection with a still greater offering up. Neither of the two forms of offering is meaningful without the other, and yet both together bring to expression how Jesus understood his death as a death for many. There is no need to credit him with a theory of atonement, worked out down to the last detail, and one must be careful about understanding his sayings directly in the sense of one or the other of the more recent theological doctrines.

The Heavenly Father and the Persecuted Son

So far we have considered different actors in the drama of Jesus' death: himself, his enemies (cooperation of different groups), and the disciples, who were with him at the last meal, but shortly thereafter let themselves be drawn to his opponents' side. But the "role" of heavenly Father is still to come, and it is his actions which will determine how Jesus' offering of himself for the many, and hence the idea of atonement, is ultimately to be understood. Since the actions of the Father appear only indirectly, in the prayer on the Mount of Olives and in the abandonment by God of the crucified one, we have to proceed very cautiously here in order not to introduce too quickly into his fate our own interpretative representations.

The Will of the Father

In great distress at the prospect of death, Jesus begged the Father that the cup should pass him by, and at the same time he put his trust in the divine will: "Yet not what I will, but what thou wilt" (Mark 14:36). Since his arrest followed the prayer, he must have acknowledged that in the mission from his Father he had to take this path. But what does the request about freeing him from the "cup" mean, if he had already at the last meal with the disciples spoken of his death for the many and dedicated it to his disciples under the symbol of bread and wine? This "contradiction" between the words at the Last Supper and the request in his prayer must be clarified if the scene at the Mount of Olives is not to become a convincing argument working retrospectively against the originality of the Last Supper sayings. Under the title "transformation of those taking part," G. Feldmeier has pointed to a decisive dimension in the Gethsemane narration. All the participating actors experience at this point a change, so that suddenly they are (or at least appear to be) in a role which is in opposition to their behavior up until now. From among the disciples who have just been with their master, now there are some who are incapable of watching with him. He himself steps out of the role of the one who resolutely walks to his death into the experience of a man who is gripped by "fear and anguish" and whose soul is "sorrowful, even to death" (Mark 14:33). And even the Father — in Feldmeier's words — becomes, from giver of the kingdom of God, the "opponent of his 'beloved Son.' "[62] This threefold transformation makes clear that

---

62. Feldmeier (1987), 118.

something fundamentally new is being portrayed in this account. The transformation cannot be explained from the theology of the post-Easter community, and therefore we have to consider that we have before us the report of a special experience which the disciples underwent with their master. Since normally in the synoptic Gospels Jesus' private feelings are hardly ever reported, the sudden alarm and horror which came over him here are particularly striking. The sadness unto death lets it appear how the power of death was beginning to spread over Jesus. Feldmeier in his interpretation emphasizes especially the silence of God, and, in contrast to those countless authors who think that it is necessary clearly to distinguish the theologically significant surrender of Jesus for sinners from a trivial and merely historical surrender to the Jewish authorities, he attempts — above all from the viewpoint of the Old Testament background — to show that the handing over by Judas is to be understood as the consequence of a divine plan and of total abandonment by the Father. "Where God takes away his protecting and sustaining hand from his Son, the Son falls prey to 'sinners' (who are already persecuting him the whole time with increasing intensity)."[63]

Since the kingdom of God was seamlessly connected with the person of Jesus, one cannot hold one set of events in his fate to be trivial, and others full of theological significance. All the elements in his drama necessarily possess a theological relevance. And yet Feldmeier's interpretation has to be taken with caution. First of all, the three synoptics nowhere speak directly of a handing over of Jesus by God, but they frequently use the passive formulation "being handed over," which allows other aspects to come into the interpretation. Even the "transformation of those taking part" analyzed by Feldmeier must be seen in a somewhat more differentiated way. Thus by sleeping the disciples did not fall into an entirely new role, as they had in the past again and again misunderstood their master (Mark 6:52; 8:14–21, 31–33). And Jesus did not experience his Father as his "opponent" in the strict sense, since he addressed him precisely at this crucial hour by the familiar name "Abba." However a profound alteration both in himself and in the disciples is unmistakable. In his suffering, Jesus experienced not only the aggression of humankind but also the absence of the heavenly Father, as his cry on the cross directly proves (Mark 15:34).

The Absence of the Father

Before his death Jesus called (in Aramaic) to his Father: "My God, my God, why have you forsaken me?" (Mark 15:34). Since Psalm 22 begins with these words, they cannot be interpreted as a cry of despair; but they

---

63. Ibid., 224.

do give expression to the way that Jesus before his death is plunged into darkness, as described by the author of Psalm 22. This experience is all the heavier as it had to be undergone by the very one who before had addressed the Father in a unique fashion as "Abba." From the viewpoint of a deep knowledge of God, abandonment by God takes on a special meaning, and for that reason the abandonment of the crucified one gains a theological dimension which goes beyond that of the psalmist. The one who was sent to proclaim by his ministry the kingdom of God, at hand and present, stepped into the opposite role. The reproach of blasphemy which his adversaries brought against him struck him in a more than purely external way. Both the prayer on the Mount of Olives and the cry of abandonment on the cross show how the dark forces struck his very soul.

The request on the Mount of Olives, therefore, does not stand in opposition to the Last Supper sayings. If what is expressed at the Last Supper was Jesus' fundamental understanding of his death, then the subsequent anguish shows how Jesus had to undergo a drama into which he was drawn with his innermost soul, and in which, therefore, something experientially new was able to come about, something which had already been made clear at the objective level. The scene at the Mount of Olives reveals how existential the drama was and that even his innermost space of belief and trust did not remain unaffected. The darkness which attacked his soul was an expression of how deeply he was struck by those forces over which he himself had pronounced judgment. He was the one taking action, and yet he became the victim of what he had released. Certainly, the dark night was possible only because the Father permitted it, but it should not be concluded from this that he was struck directly by his God, who had suddenly transformed himself from a kindly father into a despotic master. Even in this hour it was Jesus' experience and his activity (and not that of his adversaries) which portrayed God. This God showed himself on the Mount of Olives as far more mysterious than in many earlier parables, and yet he remained the "Abba" to whom Jesus entrusted himself absolutely.

The Self-Judgment of Sin in the Judgment of Jesus

The particular character of the third act in the Gospel drama results from the connection between the behavior of the opponents of God's kingdom, the activity and suffering of Jesus, and the actions of the heavenly Father. After Jesus in the second act proclaimed the judgment of God as the self-judgment of people hardening their hearts, we can now see this process of hardening of hearts beginning. If Jesus declared the justice of the Pharisees (and Israel) to be wholly insufficient and warned them above all against judging, on the grounds that the standards which they laid down would become the norm by which they themselves were measured, the Jewish authorities in their behavior toward him insisted stubbornly on their existing form of judgment. The cooperation with the pagans and the ridicule directed against Jesus crucified, in which his good deeds were thrown back at him in scorn, illustrate how the process of hardening of hearts progressed.

However it was decisive that the people who acted in this way were not aware of the process of self-judgment in themselves. There was a great gulf between their evaluation of themselves and their actual activity. They thought that they were only (with right on their side) judging Jesus, and not themselves, and it escaped their notice that their judging of him was in truth a ganging together against him. The third act reveals things in such a way that self-judgment is not direct self-judgment. Those judging intended to judge another and not themselves. But in the light of Jesus' love for his enemies which came from the heavenly Father, their activity is shown up as self-deception, by which they only shifted their own guilt. The self-judgment whose mechanism Jesus opened up and against which he warned people consists not in explicit self-accusation (such a thing, carried out in humility, would be healing), but in the contradiction between word and deed and thereby in the concealment of guilt and the shifting of evil onto others. The judgment on Jesus and the use of ridicule against him are consequently to be read as utterances which indirectly betray a truth about those responsible for these actions. They (and not the accused) are the ones who in fact blaspheme and who want to help others (in words), but cannot help themselves (by deeds). The self-deception is made complete above all in the cooperation, or better the ganging up, on the one, in which the false judgments of individuals mutually confirm one another and thus gain the appearance of factual objectivity. The one who is declared to be guilty, a blasphemer, serves the others as a scapegoat and gives to their kingdom of lies that appearance of peace and stability which every kingdom needs, even Satan's (see Mark 3:22–30 and parallels), in order to be able to continue.

The self-judgment of humankind, in which people shifted their guilt onto Jesus in self-deception, became a judgment on him. But from his viewpoint this was a judgment of a completely different sort. He allowed himself to be drawn into the process of self-judgment of his adversaries, in order, through participation in their lot, to open up for them from inside another way out of their diabolical circle and hence a new path to salvation. He did not pay back the lying judgment and violent attack with the same coin, but he turned around the intensified evil and gave it back as love redoubled. He made of himself a gift to those who judged him and burdened him with their guilt. His atoning deed was not a reimbursement for sins, so that the heavenly Father would forgive, but an act in the place of those who should have welcomed the kingdom of God, but who from the beginning rejected it. Jesus uses precisely this rejection in order to advance under its "cover" into that dark realm where people judge themselves. By allowing sinners to shift their actions onto him, he managed to be drawn into their dark world (fear of death, abandonment by God) in order from within to open up this world once more to the Father.

It is decisive in this interpretation that the handing over by the Father, which Feldmeier stresses in his interpretation of the Gethsemane narration, is seen entirely in connection with the message of the kingdom of God and with the actions of Jesus. From this perspective it cannot be said that the Father handed over the Son because he wanted to judge him and punish him in place of sinners. The judgment did not start from God but from humankind, and the will of the Father was only that the Son should follow sinners to the very end and share their abandonment, in order thus to make possible for them again a conversion from the world of hardened hearts and distance from God.

Fourth Act:
Resurrection of the Son as Judgment of the Heavenly Father

The high claim contained in Jesus' proclamation has placed our investigation before a dilemma. Since the historical judgment about questions of detail is to an important degree dependent on the total picture that one has of the figure of Jesus, the position one takes toward his message must essentially influence the historical judgment about his fate. If one holds his proclamation to be true, then his judgment sayings and his progress toward the cross are to be interpreted entirely according to the principle which he himself gave. Everything can then be seen in the light of the inseparable connection between the message of the basileia and his own person. But if one is skeptical about his claim or even rejects it, then one is forced to see him and the Gospels above all as a product of the religious world of his time. In that case one has to look in the world around him for those factors which could make the sayings of judgment and the Last Supper, as they appear in the Gospels, understandable. In view of this dilemma which concerns scholarly method itself, we have opted — analogously to Anselm of Canterbury's method — to consider his claim to be true as a hypothesis. This hypothesis must now be tested, and we shall do so in connection with the message of Easter. Before we go into the inner meaning of the witness to the resurrection, we must therefore address the question of its credibility.

The Credibility of the Easter Message

Bultmann and many of those who followed him started from the assumption that the actual claim on faith cannot be grasped by the historical-critical method. A separation was thereby advocated between the Easter kerygma and the historical Jesus precisely in the interest of faith. Efforts to show an inner connection between the post-Easter proclamation and Jesus' self-understanding — especially between the message of the cross and the understanding of his own death by the crucified one — were thrown out as invalid attempts to ground faith by human means, as "trusting in the flesh." On this principle, every attempt to demonstrate the credibility of the Easter message by historical and rational means must appear suspicious. The thesis often quoted to this effect is "that historical investigation cannot establish the actual fact of the resurrection."[1]

The principle from which such theses are drawn has shown itself in our investigation so far to be untenable. If historical method is really

---

1. Conzelmann (1959a), 650.

applied critically, i.e., if scholars are prepared, from the viewpoint of the "object" which they come across, to put in question unproved assumptions in their own method, then it is impossible to maintain an a priori contradiction between historically proved utterances and the kerygma of faith. Up to this point we have only sketched hypothetically how such a putting in question can actually happen, and the idea needs now to be worked out as a paradigm in connection with the Easter message.

A Jewish Testimony

We can begin our investigation into the resurrection of Jesus with the testimony of a non-Christian, a believing Jew. After detailed observations on the question of resurrection in the Jewish world and on the corresponding reports of visions, P. Lapide writes:

> In relation to the future resurrection of the dead, I am and remain a Pharisee. Concerning the resurrection of Jesus on Easter Sunday, I was for years a "Sadducee." I am no longer one, since the following reflection forced me to think things through again. In none of the cases in rabbinic literature where there is talk of such visions did there result an important alteration in the way of living of the one brought back to life or of those who had lived through the story. They remained at the level of visions which were retold with wonder and devotion and often also exaggerated; but there were no results that could be established. Things were different with Jesus' disciples on that Easter Sunday. Despite all legendary embellishments there remains in the oldest reports a recognizable historical core, which simply cannot be demythologized. If this shaken, anxious crowd of apostles, who were just about to throw everything away in order to flee to Galilee in utter despair, if these farmers, shepherds, and fishermen who betrayed, disowned, and then despicably denied their master, could suddenly overnight be transformed into a convinced mission group, self-confident and aware of salvation, far more effective after Easter than it had been before, no vision or hallucination is enough to explain such a revolutionary change. Perhaps a single vision would have been enough for a sect, a school, or an order — but not for a world religion, which thanks to the Easter faith was able to conquer Western civilization.[2]

This Jewish testimony proves that not merely Christian-dogmatic presuppositions, but also historical reflections in the context of the Jewish

---

2. Lapide (1977), 74f.

belief in the universal resurrection of the dead, can lead to the conviction that Jesus was raised up from the dead. Lapide assumes not only that the disciples had visions in the days after the crucifixion of their master, which is seldom disputed in modern scholarship, but he affirms unambiguously a resurrection event which occurred to Jesus himself. Since he derived his conviction precisely from the difference from other Jewish reports of visions, it should not on the one hand be put aside too quickly as uncritical; but on the other hand its justification is in need of considerable deepening and broadening, since Mohammed's visions also led not merely to a sect, a school, or an order, but to a world religion.

Psychological Interpretation

Although the special Easter experiences of the disciples are hardly in dispute, attempts are made to explain them in different ways and to decode them as wish projections, or in the language of E. Bloch as wish mysteries,[3] or as the products of some other unconscious psychic process. However, over against such attempts there is the unambiguous fact that the post-Easter community professed its belief in the resurrection only in connection with the cross. The message of the cross contrasted sharply for all the disciples with wish fulfillment, as it was in opposition to the Jews' wish for a sign and the Greeks' search for wisdom (see 1 Cor. 1:22ff.). From this message there resulted demands on the apostles and disciples, which were in complete opposition to their spontaneous wishes. Furthermore, as the Gospels testify, the twelve did not later on hush up or cover over their failure in the face of their master's death, which would be very hard to understand if at Easter they had only succumbed to wish projections. Paul, too, describes almost dramatically the sufferings and struggles which the message of the crucified one brought on him: "[We always carry] the death of Jesus in our body, so that the life of Jesus may be manifested in our bodies. For wherever we live, we are always being given up to death for Jesus' sake, so that the life of Jesus may be visible in our mortal flesh" (2 Cor. 4:10–12).[4] If one wanted to explain an experience like the one expressed in these words of Paul by illusory wish fulfillment, one would have to account for very masochistic wishes. And yet in that case how can a song of victory like Romans 8:31–39, or a song of love like 1 Corinthians 13, be explained?

Apocryphal traditions prove how the post-Easter community, assuming it had succumbed to wish projections, would have been able to handle the historical fact of the crucifixion, and indeed would have

---

3. Bloch (1968), 226–31.
4. See 1 Cor. 4:9–16; 2 Cor. 11:16–33; 13:3f.; Gal. 6:4; Phil. 3:10.

had to. Thus for example in the Acts of John, the disciple reports the crucifixion in the following way:

> When I saw him [Jesus] now suffering, I could not bear his suffering, but I fled from the Mount of Olives and wept over what was happening. And when on Friday he was hanged [on the cross] there was darkness over all the earth at the sixth hour. And my Lord stood in the middle of hell and illuminated it and said, "John, for the sake of humans below I am crucified and beaten with spears and canes and given wine and gall to drink. I speak to you, however, and what I speak, hear!"[5]

The Lord is supposed then to have announced to his disciple John in the cave on the Mount of Olives the teaching about a cross of light and about the logos, a teaching which has nothing to do with what is reported elsewhere concerning the crucified one: "Thus I have suffered nothing of that which they [the mass of believers] will say about me; but that suffering, which I have shown to you and the others in dancing, I wish to be named a mystery."[6] Here it is possible to grasp concretely how wishes took effect and how the message of the cross with all its claims was turned around into a teaching about a cross of light and a suffering which showed itself in dance. If the Easter appearances had been wish projections, then a teaching about the cross like that in the Acts of John or something similar would have fitted in well. But precisely the opposite is found in the kerygma of the early community, which testifies to an experience which cannot be explained by the categories of depth psychology. The Easter experience of the disciples was distinguished on the one hand by the fact that it took place at a distance in time from the alarming event of the cross and consequently cannot be understood as an immediate "trauma." On the other hand it preserved in full the inner connection with the cross and cannot therefore be understood as a psychological or dialectical "counterstrike."

Tradition-Historical Interpretation

Confrontation with psychological theories of projection does not by itself bring out sufficiently the special character of the message of the cross and resurrection. These theories can be seen already as unsatisfactory when faced with the intertestamental literature with its atmosphere of overflowing imagery. Certainly, on the one hand a rich fantasy may have found expression in this imagery, but on the other hand they testify to deep religious experience. Similarly, purely psychological projection

---

5. Hennecke-Schneemelcher (1959, 1964) 2:157.
6. Ibid., 158.

theories are not able to interpret comprehensively the experiences of a Mohammed. In his hearings and visions, as they are handed down in the suras of the Koran, there are many Jewish and Christian utterances. And although the prophet of Mecca was not a copier but a visionary, in practice all the great truths of the Koran can be derived from these traditions. Through his extraordinary experiences he must consequently have entered deeply into contact with the tradition which preceded him. Can the Easter experiences of the disciples be understood in a similar way as visions, in which on the one hand the long Jewish tradition and on the other the new experiences with Jesus found expression in an intensive psychic process?

In tackling this problematic we must again briefly consider something which has already appeared in Jesus' dealings with his opponents. In connection with the great eschatological proclamation of the prophets, it was the deepest wish of the devout of Israel that God in his action as judge should annihilate the criminals and godless (pagans). The intertestamental literature expressed this basic wish over and over again with powerful pictures, in which were crystalized not only private feelings but the experience and the picture of God formed during a long tradition. It was precisely this basic wish and this centerpiece of the contemporary religious world that Jesus infringed by not reacting against his enemies with force and by letting himself be handed over to the very pagans. His disciples, who were children of their religious environment, failed to understand him on precisely this point, and their flight at his arrest shows that they were driven by quite different forces. The death of their master can only have increased their confusion in this respect, since they now found themselves faced with the further scandal of public execution. Thus neither in the long tradition of Israel nor in their own immediate experience were those elements at hand which — through the mediation of the Easter visions — would have been able to explain the specific character of the message of the cross and resurrection. It would in the circumstances have been understandable if, after a lapse of time, they had found some hope again, understood Jesus better now, and perhaps even believed in a resurrection, as was possibly the case with the disciples of John with respect to their master (see Mark 6:14). But the evangelists give no report of a long process of maturation, and also that would leave out of account the specific character of the Christian Easter message, i.e., the connection with the cross, for a long maturation process would more likely have led to representations of crucifixion and resurrection like the ones in the Acts of John. That God in the premessianic period allows the just to suffer in order to pay them back with splendor was an idea familiar to a broad tendency among the devout in Israel — not of their own initiative, but rather from bitter experience. But this situation was felt as so unnatural that the messianic time took on a great significance precisely because an end had to be put to these unnatural conditions. The religious tradition of Israel is thus in no way able to explain visions from which there could have arisen the message that God has chosen for his Messiah the path of powerlessness and being handed over to the pagans. The inseparable connection of the Easter message with the ignominy of the cross and the crucified one's nonviolent love of enemies can be made comprehensible neither by psychology nor by the history of traditions, and is therefore a decisive reason for the credibility of the Easter experience.

Credibility of the Figure of Jesus

Even if the most central point of the Easter message cannot be explained from the point of view of the faith of Israel, the message is however not thinkable without its prehistory in the Old Testament. An event which was new from every aspect would have to have remained unintelligible to those affected by it. If no ideas and symbols were at hand which could be combined in a new way or transformed, the Easter experience would not have been able to find its appropriate language. Thus our line of argument sketched above stayed completely within the area marked out by the faith of Israel. Because of this inseparable connection between the Christian Easter message and its prehistory, its credibility depends in the broader sense also on the confidence that one has in the religious experience of Israel.

But the most immediate prehistory to Easter was the life of Jesus himself. His whole fate, his claim, and his unusual behavior led up, as we have seen, to his acknowledgment by the verdict of the heavenly Father. This fate offers therefore the most immediate horizon of understanding for the unique Easter message of the disciples, and it contains at the same time elements which contribute to the credibility of his figure. He made such a high claim that he would have to have been a blind fanatic to have worked himself up to this level of consciousness. But he was the very opposite of psychically tensed up, for his communicative power of belief was so great and liberating that he was able to heal the sick and release the possessed from their inner imprisonment. Just as great was the tension between his new interpretation of the law and his dealings with the lawless. Ultimately, he understood the law more radically than even the Qumran sect, and, in distinction to Qumran, he did not cut himself off from sinners and the lawless, but got completely involved with them. Religious radicalism tends normally toward isolation and violence (psychic and physical), but with Jesus precisely the opposite was the case. His radicalism engendered his nonviolence and love toward the enemies of God. These quite unusual unities-in-tension, which have nothing of anxiety about them, carry their own credibility within them.

The Election of Israel

In spite of the independence of the figure of Jesus, he was so much a part of Israel's tradition of faith which preceded him that without it he would not have been able to express his message. The truth of his proclamation, therefore, also depends — at least in part — on the trustworthiness of the religious experience of that nation which considered itself in a special way chosen. Traditional Christian theology has seen, above all in the miracles which are reported in the Old Testament, unambiguous signs that God was already dealing with Israel in a special way. In essential agreement with Jewish faith, Christians have seen especially in the mighty deeds at the exodus from Egypt, the wandering in the desert, and settlement into the promised land unambiguous signs of the specific dealings of God with his people. However, through critical exegesis the relevant narratives have become very problematical as far as their historical trustworthiness is concerned, and they are no longer suited to proving a special trustworthiness for Israel's religious experience. However, we may not simply let this question drop, as often happens in Christian theology nowadays.

Independently of the question of miracles, we can establish the fact that Israel's faith has always come to grips with reality in a radical way. It has never cast a sacred veil over its own institutions (Temple, priesthood, kingship) to make them untouchable. On the contrary, the prophetic preaching castigated all lies and injustice among the people of Israel and its sacred institutions with merciless frankness. This criticism was possible because through many different experiences the people came to believe ever more clearly in Yahweh as a reality independent of all this-worldly powers, himself in no need of gifts or sacrifices, and therefore free over against every historical event and yet able to come to grips with it. Thanks to this belief, Israel was able to survive even the catastrophe which befell it in 587 B.C. with the invasion of the Babylonian armies. At that time these same armies annihilated other small kingdoms as well, where the very faith of the people was struck and wiped out in the political and military defeat. But things went differently in Israel. Precisely because of the catastrophe in Jerusalem and the subsequent exile, faith in Yahweh's dealings in history acquired a new depth. It was inwardly so rich and strong that it was able in the following centuries to overcome every temptation to merge into the religious and cultural world of the conquering powers of the day (Persia, Hellenism, Rome). Finally, the faith of Israel also withstood the destruction of the second Temple in the year 70 C.E. and the subsequent exile of nearly two thousand years without loss of identity. Israel thus stands as a unique phenomenon in world history, for there is no other case of a people being able to live for a very long time entirely dispersed among other nations, not cutting itself off from them culturally (in distinction, for example, from Gypsies) and yet preserving in full the identity of its faith. Jews have on the one hand settled so well into the society around them at the time that almost everywhere they have become important cultural leaders. And yet they have on the other hand held on to the identity of their faith in the passage through different linguistic and cultural environments. We are thus faced with a phenomenon which cannot be explained by the usual historical categories and which must on objective consideration at least cause us to be very cautious in our judgments and not to exclude in advance unusual factors. The "dogmatic" thesis that it is only people who are the actors in history becomes problematical precisely when we come to consider the phenomenon of Israel.

Transcendental Hope of Resurrection

We first of all developed our line of thought concerning the resurrection of Jesus within the framework marked out by the faith of Israel. The particular history of this nation then led us to cast a first glance over this religious context and to compare Israel's specific history with possible analogous experiences in other religions. Now the question must be tackled again directly, whether our reflections so far are viable only against the background of the Jewish tradition or whether they possess a similar power to convince at a more universal level. In this connection we should first of all call to mind general anthropological and philosophical reflections by which the belief in resurrection can be shown to be meaningful independently of a definite religious tradition. For example, K. Rahner has developed the argument that in all human life-decisions there is a note of hope which aims above and beyond the death of the person deciding. Rahner dared to speak of a "transcendental hope of resurrection,"[7] and he was able to point to phenomena in human behavior which suggest to impartial and careful consideration that human beings cannot see themselves as the only actors in history. Since such analyses, however, always emphasize implicit elements and consequently work with analogous concepts, which leave considerable room for play, they unconditionally need the mediation of historical experience. In particular, the significant question is above all whether our reasoning, which is based in the first place on the connection between the message of resurrection and of the cross, and on the behavior of

---

7. Rahner (1976), 264.

Jesus toward the enemies of God, is viable in a more universal religious context. In order not to remain at the level of universal reflections on this important question, as a concrete alternative we must above all consider the possibility that the myth, widespread in most ancient cultures, of a dying and resurrected divinity also influenced the Christian Easter message, and ask whether its realization in history is not explicable from a flowing together of this mythical tradition with the specific Jewish tradition, as the history of religion school before the First World War was inclined to think. This problematic is all the more pressing as nowadays interpretations of the New Testament from history of religion and mythical perspectives have become popular again.

The Myth of the Slain and Resurrected Divinity

A. E. Jensen was able to detect the myth of the divinity who is killed and lives again in primitive farming societies of every part of the world.[8] Its essential content and its function can be summarized thus:

> In the great cult celebrations there stands... at the center, in connection with all manner of different occasions, the repetition of the mythical events of the origins; it emerges clearly from this that human and animal sacrifice, maturity and fertility cults and other ceremonies and ritual customs are not individual cultural elements, which have come together more or less accidentally in a cultural group, but that they are all to be derived from a central idea, namely, that of a divinity who was killed and who by his death established the present order of existence of the world.[9]

Can we assume that such concepts played a part in the Easter experience of the disciples? It is hardly possible to prove direct historical dependency, which is why the theses of the history of religion school were not able to stand firm. But what about under-the-surface contacts at the level of "archetypes" and "mythical depths of the soul," which are often talked about by the followers of C. G. Jung and others influenced by him? Are such notions able to deliver a viable explanation even where the historical connections are weak?

R. Girard has made a comprehensive study of the above-mentioned myth and other mythical narratives from the point of view both of modern literature and of ethnology, and he has proposed a theory which makes the claim that it can unlock the key to the historical origin of the great myths. According to this, human societies are continually threatened by aggression and self-destruction because of passion which keeps

---

8. See Jensen (1966).
9. Ibid., 78.

repeatedly overwhelming reason. Peace cannot be achieved by plans and intentions, but it arrives by itself in a "miraculous way" if acts of mutual aggression are turned around into the action of all against one and the doers of violence instinctively gang up against a random victim. Since the actors in such a process act in passion and blind aggression ("anger blinds"), the collective mechanism in which they are themselves playing a part remains hidden from them. They realize only that peace and calm follow the threat in an inexplicable way. They ascribe this transformation to the victim that they have driven out and killed and on which their attention was polarized at the turn-around of the aggression. In accordance with their perspective, which was alienated by passion, it was from the victim that both the threat and the miraculous peace came. Consequently it appears to the actors in the lynching as cursed and bearing blessings at the same time, an experience which exactly corresponds to what ethnology has always described as experience of the sacred. The universally found myth of the dying and resurrected divinity is according to this interpretation a veiled representation, caused by passion, of actual events, the driving out and killing of individuals as victims and their transformation into a sacred greatness.

With this theory about the origin of the socially determined perception of the sacred, Girard is able to make visible surprising parallels to as well as fundamental differences from the Christian message of the cross and resurrection of Christ. In both cases what is involved — even if in differing ways — is the driving out and killing of victims, in which those taking action do not know what they are doing (scapegoat mechanism). Against this common background the differences stand out all the sharper. In the mythic societies the collective process passes over the heads of the silent victims whose own experience is completely obscured. By contrast in the Gospels it is precisely this latest victim who is the first to speak out, and he takes up an unambiguous position with regard to the aggression threatening him. The collective process of driving out is, as we have seen, also explicitly described in this case, whereas it remains hidden under the veil of a "dying divinity" in the sacred societies. Even the connection between killing and resurrection is a completely different one in the two cases. Whereas in the myths killing goes over directly into the new revival (=turning around of mutual aggression into the unanimous violent act of all against one), in the Gospels the human act of driving out the victim is clearly separated from the divine intervention in favor of the one who is killed. At the condemnation of Jesus one cannot establish any direct situation of excitement of those taking part, even under the surface, although just as much passion and blindness were involved. The accused was however clearly seen as an empirical figure and was in no way "sacralized"; at the most one could say he was "satanized," for he was condemned as a blasphemer. The resurrection experience did not follow directly on the driving out; a fresh impetus was needed to bring the frightened disciples to a conversion. Only after that were they capable of correctly perceiving exactly what had happened before. From the point of view of a strictly comparative way of considering matters, Girard thus comes to the judgment that the Judeo-Christian tradition of faith, as it is reflected in the biblical writings, quite clearly differs from the other religious traditions by its greater realism. Revelation includes also the disclosure and criticism of the collective mechanisms for blinding oneself.

In accordance with this interpretation, there is a central difference, which can be empirically grasped, between the myths and the biblical writings in the way in which human violence is seen and how it is responded to. Since Jesus stood out in clear contrast precisely on this point from the Jewish messianic ideas, the conclusion is that the reflections set out above not only were culturally determined, but they dealt with the problematic which can be seen to be central even in a more universal framework. Girard reaches then from the starting point of ethnology the outcome that the otherwise habitual human laws of behavior are broken by the way in which Jesus reacted to the threat of violence and the way in which his fate was described in the New Testament texts. He concludes that God was at work in the fate of Jesus, and in fact that Jesus must have been in the full sense the Son of God.[10]

Even a seeming irrelevance takes on from this point of view a greater significance. In accordance with Girard's theory of the sacred, cultures were regularly erected over the graves of slain victims, as they presuppose that the society has reached an inner peace, which spontaneously sets itself up by means of the violent driving out and sacralization. The grave, which covers up the corpse, thus becomes on the one hand the symbol of that great process of veiling on which every society is based, and on the other hand the first clearly defined cultural sign, because with it the distinction between sacred and profane is symbolically pinned down: "Culture always starts from the grave. The grave is always the first human memorial, which has to be erected over the victim who has been driven out, the first, most elementary, most fundamental layer of cultural signs. No culture without a grave, no grave without culture."[11] If the sealed grave is really the great symbol of the sacred cultures, insofar as they cover something over, then it is more than an accidental detail that the accounts of Easter in the Gospels begin with the narration of the opened grave, in which there is no longer a corpse to be found.

10. Girard (1983), 222–27.
11. Ibid., 85 (with his own correction of translation errors).

The historical reliability of the tradition of the empty tomb may be greater than critical scholarship has for a long time assumed. If, instead of reasoning abstractly, one considers the available fragments logically from the point of view of Jesus' fate, then the question is not as irrelevant as was frequently maintained. In a violent conflict, the murdered corpse is the empirical sign, there from the very beginning, that there has been a victim and that someone else was the victor. Talk of an Easter victory cannot therefore lightly pass by this sign. But also, independently of the historical question, the opened grave has, against the background of Girard's theory, an important symbolic meaning. It shows that the new beginning constituted by Easter reaches so deep that the ultimate foundations of human culture itself, until now veiled, are laid bare.

Judgment and Universal History

It may be objected to the line of argument just proposed that Girard's theory is disputed and is for that reason not suited to providing a proof that the drama of Jesus' fate possesses a universal significance. Against this objection it must first of all be maintained that the problematic, as it was thrown up at the beginning of this century by the history of religion school, has not found any real solution, but that it has been more or less passed over — above all under the influence of dialectical theology. Girard has taken up again the unsolved questions, which is why his projected solution deserves attention and discussion. Problems which are repressed or displaced must recur in one form or another.

Our reflections concerning the truth of the Easter message are moreover independent of Girard's theory at the crucial point. The problematic described by him, of aggression and projection, has become so central in modern society that it is recognizable even without the mediation of a specific theory. We intend to pursue it first of all within the history of the recent philosophy of history — following on directly from a study by O. Marquard — in order then to move on to modern history itself. In *Difficulties in the Philosophy of History* Marquard sets out how the Enlightenment dogma that man is the actor in history necessarily excluded from consideration the question about responsibility for misdeeds. "Clearly man is now what, in his philosophy of history, he wanted to prevent God from being: a doer of misdeeds. How does he bear this?"[12] Men seem in fact not to have borne this, since Marquard can demonstrate how the philosophy of history has consistently sought strategies to soften the problem. "Those very philosophies of history which emancipate man and enthrone him as he wishes to be are the ones which conduct a vigorous search for 'another doer of deeds': they

---

12. Marquard (1973), 72.

need him as an alibi."[13] Marquard includes in these alibi-strategies the attempts to shift the problem onto Nature or surreptitiously onto God again, which in view of the modern thesis of radical autonomy cannot succeed. There thus remains only one way out: "In view of perennial evil, in the search for the other doer of deeds, the philosophy of history, no longer speaking of God and no longer wishing to speak of Nature, but having to speak of man, discovers as the crucial figure the others, the people who hinder the good which people intend: i.e., the opponents, the enemy."[14] And even more directly: "Where the other-worldly scapegoat is missing, there is need for a substitute, an inner-worldly one, and where Nature is considered unsuitable for it, a human scapegoat must be found."[15] The problematic of enemies and of the displacement of guilt in misdeeds is thus shown to be in no way superseded or the mere remnant of the sacred tradition. It was operative with a particular virulence in precisely those outlines of the philosophy of history which have attempted to distance themselves completely from the religious tradition of the West.

However, not only those who consider the philosophies of history, but empirical researchers into history, if they proceed in a self-critical way, face similar questions. For example, in his great study of anti-Semitism, L. Poliakov established how far the Jews during the whole history of Western Christendom were made responsible for the evils in society and were forced into the role of scapegoats.[16] In his further study *La causalité diabolique* he was also able to show that conspiracy theories played an important part in the great Western revolutions (English, French, Russian).[17] Only through the systematically stirred up suspicion that sworn enemies were everywhere present was there achieved that unity of action among rival revolutionaries, keeping a careful watch on each other, which would make effective political action possible.

The English historian H. Butterfield came to a similar insight through the study of nineteenth- and twentieth-century European history with its bitter conflicts between "civilized" nations. This history showed him, with an evidence which could not be doubted, that people and nations have again and again acted from the conviction that they themselves are the good and just ones and that they must combat evil in their neighbors. But as the neighbors thought the same, saw the guilt in others and thought they were the victims of wicked calumnies and aggression,

---

13. Ibid., 76.
14. Ibid., 78f.
15. Ibid., 77. Marquard is thinking here primarily of the Marxist philosophy of history, but also of National Socialism.
16. Poliakov (1977, 1987).
17. Poliakov (1980, 1985).

the judgments of people and nations were over and over again in sharp opposition with each other. Illusions about themselves and others must consequently play a central part in human judgments. For that reason, historians who do not come down in advance on one side out of blind partisanship, which has happened only too often even among experts,[18] do not leave on one side the problematic of aggression and projection. Butterfield concludes:

> For that reason it seems to me — although history does not pursue this problem into the deep levels in which the theologian expressed his judgments and does not lay bare the self-deceptions about our ostensible righteousness — that the historian, even already in his own area, should reach his hand to the theologian *even in the realm of observable historical events,* and the necessity of this appears even clearer today when we stand in a bitter conflict and our situation is desperate. In the world as it offers itself to me in history there is a chief sin which holds humanity fast in all its other sins and doesn't let men and nations emerge out of their difficult situation — a sin for which there is no cause if what I said above about the nature of man and his place in the world is true: self-righteousness.[19]

In order to gain insights like those put forward by Butterfield, one does not finally even need the methods of history. An attentive glance at what current history offers us shows immediately that human ways of behaving — one can with a certain justice speak of "mechanisms" — as found in conflicts over the whole earth, and independently of social classes and cultures, are very similar. Everywhere people paint pictures of themselves and of their adversaries which they consider to be objective judgments, but which in reality are opposed to one another and cannot be reconciled with each other. Everywhere also there is seen the tendency to regulate problems which cannot be resolved at the level of judgment by recourse to physical violence. The methods of history as well as immediate historical experience therefore place us before a universal problem, which cannot in any way be relativized as culturally conditioned. It is precisely the problem which was shown up as central in Jesus' proclamation and fate. With him also the issue was essentially about judgment and the question of how to meet aggres-

---

18. H. Sitta gathered in the little monograph *Geschichte und politischer Charakter der Deutschen: Ein Versuch* judgments by Germans and French on German-French conflict and, correspondingly, on German-Polish and Prussian-Bavarian conflict. One can only be amazed at how naively self-righteous and contradictory the judgments of even great people and scientists were.

19. Butterfield (1952), 50f.; see also Schwager (1987), 257–75.

sion, which arises from blind judgment. Up until now the old forms of judgment dominate history on the great and on the small scale, and for that reason conflicts continue. In the fate of Jesus, however, it became clear how, in spite of deep oppositions and smoldering conflicts, forms of cooperation and collaboration are possible if that dark element, which one cannot see and master in oneself and in one's own group, can be projected onto a "victim" (the different Jewish groups and the pagans against Jesus). This procedure has over and over again made possible human order and civilization — despite fundamental tensions. Historical experience should consequently provide the documentation that those themes in the New Testament message which distinguish the Jewish-Christian tradition from other religions and by which, within this tradition, Jesus' ministry further stands out from the Old Testament background fully maintain their outstanding significance at the universal human level.

Apocalyptic and the Self-Judgment of Humankind

The conclusions reached so far can be clarified and confirmed by a further point. The apocalyptic texts in the Gospels were exploited by a theology imprisoned in the ways of thinking of the nineteenth century, with its tendency to postulate the time-conditioned nature of Jesus' message. But in reality, it is precisely these texts that speak of the problematic of violence with that universality which imposes itself on human beings today in the most immediate way. Ever since science, which arose in partly direct, partly indirect dependence on the Christian tradition, designed weapons by which the self-destruction of the whole of humanity became a real possibility, all other questions stand under the influence of this problematic. It has become the most comprehensive this-worldly horizon of human effort. Thus the indications are — even at the empirical level — that the judgment on humankind, as Jesus announced it in his judgment sayings, is ultimately a self-judgment and can lead to a total collective self-condemnation.

> To say that we are in an objectively apocalyptic situation is in no way "to announce the end of the world." It is to say that humankind has become, for the first time, capable of destroying itself, something that was unimaginable only two or three centuries ago. The whole planet now finds itself, with regard to violence, in a situation comparable to that of the most primitive groups of human beings, except that this time we are fully aware of it. We can no longer count on sacrificial resources based on false religions to keep this violence at bay. We are reaching a degree of

self-awareness and responsibility that was never attained by those who lived before us.[20]

If the apocalyptic texts have achieved such an amazing actuality, then there is no cause from the viewpoint of this world to question that hope in the resurrection of the dead which arose precisely in the apocalyptic tradition. On the contrary, contemporary experience points back clearly — notwithstanding their once-for-all character — to those past experiences.

Place and Time

Since Reimarus, the objection has been repeatedly raised against the credibility of the Easter message that the narratives about the appearances of the risen one in the four Gospels are hard to relate to one other in terms of place and time. If our everyday experience of time and place were an absolute quantity, then a certain weight could be given to this objection. But can something be presupposed as an absolute norm, which is perhaps in need of questioning itself? Isn't scholarly research thus immunizing itself in advance against everything which could surprise it and cause it to change its thinking? Here again there can be seen the ambiguity of a historical-critical method if it is not carried out self-critically. The physical sciences today show that one has to tread carefully with the usual representations of space and time. Is not far more care required for an event which claims to be the action of God in the world? What is initially felt as disturbing with regard to place and time can be precisely a sign of how the exclusive and disturbing bounds of space and time are overcome in the power of the spirit bringing about the resurrection. For this reason, G. Wenz rightly offers this consideration:

> The living quality of this presence of the Spirit, in which Jesus himself is really present, can be seen among other things in the unanimity of the biblical message that does not destroy its pluriformity, but rather calls it forth. From the plurality of the Jesus stories, which symphonically witness to the resurrection of the crucified one, it becomes clear that in his eternal life, time and space are not abstractly negated, but are achieved in their fullness. The exclusive bounds of time and space are meanwhile negated and broken through.[21]

This is not, however, a welcome to complete arbitrariness. It is also crucial, therefore, that possible false or even mythological ways of rep-

---

20. Girard, *Things Hidden*, 260–61.
21. Wenz (1984, 1986) 2:412f.

resenting the resurrection should be guarded against. We may not then content ourselves with the question of the credibility of the Easter message, but we must make an effort to uncover its deeper meaning.

The Action of the Heavenly Father

The way to approach the inner problematic of the resurrection, arising from the consideration of Jesus' fate, was succinctly expressed in the first epistle of Peter: "When he was reviled, he did not revile in return; he suffered, but did not threaten; but he handed himself over to the righteous judge" (1 Pet. 2:23). The action of the Father at Easter is to be understood as a judgment by which he takes up a position in the conflict between the claim of Jesus and the verdict of his opponents. This statement is central and at the same time liable to misinterpretation, as it could suggest a return to traditional conceptions of judgment and thereby to a distorting horizon of interpretation. In order correctly to understand the judging activity of the heavenly Father at Easter, we must first of all remind ourselves that Jesus in his proclamation of judgment took back nothing from his message of the goodness of God, but rather uncovered the possibility which threatened that people would close themselves off absolutely. Further, we must consider that Jesus, faced with a violent death, gave himself completely for the opponents of God's kingdom, who had closed themselves off. In the resurrection brought about by the Father it is consequently not enough to see merely a verdict for his Son and against those who opposed him. Certainly, this view is correct, as Jesus' opponents are convicted as sinners. But the verdict of the heavenly Father is above all a decision for the Son who gave himself up to death for his opponents. It is therefore, when considered more deeply, also a verdict in favor of sinners. The opponents of the kingdom of God, closing themselves off, had the way to salvation once more opened for them by the Son, who allowed himself to be drawn into their darkness and distance from God. Although they had already turned their backs, as far as they were concerned, the self-giving of the Son got around this hardening of hearts once more, insofar as he allowed himself to be made the victim of their self-condemnation.

The saving dimension of the Easter message, and the revelation of God contained in it, can be clarified from yet another angle. In the parable of the wicked winegrowers (Mark 12:1–12 and parallels) a lord is presented who at first acts with unfathomable goodness, in that, after the rejection and killing of several servants, he even risks his own son. This goodness however comes to an end, for after the murder of his beloved son it is transformed into retribution, and the violent winegrowers are in their turn killed.[22] But the heavenly Father in his Easter "judgment" acted differently from the master of the vineyard in the parable. Even the murder of his son did not provoke in him a reaction of vengeful retribution, but he sent the risen one back with the message "Peace be with you!" (Luke 24:36; see also John 20:19, 26) to those disciples who at the critical moment had allowed themselves to be drawn into the camp of the opponents of the kingdom of God. The judge's verdict at Easter was consequently not only a retrospective confirmation of the message of Jesus, but it also contained a completely new element, namely, forgiveness for those who had rejected the offer of pure forgiveness itself and persecuted the Son. Through the Easter message of peace there came about a redoubling of that readiness to forgive expressed in the message of the basileia, a pardon for the earlier nonacceptance of pardon. It could be summed up in that saying from the Old Testament, which, taken together with the parable of the wicked wine-growers and seen in the light of Easter, says something quite new and can serve as the hermeneutical key to the Gospels: "The stone that the builders rejected has become the head of the corner; this was accomplished by the Lord, and it is marvelous in our eyes" (Mark 12:10). The miracle of Good Friday and of Easter once again embraces those people who hardened their hearts and made their decision against the Son. A rightly understood doctrine of the atoning death is therefore, even when seen from the viewpoint of Easter, not in opposition to Jesus' proclamation of the kingdom of God. On the contrary, it is precisely the peace of Easter which shows how the Father of Jesus willingly forgives, even in the face of people's hardened hearts.

Finally, from this perspective it is also understandable why the heavenly Father "held back" in his Easter judgment and why he did not powerfully authenticate his Son before the whole world. Jesus made the claim, by his proclamation and by his lived decision not to meet the violence of his opponents on their own level, that God's action is not identical with action on this earth which brings immediate victory. He was not able himself to prove this claim, since it led him by an inner logic to earthly defeat. But even the Father was unable to endorse him in a graphic way, since a demonstrative, public intervention in favor of the Son would have worked precisely against his message. The action of God and a historical, public victory would have appeared once again as identical values, and the way of surrender to death would have shown itself to be merely a passing episode. This style of endorsement would

---

22. In Matthew, of course, Jesus poses only the question about the action of the owner, and the hearers themselves answer that the owner will put the wretched tenants to death (21:40–41).

have contradicted what was to be endorsed. Rather, what was needed was a sign which on the one hand made explicit the unrestricted divine "yes" to Jesus and on the other hand was "reserved," so that it was not tantamount to a public victory. Both demands were met by the appearances of the risen one before the women and his disciples. What from the historical-critical viewpoint may be felt to be unsatisfying shows itself to be most appropriate at the level of the inner coherence of content. Thus it emerges once more that the cryptic presuppositions of the historical-critical method do not match the reality which came to expression for the first time in the fate of Jesus.

The Appearances of the Risen One

In connection with the Easter appearances there arise countless questions which have a certain importance for the deeper understanding of the Easter message. How are the appearances themselves to be understood? What did the risen one say in them? How are they different from later experiences of the Spirit? Behind these questions stands the even more central problem, how a transcendent reality can bring about an effect in our world.

Nature of the Easter Appearances

It is impossible to reconstruct precisely the chronology of the Easter appearances. What most likely happened is that the disciples after the crucifixion of their master fled to Galilee, their home. The visions may have begun there, to be continued later in Jerusalem. But it is also conceivable that some disciples — above all Peter and John — stayed behind in Jerusalem from the first, experienced the first appearances there, saw the empty grave, and only somewhat later went to Galilee to report their experiences to the other disciples who had fled.

Just as difficult as determining the spatial and temporal order of events is describing the exact nature of the Easter appearances. Some of the narratives set out how a strange person (traveler, gardener, wanderer by the lake) is noticed and only afterward the risen one is discovered in him (Luke 24:13–35; John 20:11–18; 21:1–14). An essential element also in Saul's vision before Damascus, even if in a completely different way, is that the exalted Lord showed himself in his unity with humans, namely, with the persecuted disciples ("Saul, Saul, why do you persecute me?" [Acts 9:4]). These narratives may suggest that the risen one was recognized through the medium of fellow human beings, preferably at a common meal (see the Emmaus narrative). The unambiguous belief in community (koinonia) with the Lord in the Eucharist, as witnessed already by Paul (1 Cor. 10:16–22), makes the assumption likely in any case that the disciples experienced the presence of their murdered and risen Lord in a powerful way at the common meal. The origin of this belief would be hard to understand merely from the brief Last Supper sayings and without the corresponding experience after Easter. However, this probable form of the appearances should not to be played off against other forms; in particular the well-attested first appearance before Peter (Luke 24:34; 1 Cor. 15:5), but also others (before the women, before more than five hundred brethren) become very hard to understand if we follow this line. For an authentic understanding of the Easter message, it is important to distinguish clearly between the transfigured body of the risen one, as he is acknowledged in faith, and what the disciples directly experienced. Since they remained people of this world, they could only take in something which lay within the receptive framework of mortal beings. How far this capacity reaches is not from the outset clear. The long tradition of visions and appearances in the history of the church — and also in other religions — has still never been systematically studied from this point of view, but above all they have still hardly been analyzed or evaluated by historical-critical exegesis. Certainly, such experiences cannot be directly transferred to the Easter reports; but a systematic evaluation of the multiplicity of witnesses in the history of piety would provide more differentiated categories than are usually employed in historical-critical and in fundamentalist exegesis. Such categories would perhaps also help us to cope with other "difficult" accounts, not considered up until now (transfiguration of Jesus, multiplication of bread, walking on the sea, raising of the dead, etc.), better than with the declaration that the narration is of legendary or midrashic type, because the element of experience should be taken more seriously.

The Sayings of the Risen One

Besides the message of peace, the risen one opened up to his disciples the meaning of the Scriptures — especially according to the tradition of Luke (Luke 24:25–27, 44–47). This utterance is usually interpreted as an attempt to legitimate the new interpretation of Scripture in the post-Easter community through Jesus himself. But this is to overlook a crucial problem, namely, the question of how a more or less unified interpretation of Scripture became possible at all in the early community after Easter. How did it come about that such differing figures as Peter, James, John, Stephen, Paul, and Barnabas, to name only the most important, were able to concur on essential questions? We know from Paul that differences of opinion quickly arose in his communities (1 Cor. 1:10–13; 2 Cor. 10:1–11) and that fundamental splits threatened, since he speaks of those who proclaim "another Jesus" (2 Cor. 11:4). In Jerusalem itself there arose early on a great argument concerning the continuing validity of the Jewish law (see Acts 6:8–7:60; 11:1ff.), and this conflict remained virulent over a fairly long period and led to "violent strife" (see Acts 15:7; Gal. 2:1–21). It seems that it was only thanks to a special vision which Peter received that it was possible to avoid an actual split (see Acts 10:9–16; 11:1–18; 15:6–11; Gal. 2:6–9). Now if the question of the law had as a consequence such a deep conflict, then it is all the more amazing that no similar arguments were reported concerning faith in Jesus as the Christ. The problems here were at least as great, in fact finally even greater. As early as the hymn of Christ in the letter to the Philippians, where we have before us "very probably . . . the oldest New Testament utterance about the preexistence of Christ,"[23] that name is attributed to the exalted one which is above all other names and before which every knee should bend (Phil. 2:5–11ff.). That such a confession, on one side bound up with the concrete historical figure of Jesus and on the other side going beyond any concepts of preexistence that can be found in the wisdom and intertestamental literature, should not lead to a split among the faithful, is more than astonishing. Despite the different tendencies within the post-Easter community there seems never to have been a big conflict over it among its authoritative leaders. This surprising fact must cause us to think hard. If one attributes to the early community the utterances in which the earthly Jesus or the risen one speaks of himself particularly clearly, this does not solve the problem, but only shifts it and creates somewhere else an even greater one: How was a unanimous confession of Christ — without fundamental conflicts and split — possible in the post-Easter community? From the Old Testament viewpoint there was no overall picture to illuminate the whole fate of Jesus. Post-Easter prophetic experiences are not able to explain in a satisfactory way the unity of the confession, since the charismatic experiences may have been very ambiguous and they were in need of interpretation and "discernment of the spirits" (1 Cor. 14:29), which presupposes on their side a clear confession of Christ. Precisely if one accepts intensive pneumatic experiences, with their strong, subjective components, it is even more astonishing that the community of the disciples after Easter did not quickly split up into different small groups. The more concretely one thinks of the post-Easter situation, the more strongly the question arises, how a confession of faith in Christ was possible — without fundamental conflicts concerning this confession. If the first efforts of the new gathering during the earthly ministry of Jesus were associated with long-lasting misunderstandings, how then was the unity after Easter made possible? One satisfactory explanation would be that it was precisely the risen one himself who with his whole

---

23. Gnilka (1968), 146ff.

authority communicated to his disciples the main lines of the new interpretation of Scripture, and that they were now capable of understanding
it in essentials on the basis of their new experience. If this explanation is not acceptable, then the only realistic alternative remaining is
to attribute the post-Easter interpretation of Scripture even more to the
earthly Jesus, as we have done further above.

In Acts 4:11 the new exegesis of the Old Testament is summarized
and brought to focus in an important passage from the psalms and applied to the new situation (resurrection of Jesus): "This one [Jesus] is the
stone rejected by your builders, but which has become the cornerstone"
(see Ps. 118:22). In this passage the lines of tradition concerning the violent fate of the prophets and the persecution of the just are brought
together with the quite different theme of the Messiah, who is to set up
the new nation. The saying about the rejected stone is found already
on the lips of the earthly Jesus, and moreover in connection with the
parable of the wicked wine-growers (Mark 12:10 and parallels). We can
assume without any great difficulty that he actually said these words. In
this case it would bear witness to his messianic consciousness of sonship
and to his knowledge of the way of suffering. If this assumption is seen
as unlikely, then the other one becomes all the more unavoidable, that
the risen one himself made clear to his disciples how the Messiah had
to suffer in order to reach his splendor. In the post-Easter situation the
disciples were certainly capable of understanding correctly the new interpretation of Israel's holy Scripture. As they had been confronted with
a new type of reality through the appearances, they were able to see the
whole tradition of Israel in a new light.

If one assumes that the risen one spoke to his disciples at the appearances, then the originality of the missionary task does not require any
further explanation. The first sending out of the disciples with the aim
of the gathering of Israel, which at first met failure, was taken up again
by the risen one to a new level and deepened. The message of the kingdom of God at hand led consequently via the drama of judgment, cross,
and resurrection to the post-Easter mission and gathering.

The End of the Easter Appearances

According to Luke, the Ascension of the risen one ended the Easter time
of appearances (Luke 24:51; Acts 1:9–11). But it is also possible that
Luke himself made up this story. G. Lohfink thinks: "It is advisable for
the historian not to differentiate too quickly between those 'vision' phenomena which led to the Easter faith and 'vision' phenomena in the
early community, or pneumatic phenomena generally."[24] This advice

---

24. G. Lohfink (1980), 165f.

may be appropriate, and yet the question arises whether one may assume that the Easter appearances flowed "without any transition into the countless ecstatic and visionary experiences of the early church."[25] Behind this seemingly trivial question lies another which was of structural importance for the coming history of faith. How did it come about that the post-Easter community separated the working of the Holy Spirit from the working of the risen one? From the point of view of the Old Testament such a distinction was in no way evident, as all utterances about the divine spirit could have been interpreted without difficulty with an eye to the pneumatic presence of the risen one. Later theology also shows that a considerable effort is needed to allot a decisive role to the Holy Spirit alongside the ministry of Christ. The post-Easter community was thus in no way forced from outside into devising its own theology of the Spirit. If, despite this, it did so and did not rest content with a confession of the Father and the Son, then this surprising fact can perhaps only be explained by an equally surprising experience. Whether sayings of Jesus relating to this played a part may remain open. In any case, only a very clear experience can have led the post-Easter community to accept a working of the Spirit on its own alongside the pneumatic presence of the risen one. Because the distinction is so familiar to us, we normally think of it as quite natural for the early community. But this is to eliminate one of their central experiences and to overlook its meaning for them. Only if one clearly puts the question of why the appearances of the risen one were separated from the pneumatic experiences do the history and theology of post-Easter become understandable.

---

25. Ibid.

Fifth Act:
The Holy Spirit and the New Gathering

The fundamental difference between the time characterized by the appearances of the risen one and the coming time of the Holy Spirit can be — at least at certain points — historically determined. The time of the appearances was still a time of uncertainty, even of fear. It is striking how strongly this element appears in practically all the Easter accounts. The women at the tomb were, according to Mark, seized with "terror and fright" and "were afraid" (Mark 16:8). At the appearance on a mountain in Galilee, some of the disciples, according to Matthew, were "uncertain" (Matt. 28:17; see also John 20:24–29). In Luke, too, we find that the disciples "were startled" at the appearances in Jerusalem, had "great fear" and thought that they "saw a spirit" (Luke 24:37). According to John they had even gathered behind locked doors "for fear of the Jews" (John 20:19, 26). In contrast to this mood of doubt and fear, from Pentecost onward the behavior of the disciples is completely different. They come out into the open and dare to profess faith in their murdered and resurrected Lord. How are we to understand this transformation more precisely and what significance does it have?

The Special Character of Pneumatic Experience

The description of the events of Pentecost in the Acts of the Apostles contains — especially in Peter's preaching — a strongly theological interpretation of what happened. "The old narrative core told of a happening in the oldest community of believers, at which, in the course of a gathering of the community, there occurred that ecstatic speech phenomenon which we call glossolalia. Glossolalia is a praising of God in stammering, unintelligible speech, which in the primitive church was understood as being seized by the Holy Spirit."[1] The new element in the experience consisted in the praise of God that broke out spontaneously from the disciples' inmost being. They had always perceived the message of Jesus from without, and even with the appearances of the risen one they encountered something which appeared to them at first as strange, as is clearly proved by their reactions of shock, fear, and doubt. Very different were the pneumatic experiences, which went together with the stepping of the disciples into the open. Although they are associated in the account of Pentecost with the picture of visible "tongues of fire," they must above all have reached the innermost being of each person and thereby have created that new certainty which made possible a confrontation with the world. The Acts of the Apostles, which repeatedly

---

1. G. Lohfink (1980), 173; see also Pesch (1986), 1:107.

emphasizes that the apostles behaved with openness (Acts 2:29; 4:13, 29, 31; 28:31), clearly distinguishes the new behavior from that reported of the disciples up until then. The time of the Spirit as a time of openness thanks to pneumatic experience transforming the inmost self thus clearly differs from the time of Jesus.

Was the proclamation of the apostles also understood in foreign languages? Objections have been raised against the relevant statement in Acts 2:6–11: "On the question of speaking in foreign languages, there is...no mention outside the account of Pentecost....In the literature of the first Christian centuries, there is no news — not even in the apocryphal Acts of the Apostles — of bestowing on the apostles the knowledge of foreign languages."[2] The talk of the endowment of the apostles with the knowledge of foreign languages shows that a misunderstanding may be creeping in here, as Acts 2:1–12 does not say that the apostles knew and spoke in foreign languages, but only that each one heard them speak in his or her own language, which is not the same. This speaking in foreign languages remains fundamentally in the realm of glossolalia. In the Jerusalem of that time countless languages were spoken, and in the young community it was easy to find Hellenists (Acts 6:1) and people from different areas (Mark 15:21; Acts 4:36; 6:5; 9:10). As the language barrier was quickly overcome, it is at least a probable assumption that this step was facilitated by glossolalia. But however the historical question stands, the praise of God "in languages" did not in any case lead to life in a sect for those who took part in it; rather it brought about the step into the open and promoted the growing mission.

The multiplicity of languages which were understood by the hearers is of fundamental significance, as the account of the Acts of the Apostles offers a counter-picture to the Old Testament legend of the tower of Babel. Whereas there understanding between people was lost, here it is won back. But the new event is not a return to the one language of the beginnings. Whereas there the multiplicity of languages is interpreted purely negatively — as loss of the possibility of understanding and as punishment for arrogance — here it wins a positive evaluation. Thanks to the working of the Spirit, from now on understanding is possible even where many languages coexist, and it becomes clear that the new unity does not violate the multiplicity, and that it comes about in a way which lies beyond human power to dispose. The path through destruction (sin) and multiplicity is not abolished by the Spirit, but is passed over on the way to a new and higher goal.

2. Kremer (1973), 201.

The New Gathering

The pneumatic phenomenon of glossolalia and of speaking "in tongues" points toward the new gathering, since these experiences could only have taken place in groups of people gathered together. How this gathering together came about in historical actuality cannot now be reconstructed in precise detail. The tradition is well attested that the young community gathered in private houses for the "breaking of bread" (Acts 2:46). But up to what size were such house communities possible? The appearance of the risen one before more than five hundred brethren, reported by Paul (1 Cor. 15:6), was certainly not possible in a private house. But in what other way could such a large number come together, perhaps in a synagogue or in the open air? Acts 6:1ff. also bears witness that problems emerged with the growing numbers (rebellion of the Hellenists because of the widows who were overlooked; neglect of the service of the word because of service at the table). Did the Hellenists and the Aramaic-speaking Jewish Christians not get on with one another from the beginning and each assemble separately?

Despite the concrete problems, the gathering of the faithful aimed at overcoming social, linguistic, gender, and religious barriers. The Acts of the Apostles emphasizes that all were "together" (Acts 2:46) and "of one heart and soul" (Acts 4:32), and according to Paul there is "neither Jew nor Greek, there is neither slave nor free, there is neither male nor female," since all are "one in Christ" (Gal. 3:28). What was behind this concern for unity was not merely the realization of a noble ethical ideal; far more crucial was that this was how God's plan for salvation was being fulfilled. The new gathering, which Jesus had begun with the message of the kingdom of God, had initially broken down because of people's resistance. There was even a counter-gathering, a cooperation of different forces against God's messenger, which Jesus answered with the surrender of his life for the many. The new post-Easter gathering — and the Spirit which made it possible — is to be understood as the fruit of this surrender. The heavenly Father answered the rejection of his Son and the Son's obedience in a double fashion: through the resurrection of the crucified one and through the sending of the Spirit into those for whom the crucified one surrendered himself. The realization which emerged from consideration of the glossolalia, that pneumatic experience did not primarily come from outside but sprang from the disciples' inner selves, thus has a deep significance. Because the crucified one let himself be drawn into the dark world of his adversaries, far from God, and there lived out his obedience to the Father, the deep godless realms of the human heart themselves became the place where the divine spirit can from now on reach and touch people. The Pentecostal gathering is for that reason not merely an outward gathering; the visible coming together of the faithful is only a sign, intelligible to our world, of that unification which, starting from the cross, finds fulfillment in the depths of people's hearts through the sending out of the Spirit.

Because of the new assembly's function as a sign, it is not identical with the final eschatological gathering. Certainly, the disciples may have experienced both the appearances of the risen one and the pneumatic experiences strongly in the context of the end-time, so that it would have been an obvious temptation to treat the split between those who joined the community and those who refused to join as if it were the final separation between God's chosen ones and those eternally rejected. But the later weakening of expectation of the end did not lead, as has frequently been remarked, to a deep crisis among the faithful, which is only understandable if temporal expectation was from the beginning given only a limited importance. The experience of the early community was in clear contrast to those expectations described in the prophetic and intertestamental texts, because it involved, instead of the one expected eschatological event, two events: the appearances of the risen Messiah/Son of God and the sending of the Spirit. Thanks to the pneumatic experiences, it was soon possible to look back on the time when the risen one appeared as something in the past, without getting the feeling of living now outside the salvation event. The faith of the early community was thus in no way exclusively directed toward the future. As the pneumatic experiences were perceived in connection with the crucified one and yet were distinguished from the appearances of the risen one, there was within the eschatological events themselves a past and therefore an interest in past history. The experience of the early community thus remained — despite the new emphasis on the present — within the great basic framework of Jewish faith, which remembers past saving deeds, asks for the present working of the divine spirit, and hopes for the speedy fulfillment of salvation.

That the new gathering had only the function of a sign must have become obvious to the young community from the very fact that there were still sins and sinners among it. As an example of this painful fact, the Acts of the Apostles tells the story of Ananias and Sapphira (Acts 5:1–11). The extent to which sin remained at work in the community, despite the pneumatic experiences, is documented above all by Paul's letters, which constantly speak of conflicts, falling back, and failure.[3] According to Paul, conflicts among the faithful must arise, so that it can be seen who among them is loyal and trustworthy (1 Cor.

---

3. 1 Cor. 1:10–13; 5:1; 6:1–11; 11:18–22; 2 Cor. 2:1–6; 7:12; 10:1–12; 12:20–13:10; Gal. 1:6–9; 2:11–14; 3:1–5; 4:8–11; see also Rev. 1:9–3:22.

11:19). In accordance with an apocalyptic expectation which Paul took over, before the second coming of Christ a great rebellion must happen: "...the defection comes first, the man of lawlessness must appear, the son of perdition who opposes and exalts himself against everything called god or sacred — so that he even sits in the Temple and proclaims himself as God" (2 Thess. 2:3-4). Although Paul proclaimed with all his might the message that the decisive saving events have already happened in the cross, in the resurrection of Christ, and in the coming of the Spirit, he awaited the final separation — in agreement with the pictures of Jewish apocalyptic — as still to come in the future. Within the eschatological events the distinction was thus made between past (death and resurrection of Christ), present (sending of the Spirit), and future (universal resurrection of the dead, final gathering and judgment). In consequence, the present gathering of the community could not possibly be understood as the final separation between the just and sinners.

But how could the new gathering inaugurated by Christ be fulfilled in the New Testament community, without the separation which thus came about being the final one? A comprehensive answer to this question would involve a whole ecclesiology and therefore exceeds the scope of this investigation. But the answer must be sought under the guiding notion that the actual salvation event took place in the surrender of Christ on the cross, in the resurrection brought about by the Father, and in the sending of the Spirit. This decisive event remained beyond empirical perception. The empty tomb, the appearances of the risen one, the pneumatic experiences of Pentecost, and the newly assembled community of believers are only signs. The fundamental salvation events are certainly present in them, but nevertheless remain different from them. Consequently, the drama of salvation after the rejection of Jesus took place on two levels: it led on the one hand into the inner, transcendental realm which is ultimately revealed as trinitarian, and on the other hand it continued in this world under the guise of signs. The starting point from which the signs and the full working of salvation were distinguished, although they remained from another point of view closely connected, was the Last Supper. There Jesus gave himself to his disciples to eat under the sign of bread and wine and thereby established both the difference between sign and intended reality and their fundamental identity.

Attributing the origins of the new gathering of the disciples to the surrender of the crucified one, to his resurrection, and to the sending of the Spirit will be rejected as naive and mythological talk by those who think that they can explain the post-Easter Jesus movement by means of sociological factors. B. L. Mack attempts this in a particu-

larly logical, almost cynical, way[4] by, quite rightly, bringing the question
of cohesion and the social identity of the Jesus movement to the center
of his reflections. From this viewpoint, he finds that there were "vo-
ciferous conflicts" both between different Christian groups and above
all between these and the Jewish world.[5] Because of the different social and religious background of their members (slaves, freemen, Jews,
pagans, etc.), the forging of an identity for the new movement was,
he says, difficult, and it could not have succeeded on a Jewish basis
alone. But it was made possible, according to Mack, by two means:
(1) by mythological glorification of the act of joining the new movement (baptism as the beginning of a new life); (2) by the creation of
the new myth of the cross. Through this Jesus is supposed, against all
historical findings, to have been made into the wholly innocent victim and into a martyr to that cause for which the Jesus movement
itself stood. From the mythical idea of the innocent martyr all the different theologies could then have arisen in a great explosion. In this
way, above all, guilt was laid on the Jews. The devastating result of
this myth was that the true persecutors disappeared from the picture
which they painted. They looked down from their viewpoint as the (supposed) just ones on the others, attributed deeds of violence to them,
even saw in this the origin of their own "grace."[6] Consequently, the
Jesus movement found its identity by hypocritically accusing others,
and the Gospels should be read as particularly perverse texts of persecution: they turn the victims into the persecutors of one innocent
victim.

We don't need to discuss at length how to respond to such a view, as
we have already established much that contradicts it. But there is one
important point which we must go into briefly, because it is frequently
put forward that the early community in its conflict with the Jews deni-
grated them and put its own aggressive verdicts into the mouth of Jesus.
Mack radicalizes this thesis by making the persecutors in the Gospels
into innocent victims; the victim (Jesus), and above all his followers, he
treats as hypocrites and the real persecutors (double scapegoat mech-

---

4. "I have read them [the Gospels] cynically so to speak, noticing only the surface
phenomena of (early) Christian social history, but not noticing my indebtedness to the
gospels as the source of my critical posture to begin with" (Mack [1985], 160).

5. Ibid., 151.

6. "The real persecutors are not in the picture, not at work during the sacrificial crisis
as it were. They were privileged to be spectators from afar, looking out from within the
borders which separate those who are right from those who are wrong, out and onto
the scene of darkness from which, by means of the violent event to be perpetrated by
others, the origination of their grace could be seen. The Jews killed Jesus, the innocent Son
of God; God raised him up, and demonstrated rightness; Christians receive the benefits"
(ibid., 156).

anism).[7] This radicalization makes it immediately clear how fragile is the thesis of the denigration of the Jews by the early community. A superficial look at the Gospels is enough to show that the disciples of Jesus, themselves Jews, of course, are portrayed there as no better than the other Jews. It is explained that they are stubborn (Mark 6:52; see also 8:17); the arrest is provoked by a traitor from their group (Mark 14:10ff., 43ff. and parallels); Peter, the leader of the post-Easter community, is addressed by Jesus as "Satan" (Matt. 16:23), and he is portrayed as someone who is full of protestations of loyalty but who at the same time betrays his master (Mark 14:29, 31, 33–40, 66–72 and parallels). How can anyone in view of such a critical self-portrayal speak of self-righteousness and denigration of others? John 8:44 is often indicated as a particularly compelling proof for the denigration of Jews by Christians ("You have the devil as a father... "). But when Jesus pronounces this saying in the Gospel, it is precisely not to the Jews in general, but "to the Jews who believed in him" (John 8:31). Even if it includes the nonbelievers and outsiders, it is nevertheless directed in the first place inward. This is not a case of the "turning back of aggression" or "introverted aggressivity," as G. Theissen — in complete opposition to Mack — would like to interpret the harsh words used against the disciples.[8] It is a historical fact that Jesus was condemned and crucified, and in his judgment sayings only those forces are named which in fact influenced his fate and to which his disciples for a time succumbed. The post-Easter communities, in which the Gospels came into being, did not distance themselves from the pre-Easter failure of their leaders. They did not say, "If we had lived in the days of our ancestors, we would not have been guilty of the death of the prophets" (Matt. 23:30). The earlier failure was not a closed matter for them, on which they could now look back self-righteously from a higher position. The drama of the fate of Jesus remained for them a present reality.

But how could communities submit themselves so relentlessly to judgment and at the same time be full of cheerful confidence in salvation? If one sees the application of the judgment sayings to themselves as merely a psychological process, then one has to admit that one is dealing with extreme masochistic tendencies of a collective nature. But on such an assumption the joy and confidence of faith shown by these same communities becomes inexplicable. A satisfactory answer only emerges, therefore, if one actually takes seriously what these communities said about their hope. They based their joy and confidence on the cross and

---

7. "The double deceit which makes this sacrifice of the surrogate victim especially dangerous is that, not only is the scapegoat mechanism fully in operation, it is carried through under the sign of innocence" (ibid., 157).

8. Theissen (1977), 96–101.

resurrection of Christ and the present working of the Spirit. Only from the viewpoint of this confession of faith does the new gathering after Easter become really understandable.

That the separation of the Christian communities from the Jews cannot be attributed to a sociologically analyzable process can be made clear once again from the epistle to the Romans. Here Paul criticizes the law's claim to bring salvation and bases his hope exclusively on the Gospel of Christ, through which he received the Holy Spirit and in which he experienced eternal election by the heavenly Father (Rom. 8:28–30). He shows himself full of overwhelming certainty that no creature can separate him from the love of God in Christ (Rom. 8:38). Despite his unlimited profession of salvation in Christ, he dares once again to "relativize" the Gospel — precisely with an eye to his fiercest opponents, his previous brothers in faith — by taking the viewpoint of God's eternal election: "With regard to the Gospel they are enemies of God for your sake; but with regard to election they are beloved for the sake of their fathers. For the gifts and the call of God are irrevocable" (Rom. 11:28–29). Although Paul freed himself from the practice of the law for the sake of the Gospel, and for that reason had to suffer persecution from many Jews, he did not make opposition to his previous brothers in faith into an absolute. God granted him to see once again against a wider horizon what he was risking his life for, and it was for that reason that he must not denigrate the opponents of the Gospel. They still remained for him people who were irrevocably loved by God. In contrast to the apocalyptic literature, where friends and enemies of God oppose each other totally, for him conflicts of faith did not lead to any absolute opposition between the just and the rejected.

Because, according to the conviction of the post-Easter communities, the final separation was still to come, as they experienced in the working of the Holy Spirit not an end to the drama of Christ, but a reliving of it, their life took on for that reason the function of sign. The decisive salvation events were present and yet still hidden and to come. The life of the communities was a sign, and it also found its fulfillment essentially in signbearing actions (baptism and Lord's Supper).

The Lord's Supper

"The Lord's Supper of the early community has three different roots, but one common origin. That means that we can consider not only the relationship of the early Christian Last Supper celebration to Jesus' Last Supper, as is often done; besides this there are the mealtime communities of the earthly Jesus and the Easter meal celebrations to take into account."[9] If Hahn, in addition to the three roots of the post-Easter Lord's Supper mentioned by him, speaks of a common origin, then he is turning against the theory of H. Lietzmann, who assumed a double form of the Christian meal celebration for the post-Easter time, a Jerusalem form (only with bread) and a Pauline one (with bread and wine).[10] That in practice there may have been a certain wavering is probable, and perhaps it is even conceivable that in the beginning the chalice was not understood as obligatory, which would explain the clearly attested celebrations of the Eucharist without wine of a later time (second century).[11] However, we must entirely agree with Hahn that one can speak of only one origin of the early Christian Lord's Supper, as is today fairly generally accepted. On the one hand the fundamental tradition, as we have already seen, goes back to Jesus himself, and on the other hand no differences can be seen on this issue between the Hebrews and the Hellenists in the Jerusalem community, as the conflict reported in Acts 6:1 presupposes a common celebration.

Bringing About the Church

The early Christian meal celebrations consisted of a genuine meal to satisfy hunger, at the start of which the bread was blessed, broken, and distributed, whereas the blessing of the cup followed after the meal. In the Pauline communities also the celebration of the Eucharist was still connected with a hunger-satisfying meal (1 Cor. 11:20ff.). It is assumed by numerous scholars that the rites of the bread and of the cup had already come together here and took place at the end of the hunger-satisfying meal, so that this part was easily separated later on, something first attested by Justin. But against this view, it could be argued with good reason that even in Corinth the blessing of the bread and of the cup framed the hunger-satisfying meal.

Independently of the historical judgment about this particular question, it seems crucial that "the feeding of the hungry" made up "an essential part of the Lord's Supper."[12] As people greeted one another at this meal "with a holy kiss" (Rom. 16:16; 1 Cor. 16:20; 2 Cor. 13:12; 1 Thess. 5:26; 1 Pet. 5:14),[13] what we have here is a religious celebra-

---

9. Hahn (1967), 338. Lohmeyer especially has made reference to the mealtime communities of the earthly Jesus: Lohmeyer (1937), 201–4. Cullmann has emphasized the connection with the meals associated with the Easter appearances: Cullmann (1956), 17–20. More recently see Klauck (1982), 330.

10. Lietzmann (1955), 238–49 (1st ed. 1926).

11. Ibid., 240–49.

12. Neuenzeit (1960), 31, 73–76; Hahn (1967), 339; Klauck (1982), 295.

13. "The very context in the letters speaks for an assignment of the holy kiss to the meal celebration and the proximity of holy kiss, anathema, and maranatha" (Klauck [1982], 356).

tion, which at the same time integrated into itself a new representation of society. Differences of social class fell away within the community assembled for the Lord's Supper, for they were all considered as brothers and sisters, and the poor were fed in the celebration itself. The new true peace among people and the care for the poor took place at the Lord's Supper itself. What lay behind this was not in the first place the fulfillment of social or humanitarian duties. The believers' service of love was understood as an answer to Jesus' handing over of himself, and the conviction of faith that in the Lord's Supper they were bringing about the church seems to have been more important than charitable concern for the welfare of the poor.

The new community fulfilling itself in the Lord's Supper was experienced as the great new sign of God in the world, as the church of Christ. How threatened this sign was from the beginning by sin is shown by the events in Corinth, where some apparently could be already drunk while others went hungry. Paul saw in this not merely a moral failure but contempt for the church and an offense against the body and blood of the Lord, in which the guilty ones incurred judgment (1 Cor. 11:22–29). He saw the judgment event quite concretely in bodily afflictions, illnesses, and early death (1 Cor. 11:30; see also 5:4ff.; Acts 5:1–11), in which the community — above all with a view to the parousia of their Lord — was weakened in its task in the history of salvation. The message of judgment, which played an important role in the proclamation of Jesus, belonged also to the Lord's Supper, and here too those present were brought to self-judgment by the word of proclamation and the "anathema" (1 Cor. 16:22).

Remembering the Saving Deeds

In the course of historical scholarship there have been not only discussions about the two possible sources for the Lord's Supper, but for a long time it was also held that besides this meal there used to be a completely separate proclamation of the word, a divine service of the word in the morning and the Lord's Supper in the evening. But this assumption could not be maintained and it was possible to prove fairly convincingly that there were "in the early church only these two celebrations of the worship of God," namely, "the common meal, in whose framework proclamation of the word always takes place, and baptism."[14] If the proclamation of the word, praise, and prayer of thanks were associated with the Lord's Supper, then the attention at this service was directed necessarily backward toward the past. As the basic structure of post-Easter experience (presence of the Spirit, backward look at

---

14. Cullmann (1956), 33; for complete documentation see also Schenk (1970).

Jesus' death and resurrection, look forward to the return of Christ) was, despite important alterations, in agreement with the fundamental structure of the Old Testament prayer of praise, thanks, and petition, the suggestion is that the prayer tradition of Israel also influenced the bread and wine rituals. As, further, the words of remembering were understandable only in connection with the events of the night of betrayal, the Lord's Supper itself imposed the necessity of keeping alive important events in the life of Jesus and of announcing them to the newly converted believers. The Lord's Supper must for that reason have been the actual place where from the beginning there existed an interest in the past and where the tradition about Jesus was passed on. If one is not to make the historically impossible assumption that the young community, among which there still lived disciples of Jesus, was content with a form of worship which was very hard to understand, then the conclusion is unavoidable that a tradition gathered around the words of remembering from the beginning, "which told of the path of Jesus to his passion in Jerusalem."[15] Accordingly, an old (pre-Marcan) passion story, which reported how and why things came to the handing over of Jesus, may have belonged to the Lord's Supper from a time early on. Besides the daily celebratory meal, the Lord's Supper on Sundays (the day of the Lord) and on special days of remembering will have been the occasion for looking back more explicitly on the fate of Jesus.

Since the community gathered together regularly at the celebratory meal, all decisive activities must have joined up here. The new converts were introduced into the faith and prepared for baptism in connection with it. Here also problems may have been talked over and "processed" (with pneumatic experiences) in prayer (see Acts 4:23–31), problems which resulted from the life of the community as well as from the missionary preaching and the reaction of the hostile surrounding world. Catechesis and missionary preaching on their side made necessary brief summaries of the profession of faith in Christ. In this way "short gospels" or "confessional formulae" arose, such as are found in Acts 10:37–43 and in 1 Cor. 15:3–7. Finally, remembering the sayings of Jesus and occurrences from his life belonged to the regular preaching in the gatherings of the community, by which questions of everyday life in the community could be illuminated and clarified; this process may have led to a collection of sayings of the Lord and of short narratives. From the old passion story, from this or that "short gospel," and from collections of sayings of the Lord, the new literary genre of gospel was able finally to come to birth.

---

15. Pesch (1974), 153.

Kerygma of the Early Community and History

In the course of our whole investigation we have come to grips at different levels with Bultmann's thesis that the kerygma of the early community had no interest in the question of history. As we have now reached this kerygma, we can briefly look back and once again bring together those elements which form the basis for our opposing thesis. We can also make it clear in what sense the post-Easter proclamation was necessarily bound up with the question of Jesus' earthly life and his fate.

If the Easter appearances and the spiritual experiences were perceived by the disciples as isolated phenomena outside the great framework of salvation history, then their faith would have depended on immediately psychological aspects of these experiences; and at the most, in such a situation, various small religious groupings might have arisen, as often happened in the history of religions. But in the context of the fate of Jesus, the Easter and Pentecost experiences led to something completely different, namely, to the recognition of an event that was no longer available to direct experience: to faith in the exaltation of the murdered Christ. This statement about the activity of God in Jesus as the Christ, which transcended all immediate experiences, became possible through the retrospective overview of the different experiences.

If the way of Jesus had been handed down independently of the Easter experience, it would necessarily have appeared quite different, not because it would have lacked some additional "illumination" from the Easter faith, as Bultmann thought,[16] but because Jesus' message would quite simply have been driven out by the opposite view of the victors. His struggle would have remained one among those many which are covered over in the march of history and are replaced by the viewpoint of the victor. Easter was not necessary in order to lend the pre-Easter way of Jesus a new (artificial) appearance in retrospect, but to protect the truth of this way from retrospective domination.

Through the resurrection of Christ a new approach to meaning was simultaneously opened up in the consideration of universal history, for it became possible from now on to see conflicts, persecutions, and defeats in a different way. No longer did immediate this-worldly success have to be decisive. History as the history of victors was, at least in principle, overcome, and the question about the truth of those judgments which at first find acceptance through victory became a real one and could from now on lead to subsequent revisions. Truth and immediate this-worldly success were separated. That Christian truth thereby became nonhistorical could only be maintained by someone who thinks that

---

16. Bultmann, "Das Verhältnis der urchristlichen Christusbotschaft zum historischen Jesus," in Bultmann (1967), 454.

history is fundamentally nothing but a narration of the prejudices of the immediate victors. Over against this presupposition, the Easter faith makes the claim that historical research which takes the activity of God into account is capable of seeing the activity of humans also in a more unprejudiced way. Historical-critical research is therefore not in opposition to the theological viewpoint; rather, the latter provides categories which enable us to grasp more precisely the historical activity of human beings.

We were able to overcome the apparent conflict between the basileia message and the Easter kerygma, on the one hand, by relying on the claim made in Jesus' proclamation and, on the other, by not judging God's activity according to fixed predetermined ideas. Instead we tried to pursue as precisely as possible the way in which Jesus' claim was transformed through conflict, the way in which it was disputed and finally confirmed by God. The basic elements of this drama can be found again — in more condensed form — in the post-Easter kerygma, which continually emphasizes the opposition between abasement and exaltation. In this way it is possible to bring out either the opposition between the people who rejected Jesus' proclamation and the activity of God ("The stone which the builders rejected has become the cornerstone")[17] or the distance between the voluntary self-abasement of Jesus and his exaltation by the Father (1 Cor. 15:3–8; Phil. 2:6–11; 1 Tim. 2:5–7). The kerygma expressly contains the four crucial actors in the drama of salvation: the Son who proclaims and surrenders himself, the people who reject him, the Father who judges, and the disciples who witness, in their respective relationships to one another. Therefore the statement of faith implies a historical statement, and vice versa.

The problematic of history and kerygma surfaces as the problematic of the divine and human actors in the drama of salvation, and thus we have arrived at that great Old Testament theme designated by the word "covenant." Although this covenant sprang from the initiative of God alone, who maintained his faithfulness even when the people failed, and although the covenant partners were not on the basis of equality, the people's yes was owed to him. On Sinai, the covenant was struck by the people answering the words and commandments of Yahweh, as they were announced to Moses on the mountain, "with one voice:" "Everything the Lord has said we will do" (Exod. 24:4). This answer was repeated in the context of ritual sacrifices (Exod. 24:7) and confirmed with the sprinkling of blood: "This is the blood of the covenant that the Lord has made with you in accordance with all these words" (Exod. 24:8). After the yes of the people, Moses climbed the mountain once again with a great crowd accompanying him, and now Aaron, Nadab,

---

17. See also Acts 2:22–24; 3:13–15; 4:9–12; 5:30–32; 7:35–39; 10:37–43.

Abihu, and the seventy elders could also see God: "They beheld God, and they ate and drank" (Exod. 24:11). Finally the splendor of the Lord appeared over the mountain also to the whole of Israel "like a devouring fire" (Exod. 24:17). But despite this sight, the people failed again immediately (Exod. 31:18–33:6), so that a renewal (Exod. 33:7–34:35) was necessary. This representation of the sealing of the Old Testament covenant contains a whole dramaturgy, in the center of which stood the offer of God and the double yes of the people to the words of Yahweh, but which also from the beginning opened the way to a long history of refusal and renewal.

Beside the dominant picture of the covenant as something which could be renewed again after a break, in the tradition of prophetic proclamation, there was also the idea that the covenant of Sinai had been completely broken in the history of Israel. For this reason, people hoped for an entirely new initiative from God and for a new covenant (Jer. 31:31–34). Even with this hope, however, human activity did not lose importance, for the hope was precisely that, thanks to the divine spirit, people would finally be capable of living up to the covenant law and of being the true people of God: "I [Yahweh] place my Spirit within you and cause you to walk in my statutes and observe my commands and fulfill them, . . . you will be my people and I will be your God" (Ezek. 36:27ff.).

In the destiny of Jesus we have been able to pursue a drama, which likewise started off from a totally new initiative of God and in the center of which stood the alternative of yes or no to God. To the proclamation of the basileia message the people should have answered — as at Sinai — "with one voice"; then they would have seen the splendor of the Lord and been able to eat and drink in his presence. But the full and unambiguous yes did not happen this time either. And yet the "new" covenant is not shattered again (which would have made it immediately an "old" covenant), for Jesus himself, through his obedience to the Father and through his surrender for the many, vicariously spoke the full and final yes of the human covenant partner to God's proposal and also suffered in delivering that reply in view of the resistance he met. The saying about "the blood of the covenant that is poured out for many" (Mark 14:24), as it is found in the Last Supper tradition, fits seamlessly into the situation of Jesus' last meal with his disciples.

At this point the question of the kerygma and history arises again in its final refinement. Bultmann objected to the new interest of his disciples in the question of the historical Jesus, saying that we could not know "how Jesus understood his end, his death."[18] This objection is in

---

18. Bultmann (1967), 452.

fact of the greatest importance, and in this respect Bultmann was more logical than those of his disciples who accepted much of the story of Jesus as historically reliable, but shared their teacher's judgment when it came to the understanding of Jesus' death. It is quite undisputed that for the later community both the confession of the redeemer's death and the Lord's Supper as remembrance and participation in it were essential elements. If this central conviction and praxis of faith had not been in agreement with the de facto behavior of Jesus in the face of his death, there would have been at the most essential point a break between message and actual history, and the talk of God's activity would have been lacking all firm outline. However it becomes clear precisely from the point of view of Jesus' self-giving that God's activity in history does not mean some purely outward mighty deeds, but starts with the awakening of a new human activity, as became visible in the Old Testament with the suffering servant ("Every morning [God] wakens my ear..." [Isa. 50:4]). The question of the continuity between the Easter kerygma and the history of Jesus is revealed as the question about the agreement between the will of Jesus in the face of death and the verdict of judgment of the Father in the resurrection. If the agreement is broken here, then continuity in other points could perhaps be historically interesting, but theologically it would be of no importance. A break between Jesus' understanding of his death and the Easter kerygma would have as a consequence that the early community would have announced a new and final covenant of God, without being able to point to any corresponding final human answer. The Old Testament understanding of covenant, and thus also the relationship of faith and history, would thereby have been totally destroyed, since an action of God would have been announced which was only outwardly connected with events in history (the fact of the arrival of a messenger), but which in essence was completely severed from it.

That the early community of Christians in fact judged quite differently should become clear once again through an example. This will allow us also to see in what sense Jesus' earthly life was seen and interpreted afresh from the viewpoint of the Easter and Pentecost experiences. Acts 4:1–22 describes how Peter and John were arrested for their preaching in the Temple, gave witness to Christ before the High Council, and were finally forbidden to preach. Under many threats, they were let free again. The continuation of the story (Acts 4:23–31) shows how the community reacted to this event in prayer, and how they were given a sign that they were heard.

The prayer handed down as connected with this event is on the one hand within the great structure of Israel's prayers: a look back at past history and a request for a new working of God in the present. But on the other hand there is an important alteration. Before the request about the present working of God ("And now, Lord, look upon their threats and grant your servants the power to speak your word..." [Acts 4:29]), there is a *double* look back, first at God's deeds, as they are reported in the Old Testament (creation and prophesying through David), and then at the fate of Jesus, in which the (Davidic) prophecy was fulfilled. Psalm 2:1ff. is quoted as prophecy, in which there is talk of the frenzy of the peoples (*ethne*), of the vain plans of the nations (*laoi*), and of the joining up (*synechtesan*) of the kings (*basileis*) and rulers (*archontes*) against the lord (*kyrios*) and his anointed (*christos*). The two verses of the psalm are then applied to Jesus, as the key words (some in a somewhat altered form) are picked up again: "For truly, Herod and Pontius Pilate, together with the gentiles and the people of Israel, joined together against your holy servant Jesus, whom you anointed, to bring about what your hand and your will predestined to take place" (Acts 4:27ff.). Consequently, by means of Psalm 2 the proceedings against Jesus are interpreted as a universal act of ganging up on the victim, which is also directed against Jesus' disciples, as the immediate continuation of the passage shows: "And now, Lord, look upon their threats...."

Compared with the condemnation of Jesus, as we saw it in the third act, there are two new elements in the description given in the Acts of the Apostles: (1) The cooperation of the Jewish groups with Pilate takes on an explicitly universal dimension. (2) The disciples no longer allow themselves to be drawn onto the side of Jesus' enemies, but, thanks to the working of the Spirit, they belong to the anointed one in such a way that persecution of him affects them (and vice versa). Universalization is achieved by seeing the rejection of Jesus in the light both of Old Testament prophecy and of the post-Easter experience, so that "the only really crucial thing about the passion event stands out clearly, i.e., that all were involved in the condemnation of Jesus."[19] Because both in the history which preceded Jesus and in that which followed, the same thing happened as before in Jerusalem, the Acts of the Apostles is able to speak of a universal ganging up.[20] This has the consequence for Jesus' disciples that they play a double role. From the viewpoint of their own tendencies and their spontaneous behavior, they continue to belong with the Jews and pagans who turned against Jesus. But through the power of the Spirit which is given to them by the exalted one, they stand on his side and share in his fate.

---

19. Radl (1988), 138.

20. This universalization can be made anthropologically somewhat more understandable by Girard's theory. If the consensus of human societies is finally based on a subterranean lynching, then all human action takes place within this frame of reference.

In accordance with this analysis, which could also be extended to 1 Thessalonians 2:14–16, the Easter and Pentecost experiences actually throw a new light on the ministry and destiny of the earthly Jesus. This is not a case of inventing new stories and projecting them back onto him, but what happened is seen with a depth and a multiplicity of levels of meaning which were not perceivable before in the immediate context of the events. This looking back allowed space for interplay between an attitude which, despite a certain freedom, placed the emphasis on a great faithfulness to the words of Jesus (synoptic Gospels) and a different attitude which wanted to bring together at the same time faithfulness to the tradition and the deeper understanding of his destiny in light of Easter and Pentecost (John's Gospel).

Part Three

SYSTEMATIC CONSIDERATIONS

We have followed the drama in the fate of Jesus primarily with the help of the synoptic Gospels. The outcome has now to be examined and deepened, first of all from the point of view of the other New Testament writings, and then it needs to be systematically evaluated in relation both to notions of God and to the Christian life. In the confrontation with the nonsynoptic New Testament writings, the main point is the interpretation of the cross, for this point will decide whether or not the different New Testament theologies, which certainly exist, are ultimately in overall inner agreement. In relation to the notion of God, the question arises whether the aspects of the divine reality which are revealed in the drama of salvation continue to exist alongside one another or whether they come together in a coherent way in a notion of God free from all contradictions. Finally, the question concerning Christian life is how far this life itself can be understood by means of the language offered by the drama of salvation.

Redemption as Judgment and Sacrifice

Like the message of the basileia, Jesus' proclamation of judgment has taken on a great importance in our investigation. But the immediate representation of judgment has undergone — in three stages — a radical deepening and reinterpretation. The judgment proclaimed by Jesus showed itself at first as the self-judgment of humankind; then from the one who spoke of judgment to the stubborn people he became one who allowed himself to be drawn into the judgment process of his opponents; finally there took place the verdict of the heavenly Father at Easter as a justification of the condemned one and as a judgment of forgiveness toward his enemies. This stage-by-stage transformation of the notion of judgment by means of the synoptic Gospels is so radical that the question must necessarily be asked whether other New Testament writings see the matter similarly, or whether in this respect they remain at a distance from the first three Gospels or even in opposition to them. Neither must we avoid the question whether from the viewpoints of Paul and John our interpretation of the synoptic Gospels as developed so far is

159

confirmed, or whether, despite the coherence which we have seen emerging, this interpretation must become subject to yet another critique. Or are we in fact dealing with an inner contradiction in the New Testament writings, which nowadays seems quite obvious to many exegetes?

The Cross as Judgment

Jesus in the first part of John's Gospel often speaks of his coming hour (John 2:4; 7:30; 8:20), but when we get to his last public appearance, this hour has become an already present reality: "Now is my soul troubled. What shall I say, 'Father, deliver me from this hour'? But for this purpose I have come to this hour. Father, glorify your name!" (John 12:27–28; 13:1). The trouble in Jesus' soul indicates that the time of suffering has already begun and that by his hour, which is now there, he can only mean his being handed over to his enemies and his exaltation on the cross. In the same connection, he interprets the event already begun as judgment over the world and its ruler: "Now is the judgment of the world; now shall the ruler of this world be cast out" (John 12:31). His hour is consequently the hour of judgment over this world. Although John's Gospel presents the condemnation of Jesus as a conspiracy rather than as an actual legal judgment, it does, however, see in his fate a larger judgment which affects the whole world. But all the same the question remains initially open: how this judgment is to be understood and why the death of Jesus can be presented in this way.

Likewise, Paul turns to the idea of judgment for his theology of the cross. In the epistle to the Romans he sets out clearly from the beginning that all humans have fallen victim to sin and cannot justify themselves through works. Only through pure grace and through faith in redemption in Christ can they become just before God. Paul describes redemption itself with several pictures and concepts. First he turns to the concept of atonement: "whom God put forward as atonement [*hilasterion*] by his blood, an atonement effective through faith" (Rom. 3:25). However, Paul does not in this context explain how this atonement is to be more closely understood. For this we find somewhat later other utterances about the event of the cross. Thus he emphasizes the willing and anticipatory love of the heavenly Father: "God has shown his love for us in that Christ died for us while we were yet sinners" (Rom. 5:8). God's loving dealings toward those people who are sinners — which means everyone — is identical with love for his enemies. Paul says this explicitly: " ... while we were enemies we were reconciled to God by the death of his Son" (Rom. 5:10). The apostle understands reconciliation on the cross as a deed of divine love for enemies.

In Romans 8:3 Paul gives more specific information relating to the way in which God's love for enemies became effective on the cross: "For

God has done what the law, weakened by the flesh, could not do: he sent his own Son in the form of sinful flesh as atonement for sin [*peri hamartias*], and he condemned sin in the flesh." Here Paul describes Christ's death for sinners (atonement) as a condemnation of sin. As with the synoptics and with John, we find with Paul too the idea of judgment. However, we have before us only a very terse formulation, and we must therefore proceed cautiously in interpreting it. The apostle at first emphasizes that Christ was sent in the form of that flesh which was powerless because of sin. Since by the word "send" he denotes above all the task given to the Son of walking the path to the cross in obedience, it belongs to his mission "in the form of the flesh" that he should be sent into the world of his opponents. In this world — in the flesh — God condemned (*katekrinen*) sin. In Romans 8:3 Paul does not explain any further how he imagines this judgment. This central question has to be answered from other passages and take into account the framework of his whole theology.

In Galatians 4:4 the apostle again speaks of Christ's mission. But he does not link it up directly with the idea of judgment, but with that of the redemption of slaves: "But when the time had fully come, God sent forth his Son, born of a woman, born under the law, to set free those who were under the law, so that we might receive adoption as sons" (Gal. 4:4–5). In a similar way to Romans 8:3, Paul stresses in this passage that for this act of redemption Christ came into that world in which people are imprisoned as sinners, characterizing this imprisonment more precisely as standing under the law. The redeemer did not free the prisoners from outside. In obedience he entered the sinful world of his opponents. What happened then, and how the redemption was actually carried out, is described more fully in another passage of the letter to the Galatians: "Christ has redeemed us from the curse of the law, having become a curse for us; for it is written, 'Cursed is everyone who hangs on a tree' " (Gal. 3:13). The "curse" is a term which belongs to the language of the law and of (religious) judgment. Consequently, Galatians also forces us to look at the problem of judgment in considering the question of the deeper understanding of the cross. In the second letter to the Corinthians, there is a further passage which has a great similarity to Galatians 3:13: "For our sake [God] made him become sin who knew no sin, so that in him we might become the righteousness of God" (2 Cor. 5:21). These texts document very clearly that for Paul the language of judgment is not the only one employed, although certainly a particularly important one, to describe redemption. Concerning the fuller understanding of this concept, everything depends on how the action of God in judgment on the cross is to be interpreted in connection with Jesus' own behavior and that of his opponents.

M. Luther, K. Barth, and H. U. von Balthasar are among the outstanding representatives of the theology of the cross. Appealing to Paul, even if with a partially different emphasis, they understood the event at Golgotha as a judgment insofar as they attributed to the heavenly Father a direct act of condemnation of his Son. Since this view does not match up with what we found in the synoptics, it becomes important to ask whether Paul and the synoptics contradict one another or whether our interpretation of the synoptics was inadequate, or whether the above-mentioned authors have interpreted Paul in a one-sided way. To answer this question, everything depends on how love and anger are seen in their relationship to one another. According to K. Barth, in the event of the cross there was revealed the "radicality of the divine love, which itself could 'do enough' only just in the complete effect of its anger against sinful man, only just in its being killed, extinguished, and removed."[1] According to Barth, judgment and anger belong to love. The wonderful thing about the divine judgment was that it was not passed on sinners, who had deserved it, but on the one pure of sin, who voluntarily took their place. The judgment process in this case was hardly different from that of other judgments, as it consisted essentially of a condemnation by a judge and the subsequent killing. And yet — according to Barth — something surprising happened. With Christ, who stood in our place, even we sinners, as well as *sin itself,* were handed over to negation and destruction: "He [Christ] has in his own person delivered us as sinners and thus also sin to destruction; he has lifted us up, negated and erased us as sinners in our sin — ourselves, sin, and with this the accusation pertaining to us, the condemnation and damnation."[2] Judgment is, according to Barth, essentially destruction. Sinners cannot be converted; they must rather be negated in Christ and created anew. The crucial thing in the Passion is then the action of God, in which he eliminates and kills sinners through his Son, and with them sin itself.

Barth's theology of the cross is essentially based on taking the Pauline utterances that God condemned sin "in the flesh" (Rom. 8:3) and made Christ "into sin" (2 Cor. 5:21; Gal. 3:13), and without further examination raising them into systematic principles. Whether this is justified must be looked at more closely. In both the above-mentioned passages, Paul speaks of Christ's mission before he takes up the idea of judgment. However this is not simply an action of the Father, as it only becomes a reality in our world insofar as Christ, by his obedience, does the will of the Father and thus gives the eternal mission a concrete form in the history of salvation. Neither does God carry out judgment directly

---

1. Barth (1932–67) 4/1:280.
2. Ibid., 278.

from heaven — somewhat on the model of the flood or the destruction of Sodom and Gomorrah — without human participation. The passion accounts in all the Gospels are unambiguous on this point. Because Barth sees this, he speaks of Jesus' opponents as the "instruments" and "agents" of the divine judgment:

> Involved in what befell Jesus were the participants, Jews and gentiles, and according to the appropriate commentary of the Acts of the Apostles (2:23; 4:28), these participants were even in their evident great guilt and the rejection their deed merited still only instruments in the hand of God, agents and executors of his "definite plan and foreknowledge."[3]

The picture of the judgment of the cross will depend on whether one should understand the opponents of Jesus as directly the agents of divine action.

In Christ's mission his human will cooperated in such a way that, in obedience, he completely followed the divine will which sent him. At the judgment on him, the will of his opponents was not similarly in agreement with that of the Father, for they acted, as Barth himself insists, in the most shameful and reprehensible way. But how could they be directly "agents" and "executors" of the divine will if their will was opposed to his? Here the further question arises as to how the divine will can be precisely recognized at all in the event of the cross. Does it reveal itself in the surrender of Jesus or in the actions of his opponents or in both? To play off the second possibility against the first would mean that Jesus had suddenly stopped being the revealer of God and instead his opponents had been entrusted with this mission, an idea which can immediately be seen as nonsense from the viewpoint of the New Testament. At the most there remains the possibility that both the surrender of Jesus and the actions of his opponents reveal in their own way something of the comprehensive will of the heavenly Father. However, since the message and surrender of Jesus (nonviolence, love of enemies, holding back from finally judging anyone) and the actions of his enemies stood in contradictory opposition, both cannot point to God under the same aspect, for in that way a contradictory opposition would arise in the idea of God, which would cancel itself. If the New Testament conviction of God's revelation is not to be destroyed, the action of God in Jesus must be clearly separated from possible "divine" actions by his opponents. But from this it becomes clear that in the principles 'God sent his Son' (Rom. 8:3; Gal. 4:4) and "God made Christ to be sin"

---

3. Ibid., 262.

(2 Cor. 5:21) or "He condemned sin in the flesh" (Rom. 8:3), the action of God is to be understood differently in each case. In the first one, the participating human will is in full agreement with the divine, while in the two other cases it pulls in the opposite direction. The utterance that God condemned sin in the flesh (Rom. 8:3) has therefore to be interpreted very cautiously, taking into account both the Old Testament background as well as the larger context of theology.

In Old Testament thinking, Yahweh is believed in as the creator of all, and yet there is much in the world that happens against his will. Thus on the one hand there is: "I am the Lord, and there is none other. I create light and make darkness, I bring about salvation and I create woe. I am the Lord who accomplish all this" (Isa. 45:6ff.). And beside this there stand many utterances which run very much as follows: "From the days that I led your ancestors out of Egypt until this very day I sent them continually all my servants, the prophets. But they did not listen to them and did not incline their ear to me; instead they remained stiffnecked and did even worse than their ancestors" (Jer. 7:25ff.). Although God brings everything about, people resist him and act against his will. But the faith of Israel never made God responsible for sin (as an act of God against God), but always only people. Belief in his omnipotence was consequently a differentiated belief, which necessarily included the idea of allowing sin. It is against this background that the utterances of Paul also should be carefully examined. Undifferentiated-sounding principles about God's working ("God made Christ to be sin," "He condemned sin in the flesh") may have been influenced by the linguistic structure of Hebrew and do not therefore a priori exclude a more differentiated thinking on the part of the apostle.

The idea of judgment stands in an immediate connection with that of divine anger. In relation to this theme, Paul offers us fortunately not merely individual utterances which are compromised and often hard to interpret, but a short articulated presentation. In Romans 1:18–32 he unfolds how the anger of God makes itself known "from heaven... against all ungodliness and unrighteousness of men" (1:18). In this way the apostle maintains firmly from the beginning that God has revealed through his works "his eternal power and deity" (1:20), that humans have not thanked him for what he has revealed and given, and because of this their thinking and their hearts have been darkened. Out of this darkening they themselves transformed the splendor of the immortal God into pictures of worthless idols (1:23). After this interpretation of human guilt, Paul proceeds to describe more precisely God's reaction to sin. He does this in a great rhythmical movement of thought, which repeats the same idea with small variations, deepening it step by step. In this way the apostle makes it clear that we are dealing with one of his absolutely central intuitions, which he formulates in the following terms: "Therefore God *delivered* [*paradidonai*] them over through the desires of their own hearts to impurity.... Therefore God *delivered* them over to dishonorable passions.... And since they refused to acknowledge God, God *delivered* them over to depraved thinking..." (1:24–28). Paul speaks three times of the divine handing over, and the consequences from it are three different but connected misdeeds which people themselves commit and by which they punish themselves, namely: (1) worship of idols; (2) distortion of human relationships in the sexual sphere; (3) total breakdown of human order (injustice, wickedness, greed, malice, envy, murder, quarrelling, cunning, and trickery). The representation of direct punishment by an external authority is not once indicated by Paul. The anger consists entirely in the fact that God hands people over to the dynamic and inner logic of those passions and of that depraved thinking which they themselves have awakened by their turning away from God. Thus God's anger means that God fully respects the evil that people do with all its consequences. By turning away from the creator, they have distorted their hearts' striving and their thinking. Sinners are now entirely handed over to and victims both of the passions which have thus arisen and of the overpowering pictures of a thought process which has lost all foundation. Their life with God, their dealings with their fellow humans, and the way they relate to themselves and to the good things of this world are ruined: for this they punish themselves (mutually).

There are only a few passages in the Pauline letters where the apostle presents an idea so explicitly and forcefully as his understanding of God's anger. From this one can deduce that it was important to him and that, in investigating his idea of judgment, which is closely connected with the theme of anger, one cannot pass over it. As anger is understood as a handing over, in Romans 1:18–32 we are prompted to interpret also the angry judging in the event of the cross as a handing over. But before we can risk a conclusion on this point, there are still further utterances to consider.

In 2 Corinthians 5:19, the apostle writes: "Indeed, God was in Christ reconciling the world to himself, not counting [*logizomenos*] their trespasses against them and entrusting to us the message of reconciliation." The apostle speaks here neither of an anger of God toward his Son nor of a destruction of sin through him. By means of the grammatical construction of the participle he characterizes reconciliation rather as not taking sin into account. This utterance is closely related to Romans 5:8–10, where Paul speaks of the anticipatory action of God and of the love in Christ, by which we were reconciled, "when we were still enemies." God's love for enemies, the refusal to take sin into account, and anger understood as handing over — these concepts create the context in which the judgment utterances are to be interpreted. The interpreter should take continual care that no contradictory opposition is introduced into God's will, in accordance with Scripture.

Starting from the presuppositions mentioned above, we can now attempt an interpretation of those utterances of Paul in which he describes reconciliation on the cross as a judgment. In Romans 8:3 he says, as we have already seen, that "God sent his Son in the form of sinful flesh" and "he condemned sin in the flesh" (*en te sarki*). By the emphasis on the "flesh of sin" and on judgment "in the flesh," a connection is established with the theme of anger, as this is also fulfilled in the flesh. According to Romans 1:18–32, this is not merely the outward place where the angry action of God takes place, but it is more that active and boundless force which holds people imprisoned in its own dynamic and ruins their life. The boundless desire which springs from sin, with all the consequences from which people suffer, is identical with the anger of God, and it is identical with the law of the flesh which holds people prisoners (Rom. 7:7–25). Through these connections it should become clear that in Romans 8:3 the flesh in which judgment on sin occurred is not thought of as a purely passive substance, on which the action of divine judgment had its effect as the only active factor. As it bears within itself a boundless dynamic of desire, it must have played a part also in the condemnation of sin that took place in it. If, according to Paul, Christ was sent into the boundless and destructive dynamic of the flesh, this should in consequence mean that also the judgment on sin was achieved thereby.

The interpretation which suggests itself so far is supported in addition by a linguistic hint in Romans 8:32. There we find: "He [God] did not spare his own Son, but gave him up [*paradidonai*] for us all..." (Rom. 4:25). The mission of the Son in the form of the flesh (Rom. 8:3) includes not sparing and surrendering or handing over (Rom. 8:32). Paul uses exactly the same word (*paradidonai*) for this giving over by the Father as he does to describe the working of the divine anger (Rom. 1:24–32). This linguistic link consequently shows how one would be justified in interpreting the judgment on sin in Romans 8:3 in the light of Romans 1:18–32.

Taking into account the outcome so far, we can now turn to 2 Corinthians 5:21: "[God] has made the one who knew no sin to become sin for us, so that we might become the righteousness of God in him." As we interpret this text, the final decision must be made as to how Paul's view of the judgment on sin is to be understood and whether one may and ought to speak of an angry and destructive direct action of God toward the crucified one. Certainly, it is hardly to be supposed that Paul is here directed by completely different concepts than in Romans 1:18–32 and Romans 8:3. But the question must once again be looked at afresh, and the essential point is whether the utterance "he has...made to become sin" is to be interpreted as an *exclusive* activity of God or whether it means that God sent the one pure of sin into that event in which he was made to be sin by sinners. This latter interpretation is suggested by the Old Testament background. But can this be confirmed from the context?

Just as 2 Corinthians 5:21 says that Christ was made into sin, so Galatians 3:13 says that he became for us a curse (*katara*). Both utterances entirely match up in subject matter. However, in Galatians 3:13, Paul additionally indicates in what way this happened, namely, through the law. All who live according to the law stand under its curse if they do not keep all its prescriptions (Gal. 3:10). It further declares each one accursed who — like the crucified one — hangs on a tree (Gal. 3:13). Galatians serves as an important complement to 2 Corinthians 5:21, and the question of how Christ was made into sin and a curse must be seen and decided from this viewpoint in conjunction with the problematic of the law, so we must also briefly go into this subject.

The letter to the Romans presents the relationship between law and sin as a complex interaction. The law is of itself "holy, just and good," and it is supposed to "lead to life" (Rom. 7:10, 12). Nevertheless, its effect in fact is the opposite, and it brings death (Rom. 7:10). This contradiction can be clarified as sin taking possession of the law and perverting its sense. Sin is so powerful that it can make use of what is good: "Did something good become death to me? By no means! But sin was bringing about my death through what is good so that it might be revealed as sin. For it was through the commandment that sin showed itself in its full measure as sin" (Rom. 7:13). If the law, which in itself is good, actually leads to death, then it follows that the law itself is not the real initiator of the event, and still less is it God, from whom it comes. What really takes action is sin, which shows its excess in knowing how to use even the good as its means and as its cover. If now even Christ became a curse through the law, then it was not the law itself and still less God who was the actor responsible. Within the Pauline world of ideas, the utterance of Galatians 3:13 can only mean that Christ became a curse through the power of sin, which made use of the law. With this insight the decision about the interpretation of 2 Corinthians 5:21 should be resolved. God was not the direct actor, but he sent his Son into the world ruled by sin, and thus, through the excess of sin making use of the law, he became sin and a curse. But who were the immediate actors in this event?

Paul's understanding of the law was conditioned by his own experience. Since he himself, in his zeal for the law, persecuted Jesus' disciples and at his conversion on the way to Damascus had to acknowledge the error of his ways, he remained throughout the course of his life constantly confronted by the fact that in his zeal for the good law he had done evil. But he could not estimate from his own experience the consequences of this fact, for that experience prevented him from developing a fundamental position toward the law. If nevertheless the apostle came to make statements concerning the law as such, he can only have drawn them where he found his new confidence in faith: in Christ. In the light of his own experience he was able to understand more deeply the fate of the crucified and exalted one. As he himself had persecuted Jesus' disciples, so had his brothers in faith already in the name of the law condemned as a blasphemer and driven out the preacher from Galilee, who at his trial made the claim to be the Messiah and Son of Man (1 Thess. 2:15). But since this claim, as his own experience on the road to Damascus confirmed, was authenticated by God, the consequence must have pressed itself on Paul that the law had totally failed not only in his life but also at the most decisive moment, namely, in the encounter with the Son of God. It had not led people to a full knowledge of the will of God, i.e., of the Son, but on the contrary it contributed to his rejection and condemnation.

The power of sin is so cunning that it can get completely within its grasp the good and holy law and can so distort it that it works against God and his envoy. If Jesus in the name of the divine law was condemned as a "blasphemer" and thus was made into a curse, even into Satan (John 10:33; 19:7), it was consequently not God, the originator of the law, who cursed his Son. The power of evil rather turned back the command which came from God against the Son. Working from this insight, we are finally led to the interpretation of 2 Corinthians 5:21, that God did not himself destroy Christ in judgment. Certainly, he sent him into the world of sin, but entirely with the aim of saving humankind. However, the power of sin was so great that it was able by means of its own mechanism and dynamic to draw him into its world and thus to make him into sin.

We started off from the question of whether there is a contradiction between the synoptics and Paul or whether our interpretation of the synoptics must be put in question again, or whether that theology which attributes to the apostle the idea of God's direct act of anger toward the crucified one has got things wrong. The result which has emerged is that Paul and the Gospels present the decisive point in a similar way. There are people who have condemned Jesus in the name of the law and branded him as a curse (Gal. 3:13), as sin (2 Cor. 5:21), and even as a satanic being (John 19:7). People have ganged up against him (Acts

4:27), projected the evil in their hearts onto him, and thus made him the bearer of sins (1 Pet. 2:22–24) and scapegoat. However, this did not free them from their sins, for the process of transference was in a double sense false. It laid on Jesus a blame which was not his, and it generated in the judges a feeling of self-certainty which was illusory and involved them still deeper in their guilt. For that reason, they had to conceal their activity from themselves by a double self-deception.

The actors immediately involved as judges in the dramatic event of the cross were human beings (the Jews and gentiles, Judas, Peter, and the other disciples). They acted in a strange blindness, so that in the end they did not know what they were doing (Luke 23:34). According to the synoptic Gospels they fell victims to a process of hardening of the heart. John sees the satanic spirit at work in this, and Paul speaks of the power of sin or of the rulers of this world (1 Cor. 2:8). People are thus caught in an evil power; on the one hand they are guilty and on the other victims of evil and therefore they also act in "roles." All the New Testament writings agree substantially on this central question, even if they use different languages and forms of presentation.

Jesus' Surrender as Identification with Sinners

Because sinners could not free themselves from their sin by transferring their guilt, only one aspect of the complex drama of salvation is settled by this process. The decisive point is how Jesus responded to this burden and how he bore it. Luther applies the church fathers' picture of a marvelous exchange between Godhead and humankind to the relationship between Christ and the sinful soul, and he speaks of a marriage in which the goods of the bride and bridegroom are mutually exchanged. The justice of Christ becomes the soul's own and he takes on himself the sin of his bride. K. Barth develops Luther's view, centered on the justification of the sinful self, into a more objective one and he speaks of the identification of Christ with sinners: "Jesus Christ battled, no, even loved his, God's, enemies — and that includes us all according to Romans 5:10 and Colossians 1:21!—to the point that he *identified* with them."[4] The identification of which Barth speaks is of great, even decisive importance in the event of the cross, and this from the perspective of the synoptics as well as of John and Paul. How radically it is to be understood will be shown step by step from the New Testament writings.

Whoever prays for his enemies, as Jesus did during his suffering (Luke 23:34), identifies himself at least in thought and in inner concern with them. However it is from the actions and words of the Last Supper that

---

4. Barth (1932–67) 4/1:268 (my emphasis).

we can conclude how deep this inner participation went. Jesus gave himself to his disciples to eat in the forms of bread and wine, and with this he interpreted his offering of himself to death. Since food and drink are completely assimilated by the eaters and drinkers into their own body, the self-giving of Christ must be understood, as it is presented in the eucharistic signs, as a bodily union with those for whom he went to his death. His self-giving for many consequently included a "bodily" identification with them. In his nonviolent love he not only became involved in their dark world, as we have seen, but he also set out, in saving them, to become "one body" with them.

In John's Gospel we find Jesus, in his announcement of the judgment on the world, making the following pronouncement: "And I, when I am lifted up from the earth, will draw everyone to me" (12:32). By exaltation is meant both the crucifixion and the resurrection. From the word "draw" it is consequently made clear that the crucified one not only outwardly — as it were juristically — stood for the many, but he took them completely to him.

The idea of a universal identification is found most directly in Paul. He speaks not only of God reconciling the world to himself when we were still sinners, but he also makes clear in detail what happened to us at the death of Christ, even if we knew nothing about it at the time: "One has died for all; therefore all have died" (2 Cor. 5:14). The utterance is surprising from the viewpoint of everyday experience. Spontaneous imagination and logic would have suggested a completely different consequence: one has died for all, so the many don't have to die anymore. If Paul on the contrary "designated Jesus' death on the cross as the death of all, then he assumed that here identification occurred."[5] Only from the viewpoint of such an identification is it correct to conclude that in the death of Jesus all others have died with him.

If we have to understand Christ's self-giving for the many, on the basis of clear New Testament witness, as an identification with sinners, still there is an important distinction to make. To speak of it in an undifferentiated way produces the logical consequence that Jesus also identifies himself with those deeds of his opponents by which they condemned and crucified him. He would then have indirectly condemned and killed himself; his apparently nonviolent self-giving would have been in reality an indirect suicide. This questionable conclusion shows how cautiously one must proceed with the analysis of the event of the cross, if one is not to ascribe to Christ — with the best of intentions — highly immoral acts.

---

5. O. Hofius, "Sühne und Versöhnung: Zum paulinischen Verständnis des Kreuzestodes Jesu," in *Versuche* (1973), 39.

Because Jesus was free of sin and at the same time was made to be sin, we have to distinguish within the sinner the responsible agent and the victim. Both aspects are found in the same person, as every agent makes himself (unintentionally) also a victim, as Psalm 7:14–17 described it in vivid and striking language: "When the wicked man sharpens his sword, his bow bent and strung, then he has prepared his deadly weapons against himself, made ready his fiery arrows.... He digs a pit, shovels it out, yet he falls into the grave he himself has made. His evil deed comes back on his own head, and on his own pate his violence descends." The concept, that every criminal ultimately damages himself (see also Prov. 26:27), is decisive for the idea of self-judgment. The doer of evil deeds always becomes also the victim of his actions. However, the distinction between responsible agent and victim should never be blurred, and it is crucial for a correctly understood doctrine of redemption. Jesus was never himself a sinner and he never agreed to others' sins.

In the petitionary prayer for his enemies during the passion we find the explicit reasoning, "...for they know not what they do" (Luke 23:34) This postscript makes it clear that Jesus, in asking forgiveness for his torturers, in no way approved their actions. He gave lack of personal responsibility precisely as a reason why he stood in for his adversaries. He represented his persecutors to the heavenly Father as the sort of people who, because of their lack of knowledge, have no genuine responsibility for their actions. Their actions arose not from their own wide-awake decision, but it just happened to them, so that they were more victims than agents.[6] The reasoning in Jesus' request also makes clear that the distinction between responsible action and being a victim is not identical with that between active deeds and passive suffering. The executioners of Jesus were certainly active at the crucifixion, but because of their lack of knowledge they were ultimately not responsible agents: in their actions they were victims. They acted under a spell and took the role of that power to which they fell victim.

Also the fact that, after the representative redeeming death, individual conversion remained necessary gives a clear indication that Jesus' solidarity with sinners is to be understood in a differentiated way. By his surrender for sinners he did not abolish their own responsibility and make their personal conversion superfluous. However much he stood in for the many, the basic freedom of those for whom he gave himself remained untouched. He himself became the victim of misdeeds, and as such he united himself in ultimate solidarity with all other people, insofar as they are struck down by their own and others' sins.

The blindness of Jesus' opponents makes evident that people at the

---

6. See also John 16:3; Acts 3:17; 13:27; Rom. 10:2.

crucial moment are likely to succumb to their own actions, that they are far more victims of their deeds than responsible initiators of them. In Pauline terms, this means that sin rules as an active force in them and that they are tied up in their own house. K. Barth saw this truth clearly, and he uncovered the deception in that enlightened, liberal theology which thought it had to criticize or tone down the doctrine of the representative redeeming death of Christ in the name of the autonomy of the moral subject. For this reason Barth rightly emphasized in his doctrine of reconciliation that Christ fought the central battle with evil in our place. Luther had already expressed a similar view, and he too stressed that the rule of sin is so comprehensive that the sinner cannot adequately distinguish between being a person and being a sinner and thus cannot distance himself from sin. Over against this, modern philosophy thought that it could explain man to a large extent from the viewpoint of his own autonomous activity and freedom. It was rightly seen that people in fact build up the picture of their existence as human and thus also their identity through their own deeds and do not find them already there in nature. But at the same time there was a widespread failure to recognize that these deeds are in no way autonomous but subject to many external and internal laws, mechanisms and compulsions. Even where alienation from self and suppression of self are explicitly discussed (Marxism, sociology of knowledge, psychoanalysis), they have not been seen in their full import. Barth is in the right, therefore, when, over against all these tendencies, he stresses Christ's deed and emphasizes that the crucified one fought the real fight with evil and by his deed identified himself with all sinners and thus opened up to them a new possibility of life. However, it would be a failure to acknowledge not only the biblical insights but also an authentic strand in modern thought, if human freedom and the irreducible core of responsibility were not equally clearly expressed. In human activity, therefore, two dimensions have always to be distinguished, alienation from self and responsibility, which are not entirely separate, and in the concrete cannot be distinguished with complete clarity, and yet at the fundamental level have to be unambiguously split from each other. Precisely in their own activity, human beings are determined by outside forces. They are "acted upon" when they think they themselves are acting; they are the victims of their own deeds when they believe that they can claim responsibility for the origin of their works.

The Sacrifice of Christ and the "Conversion" of Evil

The distinction in active deeds between responsible action and action as victim throws up a new and very subtle problem for the event of the cross. Up until now, we have maintained that Christ identified himself with sinners insofar as they are victims, but not with them as responsible agents. But if his being the victim of his opponents also had an effect in the act of crucifixion, as we see in the petition, "Father, forgive them, for they know not what they do" (Luke 23:34), then it seems to follow that he made his own the very deeds by which he was killed. He would then have been not on the side of that failing freedom which collaborated in the crucifixion, but rather of that concrete deed by which his opponents had become entrapped. His identification with those crucifying him would in that case have included agreement to their killing and his being killed.

This question cannot be put on one side as academic quibbling, for on the one hand there are scholars who unambiguously speak of an indirect self-killing by Jesus,[7] and on the other hand even vaguer ideas which point in this direction have important consequences for Christian praxis. The picture that one has of the crucified one puts a stamp on one's own behavior. If one sees in him someone who indirectly killed himself, then the following of his way must foster conscious or unconscious self-destructive tendencies. Above all since the Middle Ages "love of suffering" has been a central theme in Christian spirituality. Is this love a subtle form of masochism, as is often assumed nowadays? That such tendencies in many cases played a part should not need to be disputed. In this connection the historical question is not important. But the fundamental problem of self-destruction within Christian spirituality shows that we have to examine very precisely the behavior of Jesus in his bitter fate, so as not to admit amoral elements in the name of piety. We find ourselves in an area where the highest form of love appears very close to perversion. The same question can also run: does not self-sacrifice mean self-destruction? In theories of sacrifice in the Mass since the Council of Trent, the starting point has almost always been that the element of destruction belongs to the concept of sacrifice. Seen from this presupposition, a self-sacrifice is synonymous with self-destruction. Our analysis of the identification of Christ with the action (crucifixion) of his opponents leads directly to the often debated question of whether and how the cross of Christ may — or indeed must — be understood as a sacrifice.

In our investigation so far we have often spoken of Christ as victim.

---

7. "Jesus remained the active agent, even and precisely on his way to the cross. He allowed no one to force a given course of action on him. His death was no avoidable accident. He was obliged to die and wanted to die. Yet the timing of his death he determined himself — in agreement with the Father. It was his role to die on the cross; and it was the role of Judas to facilitate his death." Out of this the consequence is deduced that the image of "betrayer" must be radically revised, "because he, as he 'handed over' Jesus to the arresting officers, then to the Jewish high priests, acted not from his own motive *but on behalf of Jesus*" (Schwarz [1986], 237; emphasis mine).

But in doing so we have not meant the same as the tradition meant when it spoke of the sacrifice of Christ. The German word *Opfer* contains two distinct meanings which in Latin (and in many modern languages, including English) are also denoted by two distinct words, namely, *Opfer* as the object suffering from the destructive action of another (victim, Latin *victima*) and *Opfer* as an act by which someone destroys or hands over something (sacrifice, Latin *sacrificium*). That Christ was the victim of others' actions is so evident that this has never been disputed. However the question about active *Opfer* (sacrifice) is far more complex, because here, besides the theological problems already sketched out, numerous questions arise from the viewpoint of the history of religions.

Theories of Sacrifice

There is no unanimous answer as to how cult sacrifices in the different religions and in the Old Testament are to be understood. The different lines of interpretation in ethnology diverge so widely that the question could even be asked whether to bring together certain rituals under the concept of "sacrifice" is not artificial and the expression of a cultural prejudice.[8] Many nowadays think that it is impossible to bring the multiplicity of aspects in the religious rituals, found in the countless religions of the world, into a manageable order.

Previously the attempt was made to interpret cultic sacrifice primarily from the viewpoint of the ideas of sacrifice and they were found to contain the idea of exchange or *do ut des:* I give you something, so that you give me back something else. People sacrifice gifts for the gods so as to receive from them the wished for or hoped for return gifts. These ideas were in fact widespread in most religions and cultures; however, much in the ritual sacrifices remains unexplained from the viewpoint of these ideas. Why were the individual elements of the ritual, often very different from one another, fulfilled with scrupulous precision, even sacred terror? Why were they so important for the most primitive societies that in them we can hardly distinguish between ritual and societal life? Whence came the particular shudder of fear which was bound up with the act of sacrifice and killing? What was the basis for the belief that the victim was transformed by the act of sacrifice into a sacral entity? Many saw precisely in the transformation of the victim (human, beast, gift of nature) by the act of killing or destruction the decisive element of the ritual sacrifices.[9] What does it mean to believe that something profane is transformed by the sacrifice into a sacral, even divine reality? The unex-

---

8. See Jonathan Z. Smith (1987), 191–235.
9. See Hubert and Mauss (1898–99), 67–71.

plained questions led many scholars to turn their attention away from the ideas of sacrifice and toward the ritual in its material aspect.

S. Freud attempted to explain the scrupulous exactness in carrying out the rituals through the comparison with "ritual" actions by neurotics. But this interpretation depends essentially on his understanding of sexuality. Since he maintained that sexual satisfaction is first of all a private matter for the individual, he was not able from this angle to make it understandable how the rituals and cults with their eminently social character came into being. He proposed therefore a second explanatory model which was not fully adopted either in psychoanalytic circles or in ethnological research. According to this, the "sacred mystery of sacrificial death...", which unites the participants with one another and their God," is to be interpreted as a repetition of that original meal at which the brothers consumed the father after having collectively killed him (in the primal horde): "The funeral meal, perhaps humanity's first festival, would have been the repetition and memorial celebration of this memorable, criminal deed with which so much took its beginning, such as social organization, moral restraints, and religion."[10] Other scholars continued the research along the more sociological line of interpretation, which Durkheim had already begun before Freud.

For example, A. Jensen believed that he could show "that the bloody sacrifices in more recent cultures do not rest on their own idea of sacrifice, but basically represent the survival of the killing rituals."[11] But the sense or "knowledge value of the killing ritual"[12] cannot in his view lie directly in the myths which are for us unintelligible, and which essentially say "that a divinity was killed in order thereby to give reason for the reality that everything living is mortal."[13] However the myths with their strange content must contain a "message," which was important for the people of that time, and according to Jensen it runs "in its sober form, stripped of all affective values: all animal life needs organic material to survive, i.e., it only survives by destroying other life."[14] Against this interpretation the question can be asked whether the conditions of animal life were more important to people in earlier societies than the problem of their own violence.

Along the same lines as Jensen, W. Burkert also holds the act of killing in the sacrificial rites to be central:

---

10. Freud (1968), 166f., 172.
11. Jensen (1951), 218f.
12. Ibid., 222.
13. Ibid.
14. Ibid., 222f.

Not in a pious transformation of life, not alone in prayer, song, and dance is the god experienced in the most powerful way, but in the fatal blow of the axe, in the seeping away of blood, and in the burning of thigh-bones. Holy is the realm of the gods: but the "holy" action, fulfilled in the "holy" place at the "holy" time by the doer of the "holy observance" is the slaughter of sacrificial animals.... [15]

This importance of killing in the sacrifice is derived by Burkert from the hunter culture of the Palaeolithic Age, in which the killing of animals for food was at the same time a ritual process. The ritualization of the hunt was, according to Burkert, necessary because the "educational force of tradition"[16] needed it, so that people would employ their greater ability (in comparison to the anthropoid apes) to kill in the hunting of animals and not against their own species. This threat was averted by diverting outward into the dangerous and bloody hunt that fuel for conflict stored up in the interior of the group. Through ritualization, aggression was prevented from breaking out on other occasions in an uncontrolled manner. It protected human communities from self-destruction and had the effect of developing community in the highest degree.

Like Freud, Jensen, and Burkert, R. Girard also understands sacrifice first of all from the point of view of the act of killing, and he too sees the rites in connection with a fundamental human and societal issue. However, what for Burkert comes second (after the question of getting food), becomes for him central: the problematic of human rivalry and aggression.[17] In accordance with his theory of mimesis, conflicts arise spontaneously from human desire, and this is why peaceful living together is anything but self-explanatory. The hidden factor for order in precivilized societies was according to him the scapegoat mechanism. Aggression had to be, as Burkert also assumes, diverted outward; a member of the society had to be sacrificed, so that the others should have peace again. This process was played out in a state of ecstatic and violent excitement and remained for that reason hidden from those taking part. They were aware of it only in that distortion which is mirrored in the myths. In order to maintain the healing power of the original spontaneous violent driving out, it was regularly repeated in controlled form — as a ritual sacrifice. This interpretation has numerous advantages: the rite is taken seriously in its full *concreteness*, which is always different from sacrifice *as represented* by the community, and it is inter-

---

15. Burkert (1972), 9.
16. Ibid., 27.
17. For the discussion between Burkert and Girard see Hamerton-Kelly (1987), 73–188.

preted by means of a fundamental problem of society. The apparently "neurotic" seriousness in carrying out every smallest detail of the ritual includes an understandable interpretation, since the "repetition" of the original spontaneous process had to remain controlled in every detail, so that dangerous violence did not break out again in its ungovernable way. The phenomenon of transformation which H. Hubert and M. Mauss brought to the center in their interpretation of sacrifice is important also for this theory, since through the scapegoat mechanism — and through the sacrifices which imitate it — the aggression which is within the group and therefore dangerous is transformed into a frightening and salvation-bringing external force, into the sacral reality which protects the community of the tribe by means of their fear. This theory is able further to make clear why on the one hand the motive of killing plays a central role in many myths and why on the other hand the representations of sacrifice could vary quite strongly in the course of history. The myths were at first the product of collective excitement and self-deception, in which the deepest fears and desires, the wildest accusations, and the most hidden yearnings and hopes found expression. As soon as the problem of aggression was solved in a different way (by the state having the monopoly on violence), the myths were able to become the starting point for independent religious developments. Girard's anthropological theory, which refers above all to the concreteness of the ritual and to the myths of precivilized societies, does not for that reason exclude an investigation of the ideas of sacrifice in the historical religions, in fact it even demands one for its completion. The phenomenologically establishable meaning of the history of religion lies, according to Girard's theory, precisely in gradually uncovering the original distortions, in order finally to overcome them in a fundamental way.

Sacrifice in the Old Testament

In the context of our formulation of the question, we do not need to go any more closely into the discussion about the *ideas* of sacrifice in the different high religions from the viewpoint of the history of religion. But we must turn briefly to sacrifice in the Old Testament. The problematic of these rites is found at many levels. Previous attempts to explain them were mostly made by means of the *do ut des* formula. But this starting point is nowadays widely rejected. In the texts to be considered, the idea of atonement plays an important role which, of course, only won this dominant position after the exile.[18] The sacrificial rituals themselves are certainly much older, and their history cannot any longer be

---

18. See Koch (1966).

reconstructed. The Old Testament has also very little to say on how the sacrifices are to be understood. In relation to the priestly writings, in which the decisive sacrifice texts are to be found, G. von Rad says:

> All this information about sacrifices in the Priestly Code is crudely materialistic. The reader looks in vain for firm holds to enable him to rise into the spiritual realm by way of the sacrificial concepts lying behind the sacrificial practice. In itself the offering of a sacrifice, of course, left great freedom to the attitude of the worshipper, allowing room for the meanest *do ut des* disposition as well as for the most sublime spiritualization of the outward act. It was obviously entirely without P's intention to suggest to the worshipper any specific understanding of the sacrifices. The Code's concern was that where sacrifices are offered, the ritual traditions should be strictly observed. In this sense P is greatly interested indeed in the correctness and orderliness of the outward aspects of the observances of the cult. There must have been forces and spheres in old Israel which stood guard particularly over the material aspects of observances such as these, material aspects which could not be dissolved by any spirituality."[19]

The Old Testament not only has little to say about the inner attitude which sacrificers should bring to their actions; it also keeps thoroughly silent about what God makes to happen in the sacrifice:

> However deep even the most understanding interpretation of the sacrifices in the Old Testament may go, there comes an absolute limit beyond which no further explanation is possible. And the expositor must recognize that it is precisely the most important aspect of the sacrifice which takes place beyond this limit. While the Old Testament is very full of allusions to the divine activity wherever it becomes effective among men, and full too of the most intensive address and of "revelation," there is a realm of silence and secrecy in respect to what God works in sacrifice.[20]

Despite these limits, which von Rad clearly points out, H. Gese attempts a systematic interpretation of Old Testament sacrifice from the viewpoint of the idea of atonement: "The first thing that strikes one is that in P it is not only the atonement sacrifices which atone, but all sacrifices atone."[21] Gese stresses in detail two elements in particular in the sacrificial rites: the laying on of hands and the blood ritual. He interprets the laying on of hands as identification of the sacrificer with the sacrificial

---

19. Von Rad (1962), *Theology of the Old Testament*, 1:259–60.
20. Ibid., 260.
21. Gese (1983), 94.

animal, and he sees the killing in connection with the blood ritual, in which the sacrificer is supposed to have given himself up completely to the holy power by means of the animal.

> Atonement happens through the surrender of the life of the sacrificial animal, which is identified in the laying on of hands with the sacrificer. Our definition of the act of atonement regarding vicarious total surrender fits in with this. The atonement process ought not to be imagined as unloading sins with the consequent penal death of the bearer of sins, the sacrificial animal.... Neither is the surrender of life a simple annihilation. The animal is not killed in order to achieve an annihilation of the sin object or a compensating punishment of the bearer of sin, but a holy blood ritual is fulfilled. The sacrificial animal is given up to the holiness of God, it comes into contact with the holy ones.[22]

Gese sees a confirmation of this view above all in Leviticus 17:11: "I [Yahweh] have given you this blood that you may make atonement for your life on the altar; for it is the blood that makes atonement."

This interpretation of atonement in the sacrificial cult leaves many questions open. First of all it is not at all obvious that the ritual of laying on of hands is to be understood as identification. Many exegetes (e.g., P. Volz, R. Rendtorff, K. Koch) interpret it in the sense of transference of sins from the sacrificer to the sacrificial animal.[23] The question is hard to answer, and it even remains open whether a clarification of the meaning of this ritual ever emerged in Israel. Also the understanding of killing as total surrender to the sacred is very problematic. How could a killing be understood as a total surrender at a time when belief in an individual resurrection from the dead or in an immortal soul did not exist in Israel? Gese and especially Janowski adduced texts in which atonement clearly means a vengeful destruction. (Num. 25:6–15; Deut. 32:43; 2 Sam. 21:1–14; Isa. 27:9; Dan. 9:24).[24] If atonement (*koper*) in the extracultic realm can mean explicitly vengeful destruction and if a violent death in Israel was normally understood as a judgment of vengeance, then the thesis hardly stands that cultic atonement in which animals were killed did not mean penal killing. The interpretation within the framework of concepts of revenge, which we went into in the first part, is in any case a more likely suggestion. Why did the Old Testament nowhere say with

---

22. Ibid., 97.

23. "One would gladly know what special significance was imputed to laying the hands on the head of the sacrificial animal — this ritual act is expressly prescribed by P for all blood offerings. Did it signify the transferral of sins and their danger of disaster to the animal, or was it a gesture of self-identification of the sacrificer with the animal?" (Von Rad, 1:258).

24. Gese (1983), 88; Janowski (1982), 110–37.

what inner attitude the sacrifices must be brought, if its whole cult was determined by a theology of total surrender? The priestly writing was "greatly interested indeed in the correctness and orderliness of the outward aspects of the observances of the cult,"[25] and in that it was no different from the cults of other peoples. Through the idea of obedience to God, the priestly writer provided a new reason for the demand for exactness, but he remains to a great extent silent about the deeper meaning of sacrifice. So it would be asking for too much to try to find there a coherent and systematic idea of atonement. Certainly, the search for coherence should be welcomed, but it must be tackled at a deeper, more profound level, using a more dramatic model.

On the question of the understanding of sacrifice in the Old Testament there is another issue to consider, which makes things even more complex. We are faced here not only with a cultic institution which is hard to interpret, but also an equally strong criticism of sacrifice, especially by the prophets. The great crisis in Israel which manifested itself at first in the destruction of the northern kingdom (721 B.C.) and then led to the long-drawn agony which lasted until the destruction of Jerusalem and the Temple (587 B.C.), stirred up faith in Yahweh in its inmost depths and called forth the great message of the prophets. Faced with the threat, the prophets expected no help from God through the sacrificial cult; rather they saw in it an expression of that falsehood and mendacity which was responsible for the fatal crisis. In the name of Yahweh they proclaimed: "I hate your festivals, I loathe them and cannot smell your solemn assemblies. Even though you present burnt offerings to me, I take no pleasure in your gifts and I will not look at your fat peace offerings" (Amos 5:21–22).[26] Jeremiah even disputed that the sacrificial cult went back to a command of God: "Add burnt offerings to your sacrifices and eat the flesh! For I said nothing to your fathers when I led them out of Egypt and I commanded nothing concerning burnt offerings and sacrifices. Instead I gave them this command: hearken to my voice, for then I will be your God and you will be my people" (Jer. 7:21–23; 6:20; Amos 5:25). The prophets called for true knowledge of God, justice and love, not *in addition* to the sacrifices but *in opposition* to them: "I want steadfast love and not sacrifice, knowledge of God rather than burnt offerings" (Hos. 6:6; Amos 5:21–24; Mic. 6:6–8; Isa. 1:10–17; Ps. 40:7ff.).

The fundamental significance of the prophetic criticism of sacrifice has often been blunted with the reminder that the sacrificial cult became very important again for the faith of Israel in the postexilic period. The

---

25. Von Rad, 1:260.
26. See Hos. 4:11–19; 6:6; 10:1–15; Mic. 6:6–8; Isa. 1:10–17; Ps. 40:7–8.

implication is that the criticism of the prophets was directed only against shortcomings in the manner of sacrifice and not against the thing itself. The fact of postexilic sacrificial cult is certainly to be taken seriously; but one cannot derive from this a justification for playing down the criticism of the prophets in the face of their explicit words. The prophetic message was announced in crisis situations and contains essentially a verdict of judgment. The criticism of sacrifices was not intended as an abstract judgment, based on the philosophy of religion, about the cult as such, but as a historical judgment of God on the cult which was in fact practiced in Israel. The verdict was unambiguous. But it was precisely this harsh prophetic criticism which made it possible for the faith in Yahweh to survive inwardly unharmed without sacrifices during the time of exile. The postexilic sacrificial cult was carried out in a new situation, and for that reason one should not directly relate the preexilic criticism to it. It did take up certain elements of the prophetic message, but it was far from giving a comprehensive answer as to how the judgment threatened by the preexilic prophets and experienced during the exile could in the future be avoided. The possibility of atonement through cultic sacrifice, according to the explicit teaching of the priestly source, was relevant only to *unintentional* sins (Lev. 4:2, 22, 27; 5:1–5:15; Num. 15:22). Even if, from the sacred perspective, these may have been of importance, the prophetic criticism never saw in them Israel's real failure. It was always the great conscious sins which were decisive: worship of idols, systematic injustice, the more serious sexual offenses, and deliberate acts of murder. The priestly source's theology of sacrifice agreed with this evaluation, since it knew no possibility of atonement for these sins and demanded punishment by death (Lev. 20:1–27; Num. 15:30–36; 1 Sam. 3:14). The real problem thrown up by the prophetic preaching, namely, the forfeiture of salvation through the many intentional sins, was never solved by the postexilic theology of the cult. Purely theoretically, there was the possibility that the unintentional and smaller offenses were atoned for by the cult and all intentional and greater misdeeds were purified by the elimination of the evildoers from the people. Such a praxis would have taken for granted that those who had to pronounce and carry out the judgment proceeded correctly in everything, which, according to the prophetic preaching before the exile, was mostly not the case, and even later was hardly any better (Zech. 11:4–17; Mal. 2:1–9). Further, a rigorous praxis of the elimination of all major sinners would necessarily have led to much hypocrisy and to heated arguments concerning the question of what should be punished by death. If it were fully carried out, the praxis of elimination of major sinners could have had as a consequence the destruction of the whole people. The postexilic sacrificial cult was consequently unable to solve the problematic raised by the prophetic preaching of judgment. Its distinction between atonable sins and those which were to be punished by the eradication of the evildoers may indeed have contributed decisively to the development of that observance of the law which Jesus had to criticize harshly in his opponents. Sins, especially the serious and conscious ones, begin in the depths of the heart and they often have a long prehistory, in which many people bear different amounts of responsibility and in which it often depends on accidental circumstances as to whether things get as far as an outward, punishable deed and who commits it. In view of these connections, which were also to a large extent known in Israel at that time, the distinction between those sinners who were to be eliminated from the people and to be handed over to the divine judgment, and those who could find atonement through the sacrificial cult, must turn out to be arbitrary. The problem of wicked desire,[27] which became so central for the faith of Israel in light of the prophetic proclamation, was not resolved by the cult; indeed, it was only sharpened by the arbitrariness of the distinction mentioned above and by the impossibility of carrying out a coherent praxis in the eradication of evildoers. Thus it was no accident that John the Baptist, prophet to Israel, could only announce the judgment.

The Cross and the Transformation of Evil

The unsolved problem of the Old Testament sacrificial cult would seem to make it impossible to develop a systematic interpretation of the death of Christ from that starting point. Certainly, the letter to the Hebrews sees the cross explicitly against the background of the cult, and it describes Christ as a high priest who offered a sacrifice. But the letter to the Hebrews can make these statements only because, by the use of numerous antitheses, it totally alters the concepts of both priest and sacrifice. First of all it separates Christ from the great, broad tradition of the Aaronite and Levite priesthood and links him with the priest king Melchizedek (Heb. 7:1–24), who is a marginal figure in the Old Testament and is mentioned there only briefly on two occasions (Gen. 14:18; Ps. 110:4). As high priest according to the order of Melchizedek, Christ is the mediator of a different, new covenant (Heb. 7:22; 8:1–13; 9:15), and to him belongs also a quite new priestly order. He does not have to offer sacrifice day after day for himself and the people (Heb. 7:25–28), nor does he enter an earthly sanctuary in order to sprinkle it with the blood of he-goats and bulls. Rather, he brought about a redemption once for all, and entered into the heavenly sanctuary (Heb. 9:11–10:18).

---

27. See Isa. 57:5; Jer. 2:13–25; 16:12; 23:17; Ezek. 16:15–52; Sir. 18:30–33; 23:16.

From the viewpoint of this new sacrifice it can be seen that the cultic sacrifices of the Old Testament brought about atonement only in the sense that people became "purified in the flesh" (Heb. 9:13). The letter to the Hebrews, then, expressly restricts the effectiveness of the earlier sacrifices to the realm of external cultic purity, whose purpose was to remind people of sins, without being able to bring about any inner healing: "But through these sacrifices there is a reminder of sins year after year, for the blood of bulls and goats cannot possibly take away sins" (Heb. 10:3ff.). The verdict on the sacrificial cult is unambiguous: it was unable to bring about any actual purification from sins. This is why the letter to the Hebrews, despite its explicit relationship to the tradition of sacrifice, is able to take a critical line of thought on sacrifice and to note the paradoxical fact that Psalm 40:7–9 talks of God not demanding sacrifices and taking no pleasure in them, even though "these are offered according to the law" (Heb. 10:8). The letter to the Hebrews resolves the contradictory evidence of the Old Testament by relating the criticism of sacrifice directly to Christ, who with these words abolished the existing order and set up over against it obedience. The continuity of content between the Old and New Testament runs not through the cultic line, but through the line of criticism of the cult, which emphasizes obedience.

The letter to the Hebrews is able, through a massive hermeneutical reinterpretation, to take up on the one hand the whole metaphorical and symbolic meaning of the cult, but on the other hand to express something which is completely new in content. Through the confrontation of the cultic tradition with the tradition critical of sacrifice, it succeeds in creating, out of a problematic at the heart of the Old Testament, a complex symbol for the divine action and the divine will: God by the law commanded something which he himself did not specifically want, but which — in awakening consciousness of sin — was temporarily needed for humankind. This command to offer sacrifices was promulgated by the law because of its pedagogic and linguistic function and not because of its atoning effect. The new teaching is tied in with the cult only as an illustration, whereas the criticism of sacrifice is spelled out as Christ's own words (Heb. 10:8ff.). What was a tradition competing with the cult in the Old Testament becomes in the letter to the Hebrews an authoritative pronouncement about this whole past practice of sacrifice.

There is, it is true, one point where the question arises as to whether the letter to the Hebrews might, after all, recognize a certain continuity of content between the Old Testament sacrifices and the death of Christ. The cult operated through blood (Heb. 9:7, 18–22), and Christ too offered himself as a sacrifice through his blood (Heb. 9:14). The Aaronite and Levite priests sprinkled with others' blood (that of he-goats and bulls), whereas Christ entered the sanctuary with his own (Heb. 9:12;

10:19; 12:24). But does this difference (others' or one's own blood) abolish the continuity between the cult and Christ's death, or is there a certain common basis in the shedding of blood?

The issue of the shedding of blood, so important for the letter to the Hebrews, points first to the need to examine and interrogate from a Christian perspective those theories of sacrifice arising from the study of religion which also emphasize the shedding of blood (the act of killing). The explicit statement that Christ offered a sacrifice with his own blood shows, moreover, that the problematic with which we began our reflections on sacrifice is in fact central. At the beginning of this section we asked how self-sacrifice is to be understood. If Christ identified himself not with the evil will of his opponents, but with their concrete action (crucifixion), did he not therefore fully agree to his being killed? Can one not also take the statement that Christ sacrificed himself as high priest "with his own blood" as an indication of the indirect killing of himself? In considering the fate of Jesus we have often come across the theme of God's nonviolence. But now the more subtle question arises, whether we have to understand this concept in such a way that Christ, although he shunned all violence against others, finally turned that violence against himself — in self-sacrifice. Seeing things this way, could one not very easily link up the great Old Testament themes of judgment and God's vengeance, the tradition of cultic killing, and also many New Testament utterances about judgment, with the message of nonviolence (toward others)? The cross would then be a sacrifice in the sense that the priest (Christ) did in fact kill something, namely, himself. Writing about the ethics of the early community, G. Theissen speaks of a "turning-around of aggression,"[28] and he thinks that "heightened aggressivity turned in upon itself could thus paradoxically swing around into positive acceptance of the other."[29] There seem to be statements supporting such a view even in the Sermon on the Mount, which teaches nonviolence (toward others) especially clearly. If one member is seduced into evil, it should be plucked out or cut off, for it is better to be mutilated than to be damned with the whole body (Matt. 5:29ff.; 18:8ff.). Is there consequently a self-aggression in the service of a higher good? Because of this question we must once more go into the problematic of judgment at a new and deeper level. If the thesis that God in his anger directly struck and destroyed his Son by means of sinners (K. Barth) did not stand up to scrutiny, the more subtle problematic still remains, namely, whether he led the crucified one through obedience to self-aggression and thereby judged him. Christ would then have taken on himself the self-judgment

---

28. Theissen (1977), 96–101.
29. Ibid., 97.

of sinners in the sense that he did in full consciousness and freedom what sinners do in their blindness: judge and destroy themselves.

This question is not easy to answer, since we would need to feel our way into the inner attitude of Jesus, and the New Testament utterances make use of words which come up in different contexts and can therefore be interpreted in different ways. However the question is one with very great consequences. If the outcome is affirmative, then everything which we have worked out so far has to be looked at again in a completely fresh light, with considerable consequences for Christian spirituality and the practice of the faith.

In the Old Testament, with the exception of Isaiah 52:13–53:12, violent death was understood to imply only judgment and curse, while the New Testament sees the cross of Christ as positive. How is this difference to be understood? Since the Old Testament cult also attributes a positive atoning effect to the sacrificial death of animals, we must look into the question already addressed earlier in this investigation, namely, whether the formal element in atonement resides in the act of killing. The difference between the old and new order would consist in this, that in the former animals were killed daily, whereas in the latter Christ sacrificed and (indirectly) killed himself once for all.

Since the letter to the Hebrews understands Melchizedek as king of peace (Heb. 7:1ff.),[30] such a view immediately causes problems. But peace could be understood as a paradoxical result of "aggressivity turned in upon itself." A useful indication is given by the letter to the Hebrews where it takes up the Old Testament's critical line against sacrifice and, putting words into Christ's mouth, also makes him say that he comes in order to do the divine will. Subsequently, the letter goes on: "And by that will we have been sanctified once and for all by the offering of the body of Jesus Christ" (*dia tes prosphoras tou somatos Iesou Christou*, Heb. 10:10). The sanctification was brought about fundamentally through the will of God, fulfilled by Christ. The agreement of wills was decisive. But what is meant by the addition "through the offering of the body"? Could it be that God wanted not the concrete burnt offering for sin but instead that element in this sacrifice, the killing, which pointed to the self-sacrifice of Christ? Even the apparently unambiguous text about the abolition of cultic sacrifice and about sanctification through the divine will can consequently be read in two different, even opposed directions.

Another passage in the letter to the Hebrews runs:

---

30. There were some in the Council of Trent who viewed Melchizedek differently and spoke of two sacrifices: in the Last Supper Christ acted as high priest according to the order of Melchizedek (bread and wine), while on the cross he gave himself over as high priest according to the order of Aaron (blood sacrifice). See Power (1987), 82–88.

> For by a single sacrifice he has perfected forever those who are
> sanctified. The Holy Spirit also bears witness to us; for after say-
> ing, "This is the covenant I will make with them after those days,
> says the Lord: I will put my laws in their heart and write them on
> their minds"; then he adds, "I will remember their sins and trans-
> gressions no more." Where sins are forgiven, there is no longer any
> offering for sin. (Heb. 10:14–18)

The New Testament letter makes a direct connection in this passage
between the unique sacrifice of Christ and the saying of the prophet
Jeremiah about the new covenant. The will of Christ in his surrender
is hereby formally identified with the new law which God inscribes on
our innermost hearts. But self-aggression could not have a place under
this new, inner, law, for otherwise disturbing consequences would follow
for our understanding of God's kingdom and of the life of completeness
with God.

A further text finally gives us a pointer to the answer we have been
seeking: "For if the blood of goats...sanctifies for the purification of the
flesh, how much more shall the blood of Christ, who through the power
of the eternal Spirit offered himself to God as a sacrifice without blem-
ish, purify our conscience from dead works so that we may serve the
living God" (Heb. 9:13ff.). The surrender of Christ as victim was not
only identical with the law of the new covenant written on our hearts;
it came about also "by the power of the eternal Spirit." The nature of
this Spirit we have already seen fully in the second part of this work.
It is the Spirit of freedom (2 Cor. 3:17), of love (1 Cor. 13), of joy, of
peace, of forbearance, and of gentleness (Gal. 5:22ff.). It does not make
us into slaves (torturing ourselves), but into sons of God, and calls out
from within us "Abba" (Rom. 8:15). A will to self-destruction is totally
at odds with the working of this Spirit. If Christ surrendered himself
in this Spirit, then his sacrifice cannot in any way be seen as (indirect)
self-destruction. The working of the Spirit after Easter throws the decisive light on the innermost mystery of Christ's will in his passion. The
Spirit is never a spirit of aggression or self-aggression;[31] it works rather
from within the victims of violence; it stands by the persecuted in their
need and protects them from inner subjection to their adversaries (Mark
13:11 and parallels).

For the true understanding of Christ's sacrifice we must consequently
look for a different solution from that of self-destruction. The persis-
tent question is this: how was the crucified one able to identify himself
with the actions of his opponents (condemnation and crucifixion) if he

---

31. See Girard (1988), 281–300.

did not wish (indirectly) to destroy himself? Ethnology and the study of sacrificial cults in the different religions point not only to the act of killing but also to the important theme of transformation: through the killing there occurs a transformation from the profane to the sacred. Can this track perhaps take us further? One of the most central ideas in Maximus the Confessor's doctrine of redemption can as a matter of fact be understood as an analogous development of such a view. The Greek theologian and confessor says that Christ on the cross altered the "use of death."[32] By this he means that death, which was brought by God after the fall into the garden of Eden as *punishment against human nature,* was transformed by the crucified one into *a means of salvation from sin.*[33] Maximus, in order to arrive at this conclusion, directly compared the garden of Eden and the cross with one another. The profound significance of his formulation should appear even more clearly if it is understood in the light of the two opposing intentions for acting which were at work in the event of the cross. Jesus' judges and his executioners wanted to punish a criminal; he himself on the other hand wanted to give himself, as the Last Supper sayings show, for the many. These two intentions stand in contradiction to each other. It follows that if Jesus was able to identify himself with the actions of his opponents, then this was possible only because he thereby managed at the same time to *transform their actions.*

The crucified one saw in his opponents people who ultimately did not know what they were doing, who, because of blindness, even in their actions were more victims than responsible agents. He himself was a victim insofar as he was killed and they were victims in killing, insofar as they were under the spell of an external power. For him, then, killing was an act done both to him and to them, even if in very differing ways. Both together were victims of that power which in fact kills: sin. At this deeper level, Jesus no longer stood over against his opponents, but he underwent together with them the blows of a destructive power, but in such a way that he alone experienced this suffering for what it was. Through his identification with his executioners, he suffered together with them the being killed by sin. Because of this common destiny, Paul can rightly say: "One has died for all; therefore all have died" (2 Cor 5:14).

The "conversion" and transformation of evil began with Jesus including his opponents in his being killed, and thus consciously living through on their behalf that dimension in their action which enables us to say

---

32. Maximus the Confessor, *Thal.* 61 (PG 90: 633AD, 636CD).
33. See Schwager, "Das Mysterium der übernatürlichen Natur-Lehre," in Schwager (1986), 47f.

that the act of crucifying him was in fact something suffered. But he had not yet achieved the decisive act, for suffering would only have had a positive sense if we had to assume that God *directly* willed such suffering as a punishment, which, however, we have already excluded. The crucial point was the transformation of passivity through his surrender. Because of his unreserved acceptance of the suffering which came to him, it was already more than something merely undergone. Suffering which is affirmed becomes a new form of activity.

All the synoptic Gospels on the one hand emphasize the suffering of the crucified one and on the other they clearly describe his dying as an activity. We find in Mark: "Jesus uttered a loud cry and breathed out the Spirit [*exepneusen,* usually translated "expired"]" (Mark 15:37; Matt. 27:50). The loud cry was an expression of the most extreme desolation, and with the breathing out of his Spirit he indicated at the same time a revelatory event (Mark 1:11; 9:7) which went out from Jesus as bearer of the Spirit. The breathing out of the Spirit is made even clearer in Luke: "And Jesus cried loudly, 'Father, into your hands I commit my Spirit' " (Luke 23:46). Suffering is here understood unambiguously as surrendering and handing over the Spirit to the Father. Since Luke describes Jesus at the beginning of his ministry as the long awaited bearer of the Spirit (Luke 4:16–22; Acts 4:27; 10:38), the return of the Spirit to the Father means at the same time the fulfillment of the mission. The act of dying, the fulfillment of the mission, and the handing over of the Spirit to the Father consequently come together in the one event described by the letter to the Hebrews as the sacrifice of Christ.

Whoever in dying places himself in the hands of another person renounces entirely any further self-determination and hands himself over to the treatment of this other, to whom he thereby entrusts himself without reserve in love. Every act of surrender made during a person's life has its limits, arising at the least from the demands of one's own life and one's own identity. At the moment of dying, these limits can be broken down. But since in death all a person's strengths fail, death in itself is extremely ambiguous. Is it merely the passive undergoing of an inexorable limit, or can there be a surrender which goes beyond all previous limits? From the viewpoint of ordinary human experience, no clear answer is possible. However Jesus surrendered himself "by the power of the eternal Spirit" (Heb. 9:14) and, dying, entrusted his Spirit to the Father (Luke 23:46). Since the Spirit which he laid in the hands of the Father was at once his human spirit and the divine spirit bestowed on him, he was able completely to transform the ambiguous human act of dying, which is above all something suffered, into an act of surrender.

Whoever no longer determines himself by his own spirit, but entrusts this to the heavenly Father in order to allow himself to be totally determined by him, achieves a sort of openness and availability which go beyond our earthly experience and can only be hinted at by parables. The image of the clay with which the potter works can give a clue to this readiness to be shaped, and yet the one dying on the cross was much more than clay, for it was with his whole being and above all with his free will that he became a totally available "material." What at first appeared only negative in the "victim situation" was transformed with his death into a limitless opening of himself and making himself available, an abandonment of himself and total trust. His dying as total act of handing over already contains agreement in advance to that imminent sovereign action of the Father, which was realized in the resurrection of the crucified one. His will allowed itself to open up through obedience in suffering to a complete uniting in love with the will of the Father.

The will of Jesus in his passion (Heb. 10:10) has appeared to us under a double aspect: (1) as identification with his opponents, insofar as they themselves are victims; (2) as "conversion" and transformation of evil in surrender. Under the first aspect we can see Christ's love for enemies, insofar as he preferred, faced with his own will to survive, to share their destiny and to suffer in advance on their behalf those consequences of sin which necessarily result from it. This will to identification bore salvation to the extent that it was a presupposition for the second: the conversion and transformation of evil action in love. *He turned the radical delivering of himself to his enemies, as he experienced this in being executed, into a radical surrender to his Father.* Christ never consented to the lies and killing which constitute sin, but rather he dared to suffer the concrete sinful deeds (as being killed by sin) to the point where he was transformed precisely by them into a limitless surrender. Through his identification with his opponents he also infiltrated their world in which their evil will had imprisoned itself and by his transforming power opened it up once again from its new depths to the heavenly Father. Hell, toward which they were already bent, was once more broken open. What at first seemed to be something purely negative, as the rejection of love and closing in on oneself, was transformed by Christ into a surrender which bursts all dimensions of earthly existence. He is therefore both scapegoat and lamb of God; he is the one who is the one slain and the bread of life; he is the one made into sin and the source of holiness.

We asked whether it is right, in connection with Christ, to speak of a reorientation of aggression against himself, of a participation in the self-judgment of sinners, and of an (indirect) self-killing. The answer came out unambiguously negative. What appeared at first to point in that direction is seen after more precise analysis as an expression of his great love for sinners, by which he infiltrated their world. But this still leaves unexplained how Jesus during his public ministry could utter sayings which nevertheless give the impression that he summoned or appealed to self-aggression. These sayings can, however, be understood if we remember the power of sin which is so ingenious that it even knows how to make use of the command which opposes it. Sin only really becomes inflamed in direct opposition. Jesus therefore did not generally make a frontal attack on evil, but even during his public ministry he indicated how it should be dealt with and infiltrated in different ways. In the narrative of the woman taken in adultery who was caught red-handed, even he, if we follow his actual words, gives the instruction to throw stones at the guilty woman. But because he adds the condition that each one who condemns should apply the same standard to himself ("Whoever among you is without sin throw the first stone at her" [John 8:7]), his verbal instruction to kill has the exactly opposite effect in the actual context ("When they heard his answer, they left one after the other, beginning with the eldest" [John 8:9]). If Jesus had answered his opponents with a yes or a no, they would have charged him. A direct answer, whether yes or no, would have heightened their aggression. But, by taking up his opponents' suggestion of stoning, and turning it around in an unexpected way, he let their evil intention drain away.

We should understand in a similar way his call, to which we have already referred, to tear out or cut off a member of the body. In the Sermon on the Mount, the corresponding saying comes immediately after that about adultery, in which Jesus again leaves the crucial conclusion to his hearers. He mentions first what Scripture says on this subject, and then for his part he only establishes that the situation named in the law is already present in a lustful look ("Whoever even looks at a woman lustfully has already committed adultery with her in his heart" [Matt. 5:28]). The conclusion for the hearer is on the one hand clear and on the other leaves the decisive issue open. Each one should guard against the lustful look; each one should equally guard against condemning others for adultery, for who can claim for himself that he has never by a lustful look done the evil thing which he reproaches in others?

"If your right eye leads you astray, then tear it out and throw it away!" (Matt. 5:29). But how should the right eye or the right hand lead astray and not equally the left? And even if the one member was violently removed, would not the other carry on leading the person astray? Jesus expresses what should be done in all logic. But at the same time he makes clear from the harshness of the consequences that there is nothing positive to be achieved in this direction, and that the problem should be approached from a more fundamental angle. In another passage, the saying about cutting off a member is directly linked with the warning about leading little ones astray (Matt. 18:6–11; Mark 9:42–48). Are the people who are led astray by their members ultimately identical with the little ones who are ruled by a different law in their members (see Rom. 7:23)? Unambiguous answers are not possible here. But that is precisely why, given the subtlety of sin, there can be no really permanent remedy against it. Like the image of bloody sacrifice, the image of self-aggression can be used to point to depths where only the power of the Spirit can find the appropriate distinctions each time.

Substitution and the Hermeneutic of Judgment Texts

In our reflections so far, we have worked with the idea of standing in for others. But what does this mean when there always remains an irreducible element of self-responsibility? Do not people, in spite of Christ's surrender, still stand in danger of finally closing in on themselves and of a final self-condemnation? Together with this, there is the related question: what fundamental place do the pre-Easter judgment sayings have in the post-Easter proclamation?

Different forms of substitution or representation have been discussed, above all in Protestant theology. Some held to an exclusive standing in, by which was meant that Christ did something for us without any cooperation or participation on our part, namely, he paid the price for removing sins. Others spoke of an inclusive standing in. Christ acted in our place in the sense that through him we become capable of doing something similar. Others again attempted, in different ways, to understand Christ's representative deed in both the exclusive and inclusive sense.

Our investigation has led to two universal statements which directly concern the problematic of exclusive and inclusive substitution. The possibility that Christ could have acted without people's cooperation has never arisen for us; but two radically different forms of participation have emerged. God's envoy was on the one hand condemned by sinners, and on the other hand he himself acted insofar as he stood in for all.

His surrender on the cross was exclusive in the most literal sense (*excludere*, keep out, cut off, remove), since he was physically excluded from human community, cut off and removed. We have even met the statement that not only did some groups of people reject him, but the people of Israel and the gentiles in general formed an alliance against him (Acts 4:27ff.). How is such a universal statement to be understood? Does it not contain exaggeration? The Acts of the Apostles follows Jewish corporate thinking and sees in Herod a representative of all Israel and in Pontius Pilate a representative of the pagan world. Since for us this way of thinking is no longer transparent, the question arises as to how nowadays we can theologically appropriate for ourselves this statement from the Acts of the Apostles. We have already pointed earlier to one element of the answer. The corporate way of thinking is supported by the discovery that the ganging up on a victim, which played its part in the fate of Jesus, had already been described and announced in similar terms in the Old Testament (Ps. 2); similarly, it repeated itself in the fate of the community. We are dealing with a process which did not merely occur once, but which shaped people's lives within the history of revelation. It follows that the universality of the "alliance" against God's anointed one should be understood initially in the sense that such ganging up occurs over and over again in history.

But this interpretation does not fully capture the statement from the Acts of the Apostles. How can the claim be made that all people have formed an alliance against Christ, if the conspiracies and ganging up are always aimed at different victims in the course of history? In order to make this point quite clear, we must fall back on our second universal statement. Christ by his yes in the event of the cross identified himself with all other people insofar as they are victims of sin. This inclusion of all has an immediate consequence for the exclusivity of his deed: *if he identified himself with all victims of sin, then every offense against a fellow person or against one's self is aimed against him.* As Saul in his persecution of the disciples struck at Jesus himself, in a similar way every sin is targeted against him. Condemnation is always leveled against the one who was fundamentally against condemnation, and the persecution of fellow humans strikes that victim who has identified himself with all the victims of every persecution. The universality of the *expulsion* and thus the *exclusive nature of the substitution* are based on the *act of universal inclusion* of the one who stood in for all by making himself one of them.

We have before us a multilayered process and thus a correspondingly complex concept of substitution. The concrete historical rejection of Jesus achieved a universal dimension (exclusive substitution) in that the one who was driven out included all people (inclusive substitution). Since the crucified one identified himself with sinners only insofar as they are victims, all people still retain a responsibility for themselves, for which there is and can be no longer any substitution, and this responsibility makes the conversion of each individual necessary, precisely because of Christ's act of standing in for all.

What we have found so far leads to a strange conclusion: people are simultaneously involved in two situations. As responsible for sins, all belong to the great band of those who form an alliance against God's anointed, judge him, drive him out, and reject him. As victims of their own and others' sins, they find themselves part of the universal community of those with whom the crucified one identified himself and for whom, through his ordeal of being struck and killed, he turned evil actions toward the good. Consequently the fundamental line of separation between the kingdom of God and the kingdom of the princes of this world does not run primarily between groups of people, as the apocalyptic pictures of judgment repeatedly suggested. What we have is not one part of humankind standing — as sons of God — over against the other part — as sons of darkness. Such conventional notions have almost inevitably led to the spiritual self-righteousness of those who have counted themselves among the sons of light, and too often they have given rise to intolerance and aggression in God's name. The great dividing line runs rather through individual people themselves. As a responsible doer of sin each one is an enemy of Christ, and as victim of evil each one is within the domain of his redeeming power.

The division through people is clearly spoken of by Paul. Thus he warns the community in Corinth to exclude and hand over to Satan a member who has committed a sin "of a kind which is not found even among pagans" (1 Cor. 5:1–5). This measure sounds at first disturbing, and it seems to correspond to that mechanism to which Christ himself fell victim, and consequently to be a step backward in the direction of outmoded ideas. In distinction to what was demanded in the Old Testament as punishment for major conscious sins and to what took place in the fate of Jesus, the guilty member is neither killed nor entrusted to God's final judgment. He is instead handed over to Satan — self-judgment — in the hope of his salvation. The judgment aims at the destruction of all flesh, so that his spirit will be saved on the day of the Lord. Even in post-Easter times the dramatic framework of judgment remains present. But it is a drama which is to effect a separation between "flesh" and "spirit," even for a member of the community who has sinned worse than the pagans. Despite his offense, he is not counted among the sons of darkness, but handed over to a judgment which should eliminate the evil in him and save him.

In the same letter, Paul uses yet another picture for a similar judgment. He characterizes Christ as the foundation on which each believer can build "with gold, silver, precious stones or with wood, hay, straw" (1 Cor. 3:12). What the individual in fact does will be shown up in the fire of judgment. "If the work survives that he has built, he will receive a reward. If it burns down, he must bear the loss. But he himself will be redeemed, but only as through fire" (1 Cor. 3:14ff.). Although Christ is the actual foundation, each one who builds on him has a responsibility of his own. Whether he builds a work that will last or only brings about transitory and deceptive constructions, is a matter for himself. But even if he fails, he can be saved "but only as through fire." The identification of the crucified one with all victims of sin is ultimately more effective than the person's own failure. But in this case he is only saved by the skin of his teeth, for his "flesh" and his "life's work" are destroyed and only his naked existence can find salvation.

Are all people, then, at least saved by the skin of their teeth (in their bare existence)? We have repeatedly emphasized that Christ identified himself with people only insofar as they are victims. To each person there remains his or her own inviolable responsibility. As we never know exactly where given persons are victims and where their own original responsibility begins, it is only with difficulty that we can speak of this unfathomable mystery in each person. But it is so "holy" that no overpowering grace or standing in the place of another through identification can overrun it. Thus, despite all Christ's work of substitution, there is never automatic redemption. Certainly, the excess of God's love is shown in its seeking out of sinners, but it is finally always a love which woos, embraces, underpins, and supports, but never compels.

The event of the cross shows that individual people are far more victims of evil than responsible agents, for even those who condemned, handed over, and crucified the Son of God did not know what they were doing (Luke 23:34; Acts 3:17). Paul too speaks impressively of the way people are deceived by sin and its sly cunning (Rom. 7:7–25). According to John, Satan is the ruler of this world (John 12:31; 14:30; 16:11). Because of this excessive power of sin, people are — even in the case of severe misdeeds — ultimately far more victims of evil than responsible agents, and therefore the great hope persists that all are saved in Christ. But this hope is founded not in the goodness of people nor in any automatic redemption, but in the faith that although all of us may yield sooner or later to the evil aspect of our condition as victims, the evil in us is transformed by the power of the cross.

But does not the hope of universal redemption contradict unambiguous utterances from the Gospels? Do not the judgment parables show how people are rejected, and in the great speech about the final judgment are not the sheep separated from the goats (Matt. 25:31–46)? After all, does not the dividing line run according to the synoptic Gospels, as in Jewish apocalyptic, between two groups of people? This question is linked to the basic interpretation of the judgment sayings. That caution is required here is something that the Old Testament book of Jonah can teach us. There, the prophet is sent to Nineveh with the task of announcing the destruction of the city. Despite this unambiguous message, the city is not destroyed, for something has happened which was not directly contained in the message itself: the conversion of the king and his subjects. The prophet is profoundly displeased that God has not carried out what he had to announce in God's name, and he gets annoyed that Yahweh is a "gracious and compassionate God" (Jon. 3:1–4:11).

In the interpretation of the New Testament judgment sayings, we have to take great care that we too do not get annoyed because of God's mercy. Just as, after the announcement of judgment by Jonah, something happened which was not directly contained in his message, so after the judgment sayings of Jesus, something fundamentally new took place: the herald of judgment was himself judged. This fundamental fact is crucial for the hermeneutic of the New Testament message of judgment.

The sayings and parables of Jesus make extensive use, even though in a restrained way, of the vividly descriptive words of the prophetic judgment speech and of apocalyptic. However, there is here, as we have seen, a decisive alteration insofar as Jesus, by many subtle details, expressed the judgment as self-judgment. At first little is changed in the overall apocalyptic scheme, because in either case, whether God judges people or whether they do it themselves, there comes the moment of division between the sons of light and those of darkness.

But what new interpretation results from the further fact that the messenger of judgment is himself judged? In the synoptic Gospels what strikes one immediately is that the one who speaks of the driving out of hardened sinners is himself driven out. In this event we have before us not just an irony of history, for the fate of the one driven out is parallel to that of the kingdom of God. However, it would not be easy, purely from the synoptic Gospels, to gauge the precise consequences of this fact. But as Paul's teaching points in the same direction and expressly contains the idea of the identification of the crucified one with all victims, what is only briefly hinted at in the synoptic Gospels (Last Supper sayings) can be clearly brought out. In the parable of the royal wedding feast the guilty one keeps silent (Matt. 22:12); Jesus himself is silent before his judge (Matt. 26:63; 27:12–14). The unmerciful creditor is given over to the torturers (Matt. 18:34), and Jesus also was handed over to the soldiers for torture (scourging, crown of thorns). The man without a wedding garment (in the parable of the royal wedding feast) and the worthless servant (in the parable of the entrusted money) are both cast into "outer darkness." In a similar way Jesus found himself in the outer darkness of abandonment by God (Mark 15:33–37). Many parables speak of the evildoers being in different ways violently killed (Matt. 21:41, 44; 24:51; Luke 19:27), and Jesus too experienced such a death. Finally, the Son of Man, in his great speech about the final judgment, addresses the goats on his left side as "cursed" (Matt. 25:41); Jesus himself is condemned as a blasphemer, and made into sin (2 Cor. 5:21) and a curse (Gal. 3:13). Against the background of the whole dramatic structure of the Gospels and of Paul's explicit doctrine, these correspondences are far more than surprising or accidental details. They give expression in narrative form to what is contained in the fundamental statement that the one who was judged on the cross identified himself with all victims of sin. Those sinners who come under a verdict pronounced by the judgment sayings are not alone. The first act of separation of "the just" from "the rejected" is totally overturned again, as the judge himself steps in on the side of the rejected and takes over their role. It follows that the two groups which are separated by the judgment, the just and the rejected — and each person belongs to a certain degree to both — have a share in Christ, even if in quite different ways. People are called "the just" insofar as the justice of Christ is directly mirrored in their good works. The same people are "the rejected" insofar as they are victims of sin, and Christ, as equally a victim of sin, has identified himself with their fate.

Despite the inner character of the separation, the image of the external judge must be held on to. This is because the truth of self-judgment remains hidden to sinners insofar as they are sinners and deceive themselves; they must be told it over and over again from outside. Similarly, the irreducible responsibility which continues to belong to individuals in the process of redemption is not an immediate, empirical fact. They have to be told of this too — through judgment sayings — from outside. When we look at the crucified one, therefore, the unshakable hope remains that all people are saved. But when we look at ourselves, we must all work out our own salvation "in fear and trembling" (Phil. 2:12).

From a purely subjective perspective, the image of a change of mind on the part of the divine anger turns out to have a certain justification, which also explains why the corresponding images in the Christian tradition have played so great a role. For, as long as people are trapped in sin, they can perceive everything only from the perspective of their own closed worlds, and God must necessarily appear to them as an alien and hostile power. Only after a genuine conversion does their capacity to see things alter, and thus also their picture of God. Now he no longer has to appear as the angry one, but can show himself as he is, the one who is kind above all others.

The Revelation of the Triune God in the Redemption Event

So far, from a systematic viewpoint, we have examined above all the historical drama of salvation and Christ's involvement in the complex process of human self-judgment. This has not been possible without repeated references to the action of the heavenly Father in his Son and to the working of the Holy Spirit. The revelation of God in the work of salvation requires now a comprehensive consideration of its own, for only in this way can his saving action toward human beings become more deeply understandable from within.

God, Greater Than Whom Cannot Be Thought

Anselm of Canterbury understood God as that reality above which nothing greater can be thought, and which is in fact greater than anything which can be thought. He gave this abstract definition a more precise content in two ways. First of all he showed in the *Proslogion* how the divine goodness reaches beyond all human representation and that it coincides with the highest form of justice. Then in *Cur Deus Homo* he pushed the idea of justice so above every human form of justice that it is finally shown to be identical with that goodness, greater than which nothing can be thought. By this process he attempted simultaneously to overcome, through a higher synthesis, the contradiction between the set of biblical texts which speak of God's anger, revenge, and judgment and those which speak of God's eternal mercy and love. We have found a similar intensification, tension, and synthesis in the New Testament drama of salvation. Jesus proclaimed his Father as a God of love of one's enemies, who goes looking for the lost one until he finds him. This God forgives in his goodness without demanding advance concessions, but he expects in the behavior of those on whom he bestows it a corresponding response toward their fellow humans. Since this response was not forthcoming in the fate of Jesus, the question of divine goodness arose again in its final intensity. In the parable of the wicked wine-growers the owner of the vineyard acted at first with a goodness which is no longer easily imaginable for us. But after the murder of his own son, this goodness finds a limit and makes way for retributional punishment. Because in this parable goodness is limited, it remains despite its greatness within the bounds of human thought, since in this limitation it is distinguished from the weakness that gives in to everything. However, the action of God in Jesus' fate goes a fundamental step beyond the behavior of the owner of the vineyard. If the latter reacted to the killing of his son with the killing of the wine-growers (Mark 12:9), the heavenly Father sent his risen Son back to murdering humanity and to the disciples in their failure with the words: "Peace be with you" (John 20:19). If even the greatest misdeed against his own Son provoked no reaction of revenge, then there is no other thinkable deed which God would not willingly forgive. His goodness and his forgiveness are shown to be unlimited, because they have expressly stepped over the last recognizable limit. The heavenly Father revealed, then, in the fate of Jesus a goodness greater than any that can be thought.

But if this conclusion were all, then divine goodness would still be highly ambiguous for us. In this case it would almost of necessity have to be understood that human decisions are of no importance to God and that he is so far beyond our "little lives" that they simply cannot reach him. Unlimited kindness would then only be another expression of the invalidity of our representations of judgment, punishment, and retribution, because God shines eternally over everything like the sun and is moved neither by our misdeeds nor by our sufferings.

That unlimited goodness does not mean a kindness which lacks contrast, form, and color — comparable to the Buddhist nirvana — is made clear by the opposite pole, the proclamation of judgment and the judgment event. It is the theme of hell which shows above all how seriously God takes people and their decisions. Although this question is little understood outside the Christian arena and although it is often passed over in silence even in the Christian context, without it one cannot gain a correct understanding either of the divine love or human freedom. It is nonetheless necessary to see the doctrine of hell not only under the aspect of threat, but to consider it in relation to freedom. From this viewpoint it says that responsibility, even if in a different sense from God's, is limitless. As the creature depends in every dimension on its creator, the idea almost inevitably suggests itself that God must have access to the inner being of his creatures, so that — without compelling them from outside — he can lead them at will onto the correct path. In contradiction to this spontaneous idea, however, the doctrine of hell says that even the most subtle and mysterious help which God wishes people to receive ultimately needs their agreement. Even in their inmost being, people are not puppets, and there is no ever so hidden area in which the creator would tactically get around the creature's defense. Although persons are totally dependent in their being, they possess in their actions unlimited freedom toward the one without whom they are nothing. Hell is thus the symbol of the radical freedom of creatures that are able from their own inmost being to set themselves up in every thinkable aspect against the one on whom they totally depend. Despite their fundamental weakness, there is in them no crack or crevice through which they can be overpowered and forced toward the good. They can critically distance themselves from everything which presses on them, however overpowering it may be. If many think that the New Testament doctrine of hell is the more terrible counterpart to the Old Testament representations of God's violent vengeance, then there is a gross misunderstanding behind this. The doctrine of hell is on the contrary the logical development of the preaching on nonviolence. God's renunciation of physical violence in the fate of Jesus is a concrete expression of God's recognition of human beings as partners who in their freedom may not be forced by anything and therefore may not be coerced or overpowered. Because of the doctrine of hell, the spontaneous notions of creation and grace must continually be thought through again so that they don't detract from the doctrine of freedom, but bring it out clearly. The concept of dependency is in need of radical revision, and it must be conceived in such a way that precisely the utter relatedness of the creature to the creator includes an utter difference of one from the other. Although the created world points entirely toward God, and thus bears within itself a divine norm, the free creature builds "its world" again according to the standard which it sets for itself. In connection with the message of judgment, understood as self-judgment, the doctrine of hell shows clearly that freedom is not merely a question of the yes or no to commandments of God seen in isolation, but of the sort of world the free creature wants to build. Does it open itself to God's reality and, listening to God, build a heaven, or does it close itself up in its own world and thus create for itself a hell? From the viewpoint of this understanding of freedom it becomes evident why God's anger consists in handing over creatures to their own desires and their own depraved thinking. For, where these create their world without listening to God, but construct it according to the wishes uppermost in them, a contradiction arises between being and doing, which can only be suffered as "punishment" by the rebelling creature.

The doctrine of hell stands in the greatest imaginable tension with the message of God's unlimited goodness. But because the latter involves a radical doctrine of freedom, the tension makes necessary a profound transformation in the concept of goodness. For the God of Jesus Christ, respect for the freedom of his creatures is more important than their immediate well-being. If it were otherwise, the heavenly Father would have had to make his creatures happy even despite their wills. That he did not do so shows that the divine goodness, as Jesus proclaimed it, is distinguished by its respect for human freedom from a diffuse, generalized kindness. Unconditional reverence for the unprogrammable freedom of his own creatures must be so important for the God of goodness that he even exposes people to the risk of hell. This strange fact shows how far God's goodness surpasses our representation of goodness. Because we can only vaguely and with difficulty comprehend God's respect for freedom, which does not even shrink from the final consequences, it causes us great effort over and over again to harmonize the many sufferings in history with faith in unending goodness. For us, well-being is ultimately always more important than reverence for the mystery of the Thou and its freedom, which has no further basis and is therefore for us so inscrutable.

If it is the moment of respect for freedom which comes right to the fore in the doctrine of hell as derived from the concept of God's goodness, we are led to ask: Does a genuine goodness still remain? Can we understand something as grace which does not also lead to well-being? Does not respect for freedom become a cold affair, in which there may never indeed be a direct "overpowering" toward the good, but in which the divine gaze turns into implacability, and in which the creature is abandoned in all logic to its torments? As in Anselm's doctrine of redemption, goodness at first threatens to go under at the demands of divine justice, so here the question is whether a doctrine of hell understood as a radical doctrine of freedom does not erode the concept of divine mercy. If respect for freedom had in fact to be played off against human well-being, then the concept of goodness would dissolve itself. But if we could only learn from the revelation in Christ how the heavenly Father makes a radical freedom possible for people and thereby respects them, then the concept of goodness would also once more be altered, and the idea of freedom would take on quite a different quality. A freedom which is threatening and disastrous for humankind would hardly be distinguishable from abandonment to an evil power in one's inmost being, and the picture of the divine goodness would become inextricably mixed up with this satanic freedom. It would turn into a demonic idol, necessarily in possession of good and evil — as a mixture and confusion of contradictory opposites — and capable of exercising over the human soul a strange, though destructive, fascination.

That unconditional respect for human freedom ultimately coincides with care for people's well-being is shown by the cross and Easter. Insofar as God's anointed gave himself up to the judgment event, he held on to the concern for freedom with final and most bitter consequences and withstood the judgment on sin — as freedom's self-judgment. But insofar as he stood in entirely for others in this event, he revealed the very opposite of a cold divine respect. In his request for liberation from fear and death (see Heb. 5:7), which he spoke for himself and all sinners, the most radical respect for freedom coincided with the most unconditional effort for human well-being.

In the theme of hell a freedom of the creature toward his own creator is visible, which is greater than anything which can be thought. This inscrutable dimension in free creatures is not only taught theoretically, but also in fact discovered and withstood in violent death. But on the cross the counterpart is equally demonstrated, the unlimited care for the good of creatures. The Son is so determined in his search for the lost ones that he takes on himself the fate that threatens them; and the Father is so generous in his forgiveness that he forgives even the most unthinkably evil deed, the rejection and murder of his Son, and answers it with the message of peace. There is no greater care imaginable for those who are lost than that lived out by the Son on his way to the hell of judgment on the cross, for it brought him up against that night which stands in total opposition to the divine life. There is also no greater forgiving love imaginable than that which was at work in the heavenly Father's Easter deed, for it forgave the greatest misdeed imaginable. *In the message and fate of Jesus, then, there is revealed a God greater than whom it is not possible to think.*

All human concepts know a limit, since they gain their clarity precisely through contrast with other concepts and through opposition to them. Consequently, Jesus would never have been able to reveal purely through concepts a God of unlimited goodness. By the tension in what he did, but above all by what happened to him and with him, these limits were nevertheless broken down, without clarity being lost. Each act in the drama of his life had a clear shape. What necessarily appeared as a limit in one, was in each case brought into a new light in the next and broken open. The heavenly Father's unconditional readiness to forgive, which showed itself in the basileia message, had its limit first of all in the expectation and demand for human conversion. Yet this limit was shown in the judgment message as an unlimited respect for human freedom, which for its part seemed to have its inexorable limits in God's inability to be touched by the torments of those affected by the judgment. Over against this, the event of the cross became a sign that God allowed himself to be thoroughly touched and affected in his Son. But in its turn this process again had the bitter limit that it was won by means of the greatest imaginable human misdeed and lived out as suffering and torment. But in the Easter response to this misdeed there was finally revealed an eternal goodness, which cancelled out even this evil and yet did not overwhelm people with divine power, but continued to court their freedom by means of the Spirit. Unlimited goodness is shown to be truly endless goodness and is clearly separated from any vague kindness and weakness.

The dissolved limits remain in the concept of God as differences, but at the same time they point beyond themselves. The "concept" of God which is achieved in this way is a concept which differs from all others not only by its content but also by its nature. It is a concept that includes a complete event, which concerns humans, which at the same time radically surpasses them, and into which they remain drawn in under every aspect. With this event there is no longer a final external restriction, but all limits are overcome from within and remain only as a richness of differences.

The Self-Revelation of the Father

The idea of self-revelation plays a central role in recent theology. It gives expression to the conviction that God communicated to humankind not merely some (arbitrary) truths, but himself and his own being. K. Barth used this idea to criticize the distinction between the God revealed in Christ (*deus revelatus*) and a God who conceals himself (*deus absconditus*) and turned upside down the Augustinian doctrine of predestination.

By the concept of self-revelation, naturally, a comprehensive revelation of all truths in the quantitative sense cannot be meant, for in the creation there are many individual truths which were not revealed by Christ and which yet are basically accessible to people. Also within the salvation event much had to remain open for the time being, but above all God is, even in his revelation, the one who surpasses all human thinking. Should not the idea of self-revelation be rejected for this reason? In the preceding section we have seen how in the fate of Jesus the heavenly Father expressed himself as a God greater than whom cannot be thought. But if we cannot think him any greater, can he not nevertheless be greater and quite different from anything we can think of? Why must what proves to be unlimited from our perspective be identical with what God is in himself? Behind the idea of revelation does there not hide a subtle confusion of the being of God with what we are able to establish and to think?

In the consideration of Christ's saving deed, everything is finally focused on the question of how exactly his death is to be understood. From the point of view of the basileia message and of Easter it was possible to rule out the understanding that the Son was struck in anger by the heavenly Father. Similarly, starting from the experience of the Spirit, it was possible to exclude the idea that the self-sacrifice of the crucified one was to be interpreted as (indirect) self-destruction. Christ's dying was seen rather as a surrender which burst all human limits and possibilities. As long as a person is alive, all forms of surrender are limited by the conditions of the person's physical and psychic life. A complete surrender of self is therefore impossible. But in dying Jesus entrusted his spirit and his self in the power of the Spirit to the Father. A total surrender of himself was the final form taken by his revealing activity.

However, the one dying on the cross, as shown at Easter, was not carried away into the nameless Godhead, so his total self-surrender may not be interpreted purely as an overstepping of human limits. The continuing difference of the crucified and risen one from the Father demands that his surrender should not be interpreted purely from a human perspective. We should see in it rather a revelation of the one to whom Jesus totally entrusted himself. If his dying had involved only going beyond all human limits toward something unlimited and nameless, his ego would have had to have been absorbed into this unending reality. But the experience of Easter shows exactly the opposite.

At Pentecost the disciples were gripped in the depths of their own selves. If this experience had only been the transcending of their own limits, then a life based on it would surely have led to a religion of inner contemplation. But the opposite happened. Despite their overwhelming experience, the disciples proclaimed in the first place not their subjective experiences but what they had encountered in Jesus, in the crucified and risen one. The breaking out of the experience of the Spirit from the innermost self did not lead to the systematic sounding of the depths and transcending their own limits, but to the deeper perception and recognition of what they came up against.

The continuing difference of the crucified one from the Father in the context of his total surrender to him and the difference of the experience of the Spirit from the appearances of the risen one prove unambiguously that the God who expressed himself in the fate of Jesus does not merely reflect back the most sublime acts of human transcendence. The differences reveal differences in God himself, and thus talk of God's self-revelation cannot be fundamentally ruled out. Its meaning, though, must be more deeply illuminated by the revelation of the eternal Son and of the Holy Spirit.

The Revelation of the Son and Suffering

So far we have spoken now of Jesus, now of Christ or the Son. By these three titles, three different persons were not meant, but rather each description brought into the foreground another aspect of the one figure. The multiplicity of titles points to that complex problematic which is dealt with in the church's theology as the doctrine of two natures. In our context we want to indicate at least sketchily what a dramatic view of revelation can contribute to this issue.

Jesus showed himself to us on the one hand as a prophet, and yet by his message and by his behavior he stood out clearly in important points from the Old Testament prophets. He did not present his message with the distancing introduction "word of God," but he identified himself completely with it: "Amen, I say to you." He experienced his God so strongly as Father and Abba that he must also have perceived himself as Son in a special way. He justified his activity entirely from the viewpoint of the working of his heavenly Father, and he dared to "act in God's place."[34] Even in his judgment sayings he made the claim that taking up a position toward him was decisive for or against salvation. His public ministry took place, then, in a "unity of action approaching congruency"[35] with his Father. But what did his Passion mean in view of this unity of action?

At his trial, Jesus was accused of blasphemy (Mark 14:64). The Gospel of John deepens its interpretation of this accusation: the radical

---

34. Fuchs (1960), 156; see also 154.
35. Mussner (1975), 97.

reproach lay in the charge that he was only a man and made himself the Son of God and God himself (John 10:33; 19:7). Since this accusation, as we have seen, is to be understood as a mirroring of that which dwells in the depths of sinful people's hearts, Jesus' claim is necessarily exposed to the deepest misunderstandings. Not only does it contrast entirely with people's everyday experience, but in them it also comes up against a heart which is already prejudiced. In all people there lives a genuine longing for the eternal; but in all sinners there also works in a mysterious and hidden way that for which people reproached Jesus: "for you are only a human being and are making yourself God" (John 10:33). Because of this actual sinful prejudice, Jesus' claim is not only hard to understand but above all liable to misunderstanding. It can unintentionally be perceived in the sense of that satanic will which slumbers deep in each one's heart. Even where a right belief is present, the prejudices of one's own heart can manage to falsify this. That this is not merely a theoretical possibility is proved by a quick look at the history of the church, in which only too often it is precisely in the name of Christ or of the Son of God that deeds are committed, and above all justified, which are opposed to his message and behavior. And if gross misunderstandings have been possible, must we not reckon all the more with subtle distortions which can creep into the profession of the Son of God?

The temptation of the creature to make itself God is the temptation to self-sufficiency, to worship of self, and to power. The picture that we have drawn of Jesus as Son must therefore continually be checked as to whether we bring such elements into it. He himself expressly rejected the false understanding of sonship which the tempter tried to suggest,[36] and his way to the cross was the opposite of arrogance. It was a way of humiliation, of weakness, of being handed over, and of renunciation of physical force. From this way we must gauge how his claim to be a special Son of the heavenly Father is shown and is to be understood in contrast to satanic arrogance.

If there was a unity of action approaching congruency between Jesus and his Father, then we also have to take into account a unity in suffering. This issue is for the most part clearly recognized in recent theology. However, there is a tendency to treat this unity in too undifferentiated a manner. Even if the problematic of unity in suffering is rightly brought up, it is not clear in advance how one should envisage this unity in detail and in what sense one can speak of a suffering of God himself. The issue is far more complex than with unity of action. During his public procla-

---

36. "If you are the Son of God, so command. . . . If you are the Son of God, then throw yourself down" (Matt. 4:3–6).

mation, Jesus worked in *direct* obedience to his heavenly Father, but, in contrast, his suffering was essentially conditioned by the intervention of a third actor in the drama, the sinner. For this reason we need to ask here, very precisely, what belongs to the uncovering and overcoming of sin and what is to be understood as self-revelation of God. Where this question is not carefully carried through, something arising from the world of sin can easily be brought into the idea of God. As the concept of power in its application to God needs to be criticized by means of the crucified one's nonviolence and powerlessness, so the idea of suffering needs at the least just as fundamental a conversion by means of the Easter and Pentecost experience before it may be used of God himself.

Since God does not will sin, we may not treat as revelation of the Father anything which *immediately* and *directly* arises from sin, otherwise God and sinners would merge into one another. The unjust condemnation and violent death of Jesus were unambiguous fruits of sin, and therefore nothing of God — in direct fashion — was disclosed in them. But Jesus "used" the violent death which came to him, he "turned around" evil and made it into a surrender to his Father, which burst all the limits of human existence. Since his deed on the cross took place for sinners, the question arises again to what extent it should be interpreted directly as a redeeming deed and to what extent as a revealing event. Even if the revelation was fulfilled in the redemption event, the two are not in every respect identical. Together with this goes the further question as to what extent the death of the crucified one expressed the surrender of a creature to the creator and to what extent it expressed the love of the Son to the Father. The two aspects must be distinguished and yet fit seamlessly together.

Maximus the Confessor, by means of an analysis of the prayer at the Mount of Olives which went beyond the theology of the earlier fathers, moved toward a doctrine of three wills in Christ.[37] "Abba, Father, all is possible for thee. Take this cup from me! But not what I will, but what thou wilt" (Mark 14:36). In the words "take this cup from me" and "what I will" he saw an expression of a premoral striving of Christ's human nature, which instinctively drew back in terror from the suffering. The words "what thou wilt" he interpreted as a reference to the divine will. And the priority given to the divine will over his own premoral striving — expressed by the words "not what I...but what thou..." — he saw as the work of the human will. Nevertheless, in doing this, Maximus the Confessor assumed no human freedom of choice on Christ's part, but he attributed the determination of the human will

---

37. See Léthel (1979).

directly to God.[38] Important as this analysis of the Mount of Olives prayer is, it leaves two questions unanswered. Was it in fact only Christ's human premoral striving which expressed itself in the words "take this cup from me," and did he have no human freedom of choice?

Maximus the Confessor — with the whole preceding tradition — understood the choice of the human will as a decision between good and evil. Since he could not and did not want to attribute to Christ any real possibility of doing evil, he had also to deny him any genuine freedom of choice. In distinction to the theology of the fathers, Anselm of Canterbury came to a different description of human decision, and he saw in it ultimately a choice between good and better.[39] Scholastic theology did not take up this new starting point, and yet it seems to offer a crucial help for a more precise analysis of the Mount of Olives prayer. Jesus expressly prayed for the removal of the cup. Such a request could well be provoked by an impulse of his nature, but insofar as it was explicitly formulated and spoken, the thing wished for, even if the request took place in the conditional form, moved into the arena of responsibility. For this reason it would be inappropriate to see in the request to be spared the cup of suffering only something premoral.

This statement can be made firmer by means of a further observation. At his arrest, Jesus fended off the attempt of Peter to defend him with violence, and he asked his disciple: "Or don't you believe that my Father would immediately send me more than twelve legions of angels if I appealed to him?" (Matt. 26:53). By these words Jesus expressed unambiguously his conviction that fundamentally it was possible for him to escape his suffering by a request to his Father. But since God does not listen to any request that is not moral, being spared from suffering must have been a morally thinkable alternative for him. Since, after the rejection of the basileia message people have of themselves no longer any possibility of salvation, the actualization of the alternative of escape from suffering would have meant that Jesus alone would have been saved. From our standpoint, we cannot think such a possibility through to its logical conclusion, for it would have had the consequence that we remained abandoned to total disaster. In this case our picture of God would also radically change and we would only be able to see in him a cruel despot. But even if *we* are not able systematically to think through the possibility of Jesus being freed from the cup of suffering, this does not in any way exclude that it was possible *for him* just for a moment, and that it was excluded by his own decision. If we want completely to

---

38. See Schwager, "Das Mysterium der übernatürlichen Natur-Lehre," in Schwager (1986), 141–47.

39. See Schwager, "Logik der Freiheit und des Natur-Wollens," in Schwager (1986), 176f.

understand his behavior in his suffering, we must attempt as far as possible to leave behind our situation — as candidates for disaster — for a short time in order to think ourselves into the situation of his decision. He had fulfilled his Father's task by the proclamation of the basileia message, and if people had responded to him, they would also have gained their salvation thereby. The first task of his mission was consequently coherent in itself, and the request to be freed from a further, far more difficult task was in no way unmoral. If he actually spoke out this request and at the same time subordinated it completely to the will of the Father ("not what I will, but what thou wilt"), then two things are shown: (1) The way of suffering did not correspond in any way to the direct intention of the heavenly Father, for this way entirely contradicted Jesus' human nature, which in its willing, because it was sinless, directly mirrored the will of the creator. In consequence, no direct revelation of God may be seen in suffering. (2) Through the unconditional subordination of his own human will to that of his heavenly Father, Jesus showed himself ready to let his human existence be used for a task which utterly surpassed it. Consequently, the step from his unity of action with God during his public ministry to unity in suffering took place by means of an explicit decision and must also be understood from this point of view. Both the request for release from the cup and also the subordination of this request to the more comprehensive will of the Father each in their own way reveal something about God. The request shows first of all that the creator does not will the suffering of his creatures in itself and therefore should himself not be thought of as a sufferer. But the more comprehensive will to salvation reveals that God must be so pure in himself that he can "use" even the failure of his creatures in order to bestow something on them and to reveal something which goes beyond the possibilities of their nature.

As Jesus allowed himself unreservedly to be taken up and used for a task which burst the limits of his human nature, several questions arise: By what power was he able to do this? In what way was he thereby one with his Father? What did he reveal in his surrender to the Father? To the first question we have already discovered the answer that he "by the power of the eternal Spirit presented himself as an unblemished offering to God" (Heb. 9:14). But he was not merely led like a prophet by the divine spirit. Since this conceptual model has already been shown to be insufficient for his public ministry, it must be thoroughly inappropriate for the interpretation of his greater mission undertaken in obedience, the surrender on the cross. As we have further found in our reflections on the self-revelation of the Father that we have to assume differences in God himself, the creator-creature model must be extended by a fundamentally different one.

Since we may not see either Jesus' being killed or his suffering as such as a revelation of God, and given, nevertheless, that the fate he underwent is to be understood as God's self-expression, then everything focuses on the central point of his obedience. The total entrusting of himself and his being gripped by a mission which surpasses the possibilities of human nature must be understood as a direct revelation of God, in which the resurrection of the one killed shows how radically this being gripped is to be understood. Consequently we must assume in God himself a reality of receiving and being gripped. As the judgment message, with its address to people's radical freedom, brought about a first corrective to the picture of a purely active creator, so the concept of God is once again and far more radically transformed by the event of the cross. God, from whom everything comes and on whom everything is dependent, must himself be thought of as surrendering and receiving. Suffering as such may not be attributed to him, for it stems directly from sin, which God does not want. But God himself is revealed in Jesus' will to accept a mission which includes suffering, and in the way in which he is gripped by it. It is true that the radical quality of this receptivity is brought out in the medium of suffering, and yet suffering is not identical with receptivity.

If it is revealed from the viewpoint of the cross and Easter events that God is not only power, creativeness, and activity, but also unconditional surrender and receptivity, then the possibility is opened up of applying the concept "Son," which necessarily includes in it the element of receiving, beyond creatures to God himself. In being killed and raised up, which was lived out by Christ as radical surrender and being gripped by the Father, an openness and receptivity are revealed which no longer know any limits and are entirely directed toward the heavenly Father. The concepts "father" and "son" do not merely denote, then, a particular form of creator-creature relationship within the dramatic revelation event. In the action of God toward the crucified and risen one and in his being gripped they take on a meaning which involves God himself and brings to the concept of God a profound alteration and something completely new. Already during his public ministry Jesus touched on this new accent in addressing God as Abba; but it first becomes clear for us in the cross and resurrection.

As both the surrender of the dying one on the cross and the creative act of resurrection by the Father are indirectly accessible to us, we are only able — through direct questioning — to gain only a vague representation of them. In what sense "father" and "son" are to be understood in God has remained to a great extent still unanswered so far. Certainly, our gaze has shifted unambiguously from the creator-creature relationship to a polarity in God himself. In order to understand this correctly, the framework of the question must be broadened. We have already seen earlier that the surrender of Christ on the cross can only be appropriately interpreted from the viewpoint of the post-Easter experience of the Holy Spirit. Thus it should be granted that the Father-Son polarity also can only be explained more closely in connection with the problematic of the Spirit. The Holy Spirit should not be seen as something vague and extra, about which we also somehow have to speak. He is anything but an arbitrary appendage who makes no difference to the other truths of revelation. In the question about the Spirit, the actual clarification of the Father-Son relationship must rather follow, as far as this is at all possible for us humans.

The Revelation of the Holy Spirit and the Trinity

During his earthly life, Jesus spoke only very little of the Holy Spirit, and if he did so (see Mark 3:29), his words could be understood in that general sense in which the Old Testament also knew the Spirit of God and meant by it a particular near and active presence of the creator to his creatures. In view of this fact, and because of the ready possibility of relating all the Old Testament utterances about the divine spirit to the working of the heavenly Father in Christ and to the appearances of the risen one, quite particular experiences must have occurred, as we have already shown, which were able to develop into a clear profession of the Holy Spirit and to realize it without conflicts in the community.[40]

Because the Holy Spirit has awoken and awakes in faithful freedom, love, and peace, we are drawn toward understanding also the Father-Son polarity, which reveals itself in the surrender of the crucified one "by the power of the eternal spirit," as a relationship of freedom and love. Creating and taking in, giving and surrendering, bestowing and receiving are seen in this light not merely as a flux and reflux, as an impersonal surge to and fro or dialectic change in the godhead. Since the surrender was a free act of love and as the Spirit of freedom and love, who calls forth the most fundamentally personal response in the faithful, was sent from the Father to the Son, we must all correct the pictures of an impersonal flowing current and change, and think of both Father and Son as personal poles and acting persons. What a plurality of persons in one God can mean remains at first still unanswered. Equally, the role played by the Spirit in the personal Father-Son relationship requires a closer explanation; otherwise the language used remains vague and shapeless.

---

40. "He [Paul] found some disciples and asked them, 'Did you receive the Holy Spirit when you believed?' They answered him, 'We haven't even heard that there is a Holy Spirit' " (Acts 19:2).

Traditional theology has, at the level of the inner-trinitarian relationships, unambiguously placed the Holy Spirit after the Father and Son in the order of salvation events. The justification for this was the idea of the incarnation (John 1:1, 14; Phil. 2:5–8); and the revealed facts that it was first the Son and only later the Spirit who was sent and that at Pentecost Father and Son together poured out the Spirit. This view, although it is correct, remains however somewhat one-sided. In our investigations so far we have seen what an important role the Spirit played already in the event of the cross. This fact impels us to draw the conclusion in retrospect that even the synoptic report that Jesus was anointed with the Holy Spirit (Mark 1:9–11 and parallels) immediately after his baptism by John has a systematic significance, even if historical-critical exegesis likes to speak here of a later shaping by the community. Equally, it should be noted that according to all three synoptics Jesus was led into the desert by the Spirit (Mark 1:12 and parallels). According to Luke, Jesus, taking up Isa. 61:1ff. at the beginning of his public ministry, spoke himself of an anointing by the "Spirit of the Lord" (Luke 4:16–21; see also Acts 4:27; 10:38). Paul emphasizes finally that "according to the Spirit of holiness" the crucified one was designated Son in power at the resurrection of the dead (Rom. 1:4; see also 1 Pet. 3:18).[41] In accordance with these important utterances, Jesus was himself led by the Spirit of God during his whole earthly mission. From this point of view it appears that a priority of the Holy Spirit over the Son who became man is shown.

Systematic theology tried for a long time to deal with the abovementioned New Testament findings by interpreting the utterances about the working of the Spirit in Jesus in a very restrictive sense or even going against their explicit wording. In distinction to this long tradition, H. U. von Balthasar follows the biblical text more closely, and he is inspired by it to speak of a "trinitarian inversion."[42] He means by this that the order within God was turned around at the level of the economy of salvation during the earthly life of the eternal Son and that the real order only showed itself at the elevation of the crucified one. D. Coffey also pursues the same problematic, and he is led by it to a deepening of the doctrine of the Trinity within God. In an analogy with the two traditional trinitarian models, the Western which starts from the unity of the divine nature, and the Eastern which starts from the difference of the persons and from the Father's origin in himself alone, he puts forward the view that the life within God which is revealed in Christ can only be somewhat adequately described by using two complementary mod-

---

41. See O'Donnell (1989), 37–39.
42. Balthasar (1973–83), 2/2:167–75.

els. The traditional model, according to which the Father generates the Son and both together, as one principle, breathe the Spirit results from a christology from above (mission of the eternal logos into the world). The complementary christology from below, according to which Jesus is anointed by the Holy Spirit and directed in his mission, demands also another corresponding trinitarian model. Coffey describes it as the bestowal model, in accordance with which the Father grants the Spirit to his Son and the Son gives it back.[43] The fact that the Holy Spirit proceeds from the Father and the Son should be distinguished from the question as to how his proceeding and thus his own particular nature are to be understood.[44] While the origin in the Father and the Son has to be considered above all from the viewpoint of the post-Easter mission, the question about the particular nature of the Holy Spirit must be clarified in connection with his role during the earthly mission of the Son made man.

Even if in our context we are unable to look more closely into Coffey's reasoning, based explicitly on the history of theology and on exegesis, his two complementary trinitarian models are nevertheless appropriate for doing justice to what we have worked out so far. We have come to see that the surrender of the crucified one is only to be understood from the viewpoint of the Spirit, and the Spirit in return only from the point of view of Christ's ministry. Two complementary approaches are necessary in order to put into words appropriately the one mystery of redemption faith. Since, in addition, the traditional trinitarian model only suggests the concept of a common working of the Father and the Son toward the Spirit, and our investigation has nevertheless shown that the direct behavior of Jesus toward the Father (prayer, faith, surrender to death) and the Father's direct actions toward the Son (anointing with the Spirit, voice from heaven after the baptism and at the transfiguration, resurrection) are of decisive significance, it appears from this side too that a deeper analysis at the trinitarian level is needed. The procession or mission model does not by itself do justice to the fundamental biblical evidence of reciprocal behavior between Father and Son, but only when it is clarified by the complementary model of reciprocal bestowal. Finally we have to consider that our dramatic model of redemption presupposes a concept of the mission of Jesus which was not presented from the outset as a fixed thing. Since the rejection of the basileia message created a new situation, he had to discover anew in prayer and in listening to the voice of the Father how his mission con-

---

43. Coffey (1979), 11–32, 91–178.

44. "Its [bestowal model's] complementarity to the processional model is shown from the fact that whereas the latter corresponds to the fact of the procession of the Holy Spirit, the former corresponds to the manner of this procession" (ibid., 31).

tinued, and he had also to agree anew, as the prayer on the Mount of Olives makes clear, to the deeper task. If the mission that the traditional trinitarian doctrine takes as a guide cannot be described as a once for all and unilinear process but must be understood as the fruit of a reciprocal conversation, then it demands of itself a deepening analysis, by means of a model which gives expression to the reciprocal relationship of Father and Son. The unilinear movement from Father to Son and the common actions of both toward the Spirit are not enough really to do justice to the dramatic fate of Jesus.

A particular difficulty with the procession and mission model is that the Holy Spirit proceeds from the Father and the Son as one single principle.[45]

The impression is thereby given that the Holy Spirit arises from the one divine nature rather than from the two subordinated persons. This difficulty is removed by the model of bestowal, for according to that, the Holy Spirit is the reciprocal (and not merely common) love of Father and Son. The Father bestows the Spirit on the Son and the Son gives it back. But there arises now another difficulty. The suspicion can easily emerge that two origins are attributed to the Spirit, one in the Father and one in the Son, which contradicts a central principle of the ecclesiastical doctrine of the Trinity,[46] which has to be maintained if one does not wish to be lost in contradictions.

The effectiveness of the trinitarian model of reciprocal bestowal depends to a large extent on whether the difficulty just mentioned can be resolved. We will attempt to do this in such a way that at the same time further implications of our dramatic model of salvation history emerge more clearly. The Holy Spirit is the Spirit of freedom. As an essential element of freedom, we first considered freedom of choice, as it was the presupposition for Jesus' hearers being able to accept or reject his message. By means of it even he, on the Mount of Olives, subordinated his wish to be spared the cup of suffering to the will of his heavenly Father. This human freedom of choice in God corresponds in an analogous way to the freedom of his eternal counsel in creation and redemption.

But freedom of choice is not by any means the whole of what we mean by freedom. When considering the problem of judgment as self-judgment, we saw that the yes or no to God does not mean merely the following of individual commandments. It is essentially a matter of the standard by which individuals build up their world. Even in the event of the cross, Jesus lived his freedom — through and beyond his yes to

---

45. "...quod Spiritus Sanctus ex Patre et Filio aeternaliter est, et essentiam suam suumque esse subsistens habet ex Patre simul et Filio, et ex utroque aeternaliter tamquam ab uno principio et unica spiratione procedit" (DS 1300).

46. Omnia in deo "sunt unum, ubi non obviat relationis oppositio" (DS 1330).

suffering — as the surrender of his whole being to the Father. Finally, at the post-Easter sending out of the Spirit, the freedom of the disciples showed itself above all in their being inwardly grasped and liberated from compulsions and fears, and thus becoming capable of going out into the world in all openness and giving themselves up to a mission. In all these examples the same movement can be seen: a working from a person's innermost depths outward to others (be it in giving or receiving). This deeply personal working can only be designated as freedom because it includes a distinction between the action and the actor, and is therefore free from any "oppression" or "entanglement." That is, the gift of the basileia message is to be received as a person's own life principle in such a way that it renews all thinking, acting, and feeling from within, but at the same time it demands such an inner distinctness from it that all good deeds are attributed not to oneself but only to God's working. Similarly we see in the fate of Jesus on the cross how on the one hand he was gripped by the event in the depths of his soul, but on the other hand he maintained such a distinction from the powers which he encountered that he did not become their passive object, but was able actively to transform the evil into sacrificial love. His disciples also after Easter were inwardly so deeply pervaded by the Spirit that they began to speak and act in a new way, and yet they maintained in the experience of the Spirit a distinctness, so that they did not attribute the new power to themselves and they remained capable of distinguishing the good spirit from the deceiving spirits. The freedom of the Spirit, then, shows itself in the drama of salvation as a polarity, as a working from the innermost personal depths, maintaining at the same time a distinctness from the person as self.

From the viewpoint of this experience of freedom and of the Spirit in salvation history, we can to some extent feel our way toward the mystery of the Spirit within God. The Father releases from the ultimate depths of his person the Son, and the latter is entirely constituted by what he receives. Despite this, the two of them do not become absorbed into this event. The Father is not dialectically transformed into the Son, so that he ceases to be the Father, nor does the Son change back into the Father. Although the Father gives everything, he remains distinct from what he gives, and although the Son receives everything, he remains equally distinct from the giver.

What the distinctness means can be seen above all in the salvation-historical act. The Father is not the Father because Jesus announced him, but because he precedes everyone, Jesus is able to announce him. Correspondingly, the Father is not Father within God because he generates the Son, but he is once more distinct from this process, and he is himself thanks to his own origin in himself (*sine principio*). If he was a person only because of the generation, then no longer he but this act of generation would be the first in the trinitarian order. Generation itself would be the original process of distinguishing, from which — sequentially — Father and Son would arise as from the same origin (as if from one principle). In this case one could not speak of a giving and receiving, a generating and being generated, a first and a second person in God, but only of the breaking up of a distinctness, which caused two poles to arise as from the same origin. But the New Testament writings bear witness over against such a supposition to a quite different experience of salvation history. The Father releases the Son entirely from himself (*paternitas*), but he does not become so absorbed in the relationship that it becomes the reason for his existence; he exists rather because of his mysterious origin in himself. In a similar way, the Son, too, is separate from his own being as a person. It is true that he exists only because he receives his being totally (*filiatio*), but he does not become completely absorbed in this receiving. According to the witness of salvation history, his full being as a person consists neither in a merely passive state of being received, nor is there any suggestion that he would cease to exist if he were to give back all that he received. Since he can give himself back entirely and nevertheless remain himself, he must be distinct in his actions of thanking and giving back from the principle by which he receives himself as a person. Since, further, the relationship of Father to Son is not exhausted in the Father's mission to the Son, but since he continues to speak and deal with the envoy at the level of God's inner being, we have to assume, besides the relationship which constitutes the Son as a person, the Father conducts himself in yet another way, a way which is directed toward the already constituted Son. The father's origin in himself is, then, different not merely from his generation, but distinct from this again is his turning to or his love for the already generated Son. The experience of freedom in salvation history with its two poles, working from the depths of the person with a simultaneous distinctness of action from actor helps us, consequently, to perceive also within God himself very subtle but fundamental differentiations (of a logical, not temporal, order). The God of Jesus Christ is not a God in whose unsoundable depths there exists a formless "brooding" or "surging to and fro."

Thanks to the clear perception of several distinctions within God himself, the question about the *one* origin (*unica spiratio*) of the Holy Spirit from the *reciprocal* love between Father and Son can be more easily approached. Since what the Son gives back to the Father is distinct from the principle by which he is a person, he can distinguish his love from himself and let go of it. It is not identical with him in an undifferentiated way; it is in fact not even the fruit of his own person alone, for it is attracted by the other side, by the generous goodness of the Father.

The Father too distinguishes his love for the Son from the principle by which he generates and constitutes him. He too, then, can let go of his love as his own. Here again, it is not merely the fruit of his own working, for it is related to the Son, insofar as he is already constituted and it is attracted by his thankfulness. The reciprocal love is therefore not put together from the Father's own love and the Son's own love, but both let go of their love as their own, so that it becomes one common love. The Father loves the Son on account of his thankfulness, but the Son is thankful because he sees the love of the Father. Thus the Holy Spirit is the free-moving love itself.[47] The reciprocal love between Father and Son can therefore be freely active and become its own person, because both let go of it as their own.

In the history of salvation, something common and moving freely between Father and Son is seen first of all in the message of the kingdom of God at hand. Jesus announces it entirely as the kingdom of his Father and at the same time speaks completely in his own name ("Amen, I say to you"). The word of proclamation belongs entirely to both and at the same time is detached from both: "Everything is given over to me by my Father; no one knows the Father, only the Son and that one to whom the Son wants to reveal him" (Matt. 11:27). This word, which arises completely from the reciprocity of the Father and Son and speaks of it, originates from within their intimacy and is addressed to other, human hearers. The word of proclamation shows itself thus as the first figure in salvation history by which reciprocal love (Holy Spirit) becomes manifest.

Full reciprocity and commonality is revealed even more clearly in the last three acts of the drama. The Son gives himself to the Father in dying, the latter answers in the resurrection, and both together send out the Spirit. Thus the three different forms of bestowal are already repeated within each act, even if in a differing way. The Son can only entrust himself completely in dying because he is already gripped in his depths by the God who is not a God of the dead but of the living (Mark 12:26ff. and parallels). It is precisely in the act of surrender to the Father, which includes the Father's communication to him, that the Spirit springs up for humankind ("streams of living water" [John 7:37–39; 19:34–37]). Even the resurrection is not a one-sided deed of the Father, for by it he answers the Son who "with loud cries and tears offered up prayers and supplications to him who was able to save him from death" (Heb. 5:7). The immediate common fruit of the request on the part of his Son be-

---

47. "Its substance can be stated quite simply: the Holy Spirit is the mutual love of the Father and the Son. Notice that it is not said that the Holy Spirit is the result or term of this mutual love. He is the love itself" (Coffey [1984], 471).

come man and of the heeding of the heavenly Father is the pneumatic body of the risen one as "life-giving spirit" (1 Cor. 15:44ff.), which is communicated to humankind (Acts 1:2; 2:33).

The model of reciprocal bestowal proves, then, well suited to bringing out the innermost dimensions of the dramatic salvation event. At the same time it becomes clear how reciprocal love flows into such an event of release that we can no longer speak of two acts in opposing directions, from Father to Son and from Son to Father. Each one lets go of his love as his own in favor of the other, so that this love can be constituted as the one common love and can become a person.

Because the Son himself is, at one and the same time, receiving and actively letting go and because the Holy Spirit is pure letting go, the Father is able to communicate himself through them to creatures without the distinction between creator and creature being abolished. Communication takes place at the level of these persons and their free existence and not at the level of the one essential being. Since, further, the Holy Spirit according to his entire personal character is reciprocal love, letting go of itself, it is to him that the mission in salvation history falls: to unite people with Christ and with one another. This throws light on the statement that he creates the one body with many members (1 Cor. 12:4–13). His particular nature makes it also comprehensible that Christ can live as the most inner being in the faithful: "I have been crucified with Christ; no longer do I live, but Christ lives in me" (Gal. 2:19ff.).

We next ask, in whom does the Spirit work? Here there arises a problem which can show up again the consequences of the two complementary trinitarian models. If one thinks in a linear way from the viewpoint of the procession and mission model, then it is natural to suppose that the Holy Spirit only unites those people with Christ who have already heard of the crucified and risen one and believe in him (for the Son precedes the Father). That axiom with such difficult consequences, "outside the church no salvation," seems to go together with this view. In distinction to this, we have seen that one must speak of Christ already on the cross identifying with all humans. This is essentially brought about by the Spirit.

Following the transcendental christology of K. Rahner, Coffey identifies the Holy Spirit with the transcendental love of the eternal Son's human nature for the Father.[48] But this transcendental love must express itself, and during Jesus' earthly life it took shape progressively in his human acts of love for the Father and became incarnate in them. The highest act of his concrete human love took place in the surrender

---

48. Coffey (1984), 475.

to death. This is at the same time to be understood as the highest form of the "incarnation" of the Holy Spirit (or of transcendental love) in an act of Christ's human love.[49] If now the Holy Spirit from the viewpoint of his personal individual nature is a bond of love, indeed of reciprocal love, and if he incarnated himself completely for sinners in the crucified one's surrender to death, then it becomes understandable that the Son was able in dying actually to reach all people. His identification with sinners took place, then, by the power of that Spirit incarnate in his human love and whose working consists of uniting persons with one another. In the total entrusting to the Father there took place both the giving back to him of the Spirit and the releasing of the same Spirit for humankind.[50] Since the Father inspired the surrender of the Son, the Spirit through their reciprocal giving became in fact free for his working in all people. Thus the redeeming deed on the cross can reach all people, before they themselves know anything about it.

For complete unification, consent on both sides is needed. Each individual has to answer for what is offered to him as a gift. This response takes place explicitly and unambiguously in faith and in baptism. That communication of the Spirit which comes about in baptism and which — at least at the fundamental level — presupposes faith in Christ, takes place according to the procession model. But that other communication of the same Spirit, which springs forth immediately from the cross and accompanies all people inwardly from the beginning of their existence onward, takes place according to the model of bestowal. In this case also a free consent is necessary. However, since the personal character of the Spirit is clearly different from that of the Father and the Son, and since he is not a fixed term but love itself hovering where he will, consent to his working can be given in very differing ways, which are no longer verifiable by us.

The complementary trinitarian models make it to some extent understandable why on the one hand all people can be saved thanks to the hidden working of the Holy Spirit, and why on the other hand explicit faith and baptism are nevertheless necessary. They show, moreover, that the Christian proclamation has on the one hand to be directly oriented to the express message of Jesus, and on the other hand it must also seek out the hidden working of the Spirit in human beings in order to give an unambiguous incarnational form to the Spirit by relating everything back to the message of Jesus Christ.

---

49. "There can be no greater human love than a love unto death. Hence in the death of Jesus the progressive 'incarnation' of the Holy Spirit in his transcendental love of the Father attains the limit that is possible in this life" (ibid., 477; see also Kilmartin [1988], 168–70).

50. See Coffey (1979), 147–55.

The Drama of Christian Life

In our investigation, the question of redemption could not be rounded off by itself. Many further questions had at least to be touched on, and step by step a picture emerged of how the dramatic event of salvation in Christ aims at a change of human attitude and conduct toward the whole of reality. History, with the evil forces at work in it, human society with its own laws and mechanisms, and even the individual ego with its unfathomable freedom appeared in a new light. But above all our gaze did not remain finally fixed on human beings with their many problems; it was rather the threefold life of God which stepped into the foreground. Thereby a fundamental change is treated, which we must once again explicitly call to mind. The whole of modern thought has seen the human person above all as an autonomous being. From the viewpoint of the experience of evil, this view was questioned but never fundamentally broken down. The Christian message of redemption brings a new element in here. It is aimed not merely at saving people but at a total alteration in the understanding of human life.

Living in the Service of a God-Given Life

If an actor plays his part well, he steps with his whole existence into the service of the character he is to represent. This does not make him a puppet, but his own experience with its hopes and sufferings, its dreams and disappointments is expressed in a transformed way in the person who appears on the stage. The actor puts something of his own life into the service of the figure whom he has to play. Certainly, in his performance he always remains in the role, out of which he must regularly step, in order to live his own life with his own responsibilities. But his service in the role has a great symbolic power.

Christian life can be understood from the viewpoint of this parable. Christ brought us in the first place neither new knowledge nor a new ethic, although in both these realms something new was also communicated to us by him. He himself stood entirely at the service of his mission, and in the course of his existence he lived out only the drama of his mission. In the decisive moment of suffering, he was even ready to put aside his own human will to live, which was morally justified within the context of his individual fate, in order, by his surrender, to place his whole existence finally at the service of a more comprehensive plan and thereby of a higher life. In consequence, he became without reserve an instrument for the salvation of humankind and for the revelation of the divine love. This event embracing him from above was at the same time the innermost dimension of his own human life. The threefold love became visible in this world as the last radicality of a human life. As divine wisdom played on the earth and it was her delight to be with humankind (Prov. 8:31), so it is the joy of the threefold God to act out his mysterious life in the "play" of people on earth.

Even if a good actor puts everything into his part, his own life remains more important. It was different with the fate of Jesus. His human life had no aim of its own beside his mission. It was a matter of being the living flesh and dramatic instrumentality for that threefold life which had gripped him. A similar task stands before those who are ready to follow him. Given the spontaneous urge to live, all of us start with our own wishes, aims, and plans, and these, while preserving the person's own imperious will to life, can often be built into collective projects within history without any very great difficulty. Self-will thus appears as service. Christian faith demands, however, a different service and therefore includes a fundamental conversion. The decisive thing is the question of the whole understanding of life and the readiness ultimately not to live one's own life any longer, but Christ's, and to allow oneself to be led by the Spirit. One's own life becomes then a living instrument on which the melody of a higher life can be played. Such a conversion can naturally not be the fruit of one individual decision, but involves a lifelong process.

From the insight that the innermost dimension of human life is the divine life bestowed on humankind, H. U. von Balthasar distinguishes between spirit-subject and person.[51] He ascribes the spiritual individual to the creation, while he defines personal existence by means of the supernatural mission and participation in the trinitarian life of God. In the case of Christ, from whom Balthasar draws the theological concept of person, this distinction can be established fairly easily, even by means of church doctrine (anhypostasis of human nature). However Balthasar tries to understand all human persons from the viewpoint of the supernatural mission, according to the archetype of Christ: "But in Christ there is hope to be no mere individual self, but to become a person of God, with a task likewise defined through Christ."[52] Since the Christian task is always aimed at others, together with supernatural personal existence, according to Balthasar, there is at the same time implied a community among humans: "The human self, becoming a person theologically through an individual calling and mission, comes to be simultaneously deprivatized and socialized; it is made into a space and bearer of community."[53]

---

51. Balthasar (1973–83), 2/2:186–210.
52. Ibid., 202.
53. Ibid., 249.

Impressive as this view may be, it brings up a serious problem. Ecclesiastical tradition has always held on to the element of subsistence in the concept of the person. Whoever is a person is not a part or utterance or appearance of another. It was precisely Christ's existence as a human person which was denied, in order to hold on unambiguously to the proposition that as a person he did not subsist for himself, but that this person is the second divine person. If supernatural personal existence is extended also to other people, as Balthasar attempts to do, the following alternative results: Either, with this concept of person, the element of subsistence is spread more broadly and it then follows that all people who are in Christ and the Holy Spirit subsist in them and thus are also God, or the element of subsistence is removed from the supernatural concept of person, but then the doctrine of one person in Christ only says something which is valid for all the faithful. Since both alternatives are unacceptable for a Christian theology, the purely supernatural concept of person outlined by Balthasar (following Barth) is not tenable from a systematic point of view. Nevertheless this (failed) attempt articulates an issue which is very important and which we have frequently come up against in the course of our investigation. The life revealed and communicated to people in Christ is not something additional or external to their own human life. The problematic of hell as well as the surrender of the crucified one and mission of the Spirit show that the gift of God challenges people from their innermost depths. The new element consists in this, that human freedom is addressed at a radical level which is not available to it of itself. The life bestowed does not alienate people from their own life, but gives form to what is indeterminate in them and thus brings out their humanity all the more. Balthasar rightly saw this, but his mistake lay in linking the existence of the faithful directly to Christ and not sufficiently valuing the independent function of the Holy Spirit. If this Spirit is reciprocal love, then its personal character in God himself presupposes the constitution of other persons. Its function in salvation history must be thought through similarly. By the divine gift, it does not constitute human subjects as persons, but it presupposes these and unites them with the divine person in Christ.

In all this, the human person should not be understood as a fixed quantity, closed in on itself, which can be changed only from outside. It is in its whole being oriented toward God and has as a creature something indeterminate in itself. It is of itself not finally self-determining or autonomous, but — despite its subsistence — must at the same time in its innermost being be thought of on the model of a "material" which is in need of further determination. By receiving divine life it is, therefore, not alienated from itself. Existence in faith does not mean playing a role which is strange, but being addressed by the role received (mission) in the indeterminacy at the center of one's person and challenged to a new self-determination and freedom made possible by the Holy Spirit.

It may appear at first glance that such an understanding of life is in radical opposition to modern thinking, which since the Enlightenment circles around that autonomous subject which is responsible to itself and gives laws for itself. Where Christian thought has almost exclusively based itself on the autonomous moral subject, the doctrine of redemption has also in fact run into a fundamental crisis. But the history of modern thought is far more complex than the claim to self-determining freedom and moral autonomy. To this history there belong also the bitter discoveries which this thought with claim to autonomy had to make. For that reason it is acquainted with the dialectic of the Enlightenment and has dissolved into different tendencies, so that today there no longer exists a unified modern thought. There is the tendency to see autonomy only in the power of negation (deconstruction) and to renounce every attempt to build up a positive meaning of life (nihilism). There is the counter-tendency of return to old or new mythologies, by which the individual hands himself over to uncontrolled powers and, instead of service, accepts enslavement. Yet another tendency is oriented toward science and tries to explain human behavior above all from the viewpoint of biological evolution. The individual also stands according to this view — as a member in a long chain — at the service of an all-embracing process, although within his own life's horizon, he needs only to follow the immediate urge to live. Besides these tendencies, there are many people who think themselves to be at the service of a higher truth. It is therefore far from the case that there exists today a coherent philosophy of autonomy over against the Christian understanding of life. The experience of different forms of heteronomy is on the increase rather than on the wane, and if one looks less at the great cultural trends and more at everyday life, then it clearly becomes apparent how strong is the tendency to seek happiness not in autonomy but in losing oneself, in the different forms of "fix" (work, aggression, music, sport, drugs, sexuality, consumer goods, etc.). The act of giving oneself away seems to correspond to a deep inclination in people, and thus heteronomy actually lived easily gains the upper hand over the theoretical claim to autonomy. But Christian life correctly understood is neither autonomous nor heteronomous, for it is precisely the gift received which makes possible a radical freedom.

How does the new life bestowed on people, which is experienced in the inmost depths of freedom and at the center of the person, express itself concretely? How does it incarnate itself in Christian life and how can it become a clear witness? In recent decades there has been a great discussion about the problematic of theory and praxis. A notable tendency in recent theology holds the correct teaching, orthodoxy, to be too weak and too ambiguous to give an authentic witness of the new life. For this reason orthopraxis is favored. But what praxis is meant by this? Can the moral praxis of individual Christians and of the Christian community be an unambiguous expression of the biblical message? Does not the long history of the Christian churches show that the faithful for long periods were hardly better than people of other religions or humanistic philosophies? Their praxis has long since proved unable to give any unambiguous witness. And even the shift of emphasis from individual to political praxis is hardly likely to bring about a fundamental solution. Is not the old problematic of the Enlightenment still at work, (mis)understanding Christianity as educational material for humankind?

Already in Maximus the Confessor we can find observations which point to the formulation of the question current today. Whereas the Old Testament tried above all to foster virtue, the New Testament unites both praxis and "theoria": "The performance of the Word is life; but the splendor of living is the Word. Praxis is 'theory' in its actuality; and 'theory' is a mysterious praxis."[54] Maximus recognizes, then, a reciprocal relationship of theory and praxis, and his "theoria" is more comprehensive than modern theory. He sees in it the deepest praxis. How he understood the interplay of the two in detail is, however, not easy to ascertain. The whole context of this thought and the clear mention of the showman's art and of the mysterious indicate that we are not merely dealing here with a Platonic view, which is treated as a mysterious praxis. Rather he seems to have addressed a third dimension in human activity, which to a certain extent unites theory and praxis: *performance*.

The importance of the function of performance is shown not only in the human urge to play of children (and adults). In precivilized societies, masks, jewelry, body-painting, and dress had a great importance in all public and cultic actions. Even in the high religions and in civilized societies, performance kept its great importance, even if it showed itself partly in new forms (e.g., buildings). Where cultic performance no longer dominated the entire life of the society, other forms of performance were able to arise, for example, the theater (and secular dance), which take into account the vital need for display. Also performance plays an important and conspicuous part in many areas of everyday life today.

If Maximus the Confessor speaks of a performance of the Word and sees the quintessence of "theory" in a praxis bound with mystery, this suggests that he was referring to a praxis of representation which gives

---

54. Maximus the Confessor, *Quaest. ad. Thal.* 63 (PG 90:691A).

expression to the hidden threefold life in the faithful. In the realm of faith, such a praxis of representation can only be the liturgy. And in this regard there is actually a long theological tradition which speaks of a certain precedence of praxis to theory: *lex orandi — lex credendi* (the law of prayer is the law of belief). Our investigation leads consequently to the concluding question, whether the hidden divine life finds clear expression preeminently in the liturgy of the church and whether this liturgy can be understood as the dramatic performance of the dramatic event of salvation in Jesus Christ.

Liturgical Drama

If one asks the question about a dramatic understanding of liturgy, from the outset a possible misunderstanding must be avoided. The eucharistic celebration is naturally not an imitation of individual events in the life of Jesus, as one influential allegorical explanation of the Mass from the early Middle Ages opined (see Amalarius of Metz). The question about its dramatic character can be raised only in the sense of whether it — like the fate of Jesus — may be understood essentially as an event of the transforming interaction between different actors.

Although in the actual course of the eucharistic celebration the priest has a predominant role, the cooperation of the faithful community is fundamentally indispensable. It depends on their regular affirmation (Amen) that the process of the action continues, and their listening and praying together, their bringing of the gifts, their reception of the sacraments, and their being sent out into the world give the celebration its concrete form. The Word of Scripture is not proffered in the liturgy for private meditation. It also offers more than the material and examples for instruction and education. Rather, the Word of Scripture is publicly presented and announced as the Word of God. By this is meant that in reading the Scriptures and interpreting them, something crucial takes place. God himself is believed to be working through the Spirit, so that the result is not merely instruction about him, but he himself speaks to the hearers.

Remembering (*memoria*), as a further essential dimension of the liturgical celebration, does not take place in a subjective recalling to mind. In the Eucharist it is completely integrated into the great prayer of thanksgiving (preface and canon), by which the faithful community under the invocation of the Holy Spirit (*epiklesis*) turns to the Father and prays for the living and the dead. The remembering of the past saving deed of Christ takes place within the framework of an interaction between the thanking and asking church and the Father who answers in the Spirit. The consequences of this statement become fully clear if they are deepened by the question about the effectiveness of the liturgical celebration.

In recent theology there are two great tendencies concerning the interpretation of the way sacraments have their effect. Analogously to christology from above and from below, there are also two opposite directions in sacramental theology, which lead to the question, as formulated by W. Averbeck: "Is the Word as constitutive of the sacrament intended as a word addressed from God (the Father, through Christ, the church, the donor) to the receiver? Or is it essentially a prayer of the church (the donor) with Christ to the Father?" Following M. Schmaus, E. H. Schillebeeckx, H. Fries, and O. Semmelroth, Averbeck advocates the second view.[55]

Making recourse to the theology of Coffey, E. J. Kilmartin has developed a rigorous trinitarian theology of the liturgy. By means of the Australian theologian's two trinitarian models he integrates a christology from above (prayer and surrender of Jesus to the Father) into one from below and thus comes to the conclusion that the liturgy (Eucharist and sacraments) is to be understood as prayer of the church, to which is promised a sure hearing, because it is spoken in Christ and in the power of the Holy Spirit.[56] This view, which we do not need here to go into in more detail, seems convincing, and it points to the fundamental dialogical structure of the liturgy.[57] But precisely with such an interpretation it is important to consider that all human action has a function of performance, so as to avoid misunderstandings. The prayer to which a sure hearing is promised is not only thanks and request, but as such an enactment of that which is promised to it, namely, the divine life and grace. The upward direction of the official prayer of the church, because it takes place in Christ and in the Holy Spirit, acts out simultaneously the gift of God to human beings. Therefore in the liturgy the most central sacramental words can be spoken both in the indicative and in the mode of prayerful request.

The indications so far should show clearly that the liturgy, according to its deepest character, is to be understood as an interpersonal event. Is a dialogical model not sufficient adequately to describe it? In the consideration of Jesus' fate, we were led finally to the category of drama,

---

55. Averbeck (1981), 54–58.

56. "The prayer of the Church on earth is a prayer made with the confidence of faith it will be heard. The ground for this confidence is the belief that it is made through, with, and in Christ, in the power of the Holy Spirit" (Kilmartin [1988], 173). "The epiklesis is thus, so to say, the *inner soul of the Eucharist*" (Kasper [1987], 311).

57. "It is this personalistic explanation of the efficacy of the sacraments, *ex opere operato*, that accounts for the dialogical structure of the liturgy and the essentially christological-Trinitarian dimension of Christian liturgy in all its forms" (Kilmartin [1988], 174).

because we are dealing — over and above the interaction of several actors — with a fatal conflict, which has its climax in the surrender of the crucified one (sacrifice). If this aspect were to come to real enactment in the eucharistic celebration, then it would immediately become clear that the category of the dialogic is not enough fully to characterize the liturgy. The recourse to the model of drama would then be inevitable. The question of a dramatic understanding of liturgy should, then, be answered in the light of the question about the sacrificial character of the Eucharist.

The Catholic Church does in fact teach that the Mass is a sacrifice, and she defended this doctrine at the Council of Trent against the attacks of the reformers (DS 1738–59). Because at that time people meant by the concept of sacrifice without exception an act of destruction, the posttridentine theories of the Mass searched in the Mass also for a corresponding occurrence. In this way they made many undoubted errors. In opposition to this concept, we have seen that Christ's actual sacrifice may not be seen as an act of destruction even in the case of the cross, although it was a bloody occurrence, for neither did God slaughter his Son (by means of sinners) nor did the Son kill himself (indirectly) as sacrificial priest. With the question about the sacrificial character of the eucharistic celebration, we need consequently to explain over again how sacrifice is to be understood in this context.

Trent teaches that the same sacrificial priest is at work on the cross and in the Mass, namely, Christ, and that on each occasion he offers himself as victim (DS 1743). The question whether the act of sacrifice is also the same is left unanswered by Trent, and indeed intentionally so. D. N. Power has gone into the long discussions of the council in detail, and he is able to show that at that time there was no clear and unified theology of sacrifice in the Catholic Church. Most theologians and council fathers thought that the Last Supper also had been a sacrifice.[58] But because they were not able to explain clearly the relationship of the Last Supper to the cross, over against the objection of the reformers that Christ offered himself once for all (Heb. 7:27; 10:12, 14), this question was finally left unanswered.[59] Similar confusions ruled concerning the relationship between the sacrifice of the Mass and the sacrifice of the cross. The council wanted to defend the dominant liturgical praxis of a multiplicity of Masses for the living and the dead, for which Mass stipends were received. This practice included a theory of the *limited* fruits of the sacrifice of the Mass, which the priest by the power of his official function can apply to one person or another, living or dead. But

---

58. Power (1987), 76f., 87f., 100, 105–14.
59. Ibid., 102f., 107–14.

a convincing explanation for these limited fruits of the sacrifice of the Mass could not be found in the discussions of the council.[60] They contented themselves with a vague idea of a sacrifice which began at the Last Supper, reached its climax on the cross, continues in heaven, and is made present in the Eucharist,[61] and, based on this presupposition, they taught that the Mass was a "real sacrifice of atonement" (DS 1743).

In modern theological discussions, in response to research in the scientific study of religions which we went into earlier in this investigation, the concept of sacrifice is used with quite differing meanings. And frequently a difficult sense is not explained at all. Thus it is not surprising that much in the question about the sacrificial character of the Mass remains still unanswered, even if this problematic does not have the same consequences as at the time of the Reformation. However, on one important point, which was uncontested even by Trent, ecumenical agreement is beginning to emerge. The anamnesis, or remembrance, in the Eucharist is understood as a real making present again of the whole of Christ's work of salvation. The Lima Document emphasizes that the Eucharist is the memorial of the one crucified and risen and that Christ offers community with himself through this anamnesis.[62] If Christ is present in the anamnesis, which takes place in a great prayer of thanks and asking by the church, then this means that this prayer is not promised a certain hearing purely because of the merits of the crucified one. Rather, his own surrender is effectively present in the prayerful surrender of the church. As he entrusted himself to the Father by the power of the Spirit, so the same Spirit who is invoked in the epiklesis unites the surrender of the head of the church with that of its body. Consequently, prayer in the name of Jesus does not mean merely a meritorious referral back to him; rather, the act of the church is inwardly determined by his act of surrender.

The Lima document further emphasizes that the anamnesis relates to Jesus' whole mission of salvation. With this statement we have reached the most essential point in our own formulation of the question. If the

60. "Thus the discussion ended with much the same kind of confused statement that had marked its entire course. The Fathers of the Council found themselves in something of a dilemma. They recognized that the one unique sacrifice of redemption was the cross and death of Jesus Christ, and they also recognized that the reality of the Mass lay in its representative character and that all its value came from the cross. At the same time, they were much moved by the desire to play up its sacrificial character, since this was fundamental to the needs of application of the fruits of the cross, as they saw the Christian dispensation, and they also seem to have been convinced that the true religion needed true sacrifice as part of its cult" (ibid., 114).

61. Ibid., 87, 102–14.

62. "Taufe, Eucharistie und Amt: Konvergenzerklärung der Kommission für Glauben und Kirchenverfassung des Oekumenischen Rates der Kirchen" (Lima-Dokument) 1982 (FO/E II B 5f.), in H. Meyer, et al., eds. (1983), 559.

whole drama of Jesus' life ("in his becoming man, his humbling of himself, his service, his teaching, his suffering, his sacrifice, his resurrection and ascension, and in that he sent the Spirit") is present in the eucharistic remembrance, then the liturgy itself participates in the dramatic character of his destiny. This means nothing more nor less than that in the church's sacrifice of praise and petition, the whole sacrifice of Christ's life (in all its five acts) is effectively made present again.

What is the concrete significance of a liturgy understood dramatically (or of the sacrificial character of the eucharistic celebration)? Although all the sacraments are effective as prayers of the church (in the name of Christ and by means of the Holy Spirit), in the individual sacraments the intention of prayer for one or more people in a concrete situation stands symbolically in the foreground. Baptism, confirmation, reconciliation, ordination, matrimony, and anointing of the sick are sacraments which are always dispensed with a view to one quite definite person. The eucharistic celebration is quite different. In it, Christ's entire work of salvation is made present, insofar as it reveals the triune God and is directed at the good of the whole of humanity. Instead of "for myself and my salvation" there stands the effective making present again of the event of revelation and salvation in its "objective" greatness, as it were, i.e., in its orientation toward all the actors in the drama. The anamnesis is, then, essentially thanksgiving for what God has done and does, not for me but for the whole of humanity and creation, and it is not only a request for my salvation but in the first place for the completion of the whole body of Christ. The eucharistic celebration as a sacrifice acts out in a most impressive way the unconditional priority of Christ's deed above all human works. The individual sacraments have a share in this universal and dramatic character insofar as they also, each in its own way, point toward the eucharistic celebration.

If we only had the individual sacraments, in which the concern for the salvation of individuals is always in the foreground, then the liturgy of the church could well be adequately described on the model of dialogical or communicative action. But it is different if one looks at the center of the liturgy, the eucharistic celebration. Here the universal drama of salvation is made present precisely in its universality, which embraces the individual and the assembled community. As such it calls the faithful away from their ego and its cares and invites to adoration, praise, and thanks to him who is in himself threefold love.

Two further points are still to be mentioned briefly, which are no longer crucial for our formulation of the question, but which again freshly highlight the dramatic character of the liturgy. The observations so far could give the impression that the drama of Jesus' destiny with its fatal conflict is enacted in the liturgy only in a very "muffled" fashion, by means of the interaction of those who are praying and of the God who answers the prayer. For that reason we can ask further whether there is also anything of the specific manner of Jesus' death, his surrender in blood (Heb. 9:11–14), which is made present in the eucharistic celebration. For the sacrifice on the cross, we arrived at the interpretation of a transforming identification (and not an indirect self-killing). Jesus transformed the evil that was done to him in a total surrender. Transformation now plays a decisive role, although in a different sense, in the eucharistic celebration, since it is precisely by it, by the transformation of the gifts, which takes place by the power of the Holy Spirit, that Christ's surrender of his life is really present in the anamnesis, and it is aimed at the change of heart of all taking part. Consequently, with the sacrificial character of the eucharistic celebration, the element of transformation should also be addressed. As Christ on the cross fundamentally transformed the power of evil in surrender, so also in the eucharistic celebration a transformation of the gifts occurs through the Holy Spirit; this transformation aims at a step by step conversion of the whole of humanity into his surrender.

With the mention of conversion of hearts, a final point is touched on which must be noted in order to avoid misunderstandings. The church's liturgy, which is understood as performance and effective representation of the dramatic event of salvation in Christ, may not in any way be played off against ethical action. This already follows from what we said earlier about the post-Easter Lord's Supper. In the beginning religious-social differences were cancelled out in the celebration itself (see Gal. 3:28). The poor were fed and conflicts were resolved. Even if these duties are nowadays largely separated in time from the liturgical celebration, their objective relatedness to it remains fully preserved. If the connection were to be lost, prayer in the liturgy would also necessarily degenerate into a magic recitation of formulas. The relation to the drama of life is therefore essential for the liturgy as dramatic action. Because it is not just any sort of play, but the performance and making present of the drama of salvation in Christ, it summons to decision-making. It sets in motion a process of judgment as self-judgment:

> Whoever eats of the bread and drinks of the cup unworthily will be guilty of the Lord's body and blood. Let everyone examine himself, and only then eat of the bread and drink of the cup. For whoever eats and drinks without discerning the body of the Lord, that person eats and drinks judgment upon himself. Because of this some among you are weak and ill, and not a few have passed away. But if we judged ourselves, then we would not be judged." (1 Cor. 11:27–31)

The eucharistic celebration demands a self-examination. If this is not carried out in sufficient depth, then there necessarily results an involuntary process of self-judgment, which according to Paul reaches even into a person's bodily existence. The liturgy is, then, not only the performance of a drama; as effective representation it releases a process of judgment and provokes decisions which reach into the inmost depths of the participants.

BIBLIOGRAPHY OF CITED AUTHORS AND WORKS

(If an English translation of a particular title was known or found, it is given after the initial entry.)

Anselm of Canterbury. *Cur deus homo: Warum Gott Mensch geworden.* Trans. F. S. Schmitt. Darmstadt, 1956. *Why God Became Man, and The Virgin Conception and Original Sin.* Albany, N.Y.: Magi Books, 1969.

————. *L'oeuvre de S. Anselme de Cantorbéry.* Vol. 1: *Monologion, Proslogion.* Ed. and trans. M. Corbin. Paris, 1986. Vol. 3: *L'incarnation du Verbe, Pourquoi un Dieu-homme.* Ed. and trans. M. Corbin and A. Calonnier. Paris, 1988.

Augustine. *Zweiundzwanzig Bücher über den Gottesstaat.* Trans. A. Schröder. 3 vols. Kempten, 1911–1916. *The City of God against the Pagans.* Cambridge, Mass.: Harvard University Press; London: Wm. Heinemann, 1957–72.

Averbeck, W. "Sakramente – neu verstanden?" *Münchener theologische Zeitschrift* 32 (1981): 46–58.

Balthasar, H. U. v. *Theodramatik.* 4 vols. Einsiedeln, 1973–83. Vol. 1: *Prolegomena* (1973); vol. 2: *Die Personen des Spiels,* part 1, 1976; part 2, 1978; vol. 3: *Die Handlung* (1980); vol. 4: *Das Endspiel* (1983).

————. *Theo-Drama.* 4 of 5 vols. so far published. San Francisco: Ignatius, 1988–94.

————. *Was dürfen wir hoffen?* Kriterien 75. Einsiedeln, 1986.

————. *Kleiner Diskurs über die Hölle* (Anstösse). 2d ed. Ostfildern, 1987.

Barth, K. *Die Kirchliche Dogmatik.* 4 vols. Zollikon, 1932–67. *Church Dogmatics.* Edinburgh: T. & T. Clark, 1936–77.

Becker, J. *Johannes der Täufer und Jesus von Nazareth.* Neukirchen-Vluyn, 1972.

Berger, K. "Die königlichen Messiastraditionen des Neuen Testaments." *New Testament Studies* 20 (1974): 1–44.

————. *Die Auferstehung des Propheten und die Erhöhung des Menschensohnes: Traditionsgeschichtliche Untersuchungen zur Deutung des Geschickes Jesu in frühchristlichen Texten.* Göttingen, 1976.

Blank, J., and J. Webick, eds. *Sühne und Versöhnung.* Theol. z. Zeit 1. Düsseldorf, 1986.

Blinzler, J. *Der Prozess Jesu.* 4th ed. Regensburg, 1969. There is an Eng. trans. of the shorter 2d ed.: *The Trial of Jesus.* Westminster, Md.: Newman, 1959.

Bloch, E. *Atheismus im Christentum: Zur Religion des Exodus und des Reichs.* Gesamtausgabe 14. Frankfurt a. M., 1968. *Atheism in Christianity: The Religion of the Exodus and the Kingdom.* New York: Herder and Herder, 1972.

Bornkamm, G. *Jesus von Nazareth.* 8th ed. Stuttgart, 1968. *Jesus of Nazareth.* New York: Harper and Row, 1960.

———, ed. M. *Dibelius, Die Formgeschichte als Evangeliums.* 3d ed. Tübingen, 1959.

Bultmann, R. *Jesus.* Tübingen, 1926. *Jesus and the Word.* Tübingen, 1926. New York: Scribner's, 1934, 1958.

———. *Das Urchristentum im Rahmen der antiken Religionen.* 2d ed. Zurich, 1954. *Primitive Christianity in Its Contemporary Setting.* London and New York: Meridian, 1956.

———. *Die Geschichte der synoptischen Tradition.* 6th ed. Forschungen zur Religion und Literatur des Alten und Neuen Testaments 29. Göttingen, 1964. *The History of the Synoptic Tradition.* Oxford and New York: Harper and Row, 1963.

———. *Exegetica: Aufsätze zur Erforschung des Neuen Testaments.* Ed. E. Dinkler. Tübingen, 1967.

Burkert, W. *Homo necans: Interpretation altgriechischer Opferriten.* 32. Berlin, 1972.

Butterfield, H. *Christentum und Geschichte.* Trans. S. Erdmann. Stuttgart, 1952. *Christianity and History.* Cambridge: Cambridge University Press, 1949.

Catchpole, D. E. *The Trial of Jesus: A Study in the Gospels and Jewish Historiography from 1770 to the Present Day.* Leiden, 1971.

Christ, F. *Jesus Sophia: Die Sophia-Christologie bei den Synoptikern.* Abhandlungen zur Theologie des Alten und Neuen Testaments 57. Zurich, 1970.

Clement of Alexandria, Teppiche. *Wissenschaftliche Darlegungen entsprechend der wahren Philosophie (Stromateis).* Trans. O. Stählin. 3 vols. Kempten, 1936–38. *Stromateis: Books One to Three.* Washington, D.C.: Catholic University of America Press, 1991.

Coffey, D. *Grace: The Gift of the Holy Spirit.* Faith and Culture 2. Sydney, 1979.

———. "The 'Incarnation' of the Holy Spirit in Christ." *Theological Studies* 45 (1984): 466–80.

Conzelmann, H. "Jesus Christus." *Die Religion in Geschichte und Gegenwart* (1959a): 619–53.

———, "Geschichte und Eschaton nach Mc 13." *Zeitschrift für die neutestamentliche Wissenschaft* 50 (1959b): 210–21.

Cullmann, O. *Urchristentum und Gottesdienst.* 3d ed. Zurich, 1956.

———. *Die Christologie des Neuen Testaments.* Tübingen, 1957. *Early Christian Worship.* London, 1987.

Dunn, J. "Prophetic 'I'-Sayings and the Jesus Tradition: The Importance of Testing Prophetic Utterances within Early Christianity." *New Testament Studies* 24 (1978): 175–98.

Erlemann, K. *Das Bild Gottes in den synoptischen Gleichnissen.* Beiträge zur Wissenschaft vom Alten und Neuen Testament 126. Stuttgart, 1988.

Feldmeier, R. *Die Krisis des Gottessohnes: Die Gethsemaneerzählung als Schlüssel der Markuspassion.* Wissenschaftliche Untersuchungen zum Neuen Testament 2/21. Tübingen, 1987.

Fiedler, P. *Jesus und die Sünder.* Frankfurt a. M., 1976.

————. "Probleme der Abendmahlsforschung." In *Archiv für Liturgiewissenschaft* 24 (1982): 190–223.

Freud, S. *Totem und Tabu: Einige Übereinstimmungen im Seelenleben der Wilden und der Neurotiker.* 4th ed. Gesammelte Werke 9. Frankfurt a. M., 1968.

Fuchs, E. *Zur Frage nach dem historischen Jesus.* Gesammelte Aufsätze II. Tübingen, 1960. *Studies of the Historical Jesus.* London, 1964.

Gerhardsson, B. *The Gospel Tradition.* Lund, 1986.

Gese, H. *Zur biblischen Theologie: Alttestamentliche Vorträge.* 2d ed. Tübingen, 1983. *Essays on Biblical Theology.* Minneapolis: Augsburg Fortress, 1981.

Girard, R.* *Mensonge romantique et vérité romanesque.* Paris, 1961. *Deceit, Desire, and the Novel.* Baltimore: Johns Hopkins, 1966.

————. *To Double Business Bound: Essays on Literature, Mimesis and Anthropology.* Baltimore, 1978.

————. *Das Ende der Gewalt: Analyse des Menschheitsverhängnisses.* Trans. A. Berz. Freiburg i. Br., 1983. The German trans. is an abridgment of *Des Choses cachées depuis la fondation du monde.* Paris: Grasset, 1978. The Eng. trans. of the latter is *Things Hidden Since the Foundation of the World.* London and Stanford: Athlone and Stanford University Press, 1987.

————. *Das Heilige und die Gewalt.* Trans. E. Mainberger-Ruh. Zurich, 1987. *Violence and the Sacred.* Baltimore: Johns Hopkins, 1977.

————. *Der Sündenbock.* Trans. E. Mainberger-Ruh. Zurich, 1988. *The Scapegoat.* Baltimore: Johns Hopkins, 1986.

Gnilka, J. *Der Philipperbrief.* Herders theologischer Kommentar zum Neuen Testament. Freiburg i. Br., 1968. *Philippians.* New Testament for Spiritual Reading. New York: Herder and Herder, 1971.

————. *Das Evangelium nach Markus.* Evangelische Katholischer Kommentar zum Neuen Testament II/1: Mark 1–8:26; II/2: Mark 8:27–16:20. Zurich 1978, 1979.

Green, J. B. *The Death of Jesus: Tradition and Interpretation in the Passion Narrative.* Tübingen, 1988.

Gundry, R. H. "The Hellenization of Dominical Tradition and Christianization of Jewish Tradition in the Eschatology of 1–2 Thessalonians." *New Testament Studies* 33 (1987): 161–78.

Güttgemanns, E. *Offene Fragen zur Formgeschichte des Evangeliums: Eine methodologische Skizze der Grundlagenproblematik der Form- und Redaktionsgeschichte.* Munich, 1970. *Candid Questions concerning Gospel Form Criticism.* Pittsburgh, 1979.

Haag, H. "Der 'Gottesknecht' bei Deuterojesaja im Verständnis des Judentums." *Judaica* 41 (1985): 23–36.

---

*On Girard see *The Girard Reader,* ed. J. G. Williams (New York: Crossroad Herder, 1996).

Hahn, F. "Die alttestamentlichen Motive in der urchristlichen Abendmahlsüber-lieferung." *Evangelische Theologie* 27 (1967): 337–74.

———. "Zum Stand der Erforschung des urchristlichen Herrenmahls." *Evangelische Theologie* 35 (1975): 553–67.

———. "Die Formgeschichte des Evangeliums: Voraussetzungen, Ausbau und Tragweite." In *Zur Formgeschichte des Evangeliums.* Ed. F. Hahn. Darmstadt, 1985, 427–77.

Hamerton-Kelly, R. G., ed. *Violent Origins: W. Burkert, R. Girard, and J. Z. Smith on Ritual Killing and Cultural Formation.* Stanford, 1987.

Hengel, M. *Die Zeloten: Untersuchungen zur jüdischen Freiheitsbewegung in der Zeit von Herodes I. bis 70 n.Chr.* Arbeiten zur Geschichte des späteren Judentums und des Urchristentums 1. Leiden, 1961. *The Zealots: Investigations into the Jewish Freedom Movement in the Period from Herod I until 70 A.D.* Edinburgh: T. & T. Clark, 1997.

Hennecke-Schneemelcher. *Neutestamentliche Apokryphen.* Vol. 1.: *Evangelien.* Vol. 2: *Apostolisches, Apokalypsen und Verwandtes.* 3d ed. Tübingen, 1959, 1964. *New Testament Apocrypha.* 2 vols. Philadelphia: Westminster, 1963, 1965; rev. ed. of vol. 1, 1991.

Henrich, F., ed. *Theater als Aergernis?* Munich, 1969.

Hoffmann, P. *Orientierung an Jesus: Zur Theologie der Synoptiker* (Schmid Festschrift). Freiburg i. Br., 1973.

Hofius, O. "Sühne und Versöhnung: Zum paulinischen Verständnis des Kreuzestodes Jesu." In *Versuche, das Leiden und Sterben Jesu zu verstehen.* Ed. W. Maas. Munich, 1973, 25–46.

Holtzmann, H. J. *Lehrbuch der Neutestamentlichen Theologie.* 2 vols. 2d ed. Ed. A. Jülicher and W. Bauer. Tübingen, 1911.

Hooker, M. D. *The Son of Man in Mark: A Study of the Background of the Term "Son of Man" and Its Use in St. Mark's Gospel.* London, 1967.

Hubert, H., and M. Mauss, "Essai sur la nature et fonction du sacrifice." *L'année sociologique* 3 (1898–99): 29–138.

Iber, G. "Zur Formgeschichte der Evangelien." *Theologische Rundschau* (Neue Folge), 24 (1957–58): 283–338.

———. *Neuere Literatur zur Formgeschichte, Nachtrag.* In *M. Dibelius, Die Formgeschichte des Evangeliums.* 3d ed. Ed. G. Bornkamm. Tübingen, 1959, 302–12.

Irenäus. *Fünf Bücher gegen die Häresien.* Trans. E. Klebba. 2 vols. Kempten, 1912. *Against the Heresies.* New York: Paulist Press, 1992.

Jäger, W. *Paideia: Die Formung des griechischen Menschen.* 3 vols. Berlin, 1954, 1954, 1955.

Janowski, B. *Sühne als Heilsgeschehen: Studien zur Sühnetheologie der Priesterschrift und zur Wurzel KPR im Alten Orient und im Alten Testament.* Wissenschaftliche Monographien zum Alten und Neuen Testament 55. Neukirchen-Vluyn, 1982.

Jensen, A. E. *Mythos und Kult bei Naturvölkern: Religionswissenschaftliche Betrachtungen.* Studien zur Kulturkunde 10. Wiesbaden, 1951. *Myth and Cult among Primitive Peoples.* Chicago: University of Chicago Press, 1963.

———. *Die getötete Gottheit: Weltbild einer frühen Kultur.* Stuttgart, 1966.

Jeremias, J. *Heiligengräber in Jesu Umwelt (Mt. 23,29; Lk. 11,47): Eine Untersuchung zur Volksreligion der Zeit Jesu.* Göttingen, 1958.

———. *Abba, Studien zur neutestamentlichen Theologie und Zeitgeschichte.* Göttingen, 1966.

———. *Die Abendmahlsworte Jesu.* 4th ed. Göttingen, 1967. *The Eucharistic Words of Jesus.* Trinity Press, 1990.

———. *Neutestamentliche Theologie.* Part 1: *Die Verkündigung Jesu.* Gütersloh, 1971. *New Testament Theology.* New York: Scribner's, 1977.

Jülicher, A. *Die Gleichnisreden Jesu.* Part 2: *Auslegung der Gleichnisreden der drei ersten Evangelien.* Freiburg i. Br., 1899.

Jüngel, E. *Paulus und Jesus: Eine Untersuchung zur Präzisierung der Frage nach dem Ursprung der Christologie.* 2d ed. Tübingen, 1964.

Käsemann, E. *Exegetische Versuche und Besinnungen.* 2 vols. Tübingen, 1960, 1964.

Kasper, W. *Theologie und Kirche.* Mainz, 1987.

Kertelge, K. *Rückfrage nach Jesus: Zur Methodik und Bedeutung der Frage nach dem historischen Jesus.* Freiburg i. Br., 1974.

———. *Der Tod Jesu: Deutungen im Neuen Testament.* Freiburg i. Br., 1976.

Kertelge, K., ed. *Der Prozess gegen Jesus: Historische Rückfrage und theologische Deutung.* Freiburg i. Br., 1988.

Kienecker, F. "Theater–Tribunal der Zeit." In *Theater als Aergernis?* Ed. F. Henrich. Munich, 1969, 11–37.

Kilmartin, D. J. *Christian Liturgy: Theology and Practice.* Vol. 1: *Systematic Theology and Liturgy.* Kansas City, 1988.

Klauck, H.-J. *Herrenmahl und hellenistischer Kult: Eine religionsgeschichtliche Untersuchung zum ersten Korintherbrief.* Münster, 1982.

Koch, K. "Sühne und Sündenvergebung um die Wende von der exilischen zur nachexilischen Zeit." *Evangelische Theologie* 26 (1966): 217–239.

———. "Messias und Sündenvergebung in Jesaja 53– Targum: Ein Beitrag zu der Praxis der aramäischen Bibelübersetzung." *Journal of the Study of Judaism in the Persian, Hellenistic, and Roman Period* 3 (1972a): 117–148.

———, ed. *Um das Prinzip der Vergeltung in Religion und Recht des Alten Testaments.* Darmstadt, 1972b.

———. "Gibt es ein Vergeltungsdogma im Alten Testament?" In Koch, ed., *Prinzip der Vergeltung* (1972c): 130–80.

———. "Die israelitische Auffassung vom vergossenen Blut," In Koch, ed., *Prinzip der Vergeltung* (1972d): 432–56.

Kremer, J. "Was geschah Pfingsten? Zur Historizität des Apg 2,1–13 berichteten Pfingstereignisses." *Wort und Wahrheit* 28 (1973): 195–207.

Kuhn, H. W. *Enderwartung und gegenwärtiges Heil: Untersuchungen zu den Gemeindeliedern in Qumran mit einem Anhang über Eschatologie und Gegenwart in der Verkündigung Jesu.* Göttingen, 1966.

Kümmel, W. G. *Jesus der Menschensohn.* Stuttgart, 1984.

Lamarche, P. "Le 'blasphème' de Jésus devant le sanhédrin." *Recherches de Science Religieuse* 50 (1962): 74–85.

Lapide, P. *Auferstehung: Ein jüdisches Glaubenserlebnis.* Stuttgart, 1977. *Resurrection of Jesus: A Jewish Perspective.* Minneapolis: Augsburg Fortress, 1983.

Laufen, R. *Die Doppelüberlieferung der Logienquelle und des Markusevangeliums.* Königstein / Ts. 1980.

Lemaire, A. "Vengeance et justice dans l'Ancien Testament." In Verdier, *Vengeance* (1984), 3:13–33.

Léthel, F.-M. *Théologie de l'Agonie du Christ: La liberté humaine du Fils de Dieu et son importance sotériologique mises en lumière par saint Maxime Confesseur.* Théologie Historique 52. Paris, 1979.

Lietzmann, H. *Messe und Herrenmahl: Eine Studie zur Geschichte der Liturgie.* 3d ed. Berlin, 1955.

Linnemann, E. *Gleichnisse Jesu: Einführung und Auslegung.* 3d ed. Göttingen, 1964. *Jesus of the Parables.* New York: Harper and Row, 1966.

Lohfink, G. "Der Ablauf der Osterereignisse und die Anfänge der Urgemeinde." *Theologische Quartalschrift* 160 (1980): 162–76.

———. *Wie hat Jesus Gemeinde gewollt? Zur gesellschaftlichen Dimension des christlichen Glaubens.* Freiburg i. Br., 1982. *Jesus and Community.* Philadelphia: Fortress, 1984.

Lohmeyer, E. "Vom urchristlichen Abendmahl." *Theologische Rundschau* (Neue Folge) 9 (1937): 168–227 ("Das letzte Mahl Jesu"), 273–312 ("Das Mahl in der ältesten Christenheit").

Lohse, E. *Märtyrer und Gottesknecht: Untersuchungen zur urchristlichen Verkündigung vom Sühntod Jesu Christi.* 2d ed. Göttingen, 1963.

———. *Grundriss der neutestamentlichen Theologie.* Stuttgart, 1974.

Maas, W., ed. *Versuche, das Leiden und Sterben Jesu zu verstehen.* Munich, 1973.

Mack, B. "The Innocent Transgressor: Jesus in Early Christian Myth and History." In *René Girard and Biblical Studies.* Ed. A. McKenna. Semeia 33 (1985), 135–65.

Mantel, H. *Studies in the History of the Sanhedrin.* Cambridge, Mass., 1961.

Marquard, O. *Schwierigkeiten mit der Geschichtsphilosophie.* Frankfurt a. M., 1973.

Merklein, H. *Die Gottesherrschaft als Handlungsprinzip: Untersuchung zur Ethik Jesu.* Würzburg, 1978.

Metz, J. B. "Erlösung und Emanzipation." *Stimmen der Zeit* 191 (1973a): 171–84.

Meyer, H., et al., eds. *Dokumente wachsender Übereinstimmung: Sämtliche Berichte und Konsenstexte interkonfessioneller Gespräche auf Weltebene 1931–1982.* Paderborn, 1983.

Müller, K. "Menschensohn und Messias: Religionsgeschichtliche Vorüberlegungen zum Menschensohnproblem in den synoptischen Evangelien." *Biblische Zeitschrift* (Neue Folge) 16 (1972): 161–87; 17 (1973): 52–66.

———. "Der Menschensohn im Danielzyklus," in R. Pesch and R. Schnackenburg, eds., *Jesus und der Menschensohn* (1975), 37–80.

———, ed. *Die Aktion Jesu und die Re-Aktion der Kirche: Jesus von Nazareth und die Anfänge der Kirche.* Würzburg, 1972.

Müller, M. *Der Ausdruck "Menschensohn" in den Evangelien: Voraussetzungen und Bedeutung.* Leiden, 1984.

Mussner, F. "Gab es eine 'galiläische Krise'?" In Hoffmann (1973).

———. "Ursprünge und Entfaltung der neutestamentlichen Sohneschristologie: Versuch einer Rekonstruktion." In *Grundfragen der Christologie heute.* Ed. L. Scheffczyk. Freiburg i. Br., 1975, 77–113.

———. *Traktat über die Juden.* Munich, 1979.

"Der Prozess gegen Jesus von Nazareth." In *ThRv* 84 (1988): 353–60.

Neuenzeit, P. *Das Herrenmahl: Studien zur paulinischen Eucharistieauffassung.* Studia Antoniana 1. Munich, 1960.

Oberlinner, L. *Todeserwartung und Todesgewissheit Jesu: Zum Problem einer historischen Begründung.* Stuttgart, 1980.

O'Donnell, J. "In Him and over Him: The Holy Spirit in the Life of Jesus." *Gregorianum* 70 (1989): 25–45.

The Old Testament Pseudepigrapha. Vol. 1: *Apocalyptic Literature and Testaments.* Vol. 2: *Expansions of the "Old Testament" and Legends, Wisdom and Philosophical Literature, Prayers, Psalms, and Odes, Fragments of Lost Judeo-Hellenistic Works.* Ed. J. H. Charlesworth. London, 1983, 1985.

Origenes. *Vier Bücher von den Prinzipien.* Ed. and trans. E. Görgemanns and H. Karpp. Darmstadt, 1976. *On First Principles.* New York: Harper and Row, 1966.

Pannenberg, W. *Grundzüge der Christologie.* Gütersloh, 1964.

Patsch, H. *Abendmahl und historischer Jesus.* 1. Stuttgart, 1972.

Pawlowsky, P., and Ed Schuster, eds. *Woran wir leiden.* Innsbruck u.a., 1979.

Pesch, R. "Die Überlieferung der Passion." In *Rückfrage nach Jesus: Zur Methodik und Bedeutung der Frage nach dem historischen Jesus.* Ed. K. Kertelge. Freiburg i. Br., 1974.

———. "Die Passion des Menschensohns: Eine Studie zu den Menschensohnworten der vormarkischen Passionsgeschichte." In *Jesus und der Menschensohn.* Für Anton Vögtle. Ed. R. Pesch and R. Schnackenburg. Freiburg i. Br., 1975, 166–95.

———. *Das Markusevangelium.* Herders theologischer Kommentar zum Neuen Testament. Vol. 1: *Kap. 1,1–8,26.* Vol. 2: *Kap. 8,27–16,20.* Freiburg i. Br., 1976, 1977.

———. *Das Abendmahl und Jesu Todesverständnis.* Freiburg i. Br., 1978.

———. "Das Evangelium in Jerusalem: Mark 14,12–26 als ältestes Überlieferungsgut der Urgemeinde." In *Das Evangelium und die Evangelien: Vorträge zum Tübinger Symposium 1982.* Ed. P. Stuhlmacher. Wissenschaftliche Untersuchungen zum Neuen Testament 28. Tübingen, 1983, 113–55.

———. *Die Apostelgeschichte.* Evangelisch-katholischer Kommentar zum Neuen Testament. Vol. 1: *Apg 1–12.* Vol. 2: *Apg 13–28.* Zurich, 1986.

———, and R. Schnackenburg, eds. *Jesus und der Menschensohn.* Für Anton Vögtle. Freiburg i. Br., 1975.

Polag, A. *Die Christologie der Logienquelle.* Neukirchen-Vluyn, 1977.

Poliakov, L. *Geschichte des Antisemitismus.* Trans. R. Pfister. Vol. 1: *Von der Antike bis zu den Kreuzzügen,* 1977. Vol. 2: *Das Zeitalter der Verteufelung und des Ghettos,* 1978. Vol. 3: *Religiöse und soziale Toleranz unter dem*

Islam, 1979. Vol. 4: *Die Marranen im Schatten der Inquisition,* 1981. Vol. 5: *Die Aufklärung und ihre judenfeindliche Tendenz,* 1983. Vol. 6: *Emanzipation und Rassenwahn,* 1987. Worms, 1977–1987. *The History of Anti-Semitism.* London: Routledge & Kegan Paul, 1974.

————. *La causalité diabolique: Liberté de l'esprit.* Vol. 1: *Essai sur l'origine des persécutions.* Vol. 2: *Du joug mongol à la victoire de Lénine.* Paris, 1980, 1985.

Power, D. N. *The Sacrifice We Offer: The Tridentine Dogma and Its Reinterpretation.* Edinburgh, 1987.

Rad, G. v. *Theology of the Old Testament.* Vol. 1: *The Theology of Israel's Historical Traditions.* Trans. D. M. G. Stalker. New York: Harper & Row, 1962.

Radl, W. "Sonderüberlieferungen bei Lukas? Traditionsgeschichtliche Fragen zu Luke 22,67f.; 23,2 und 23,6–12." In *Der Prozess gegen Jesus: Historische Rückfrage und theologische Deutung.* Ed. K. Kertelge, Freiburg i. Br., 1988. 131–47.

Rahner, K. *Grundkurs des Glaubens: Einführung in den Begriff des Christentums.* Freiburg i. Br., 1976.

Riesner, R. *Jesus als Lehrer.* Tübingen, 1981.

Riessler, P., trans. and comment. *Altjüdisches Schrifttum ausserhalb der Bibel.* 2d ed. Heidelberg, 1966.

Robinson, J. M. *Kerygma und historischer Jesus.* 2d ed. Zurich, 1967.

Roloff, J. *Das Kerygma und der irdische Jesus: Historische Motive in den Jesus-Erzählungen der Evangelien.* Göttingen, 1970.

Ruppert, L. *Der leidende Gerechte: Eine motivgeschichtliche Untersuchung zum Alten Testament und zwischentestamentlichen Judentum.* Stuttgart, 1972.

Russell, B. *Warum ich kein Christ bin?* Rororo Taschenbuch 1019/20. Trans. M. Steipe. Hamburg, 1969. *Why I Am Not a Christian.* New York: Simon and Schuster, 1976.

Schaeffler, R. "Logisches Widerspruchsverbot und theologisches Paradox: Überlegungen zur Weiterentwicklung der transzendentalen Dialektik." *Theologie und Philosophie* 62 (1987): 321–51.

Scheffczyk, L., ed. *Grundfragen der Christologie heute.* Freiburg i. Br., 1975.

Schenk, W. "Die Einheit von Wortverkündigung und Herrenmahl in den urchristlichen Gemeindeversammlungen." In *Theologische Versuche.* Vol. 2. Ed. J. Rogge and G. Schille. Berlin, 1970.

Schillebeeckx, E. *Jesus: Die Geschichte von einem Lebenden.* Trans. H. Zulauf. Freiburg i. Br., 1976.

Schnackenburg, R., and R. Pesch, eds. *Jesus und der Menschensohn.* Für Anton Vögtle. Freiburg i. Br., 1975. (See also Pesch, R.)

Schürmann, H. *Traditionsgeschichtliche Untersuchungen zu den synoptischen Evangelien. Beiträge.* Düsseldorf, 1968.

————. *Jesu ureigner Tod: Exegetische Besinnungen und Ausblick.* Freiburg i. Br., 1975.

————. *Das Gebet des Herrn als Schlüssel zum Verstehen Jesu.* 4th ed. Freiburg i. Br., 1981.

————. *Gottes Reich–Jesu Geschick: Jesu ureigner Tod im Licht seiner Basileia-Verkündigung.* Freiburg i. Br., 1983.

Schwager, R. *Das dramatische Kirchenverständnis bei Ignatius von Loyola: Historisch-pastoraltheologisch Studie über die Stellung der Kirche in den Exerzitien und im Leben des Ignatius.* Zurich, 1970.

————. *Brauchen wir einen Sündenbock? Gewalt und Erlösung in den biblischen Schriften.* Münden, 1978.

————. "Geschichtsphilosophie und Erlösungslehre," *Zeitschrift für katholische Theologie* 102 (1980): 14–23.

————. *Der wunderbare Tausch: Zur Geschichte und Deutung der Erlösungslehre.* Munich, 1986.

————. "Theologie – Geschichte – Wissenschaft," *Zeitschrift für katholische Theologie* 109 (1987): 257–75.

Schwarz, G. *Jesus der "Menschensohn": Aramäistische Untersuchungen zu den synoptischen Menschensohnworten Jesu.* Stuttgart, 1986.

Schweitzer, A. *Geschichte der Leben-Jesu-Forschung.* 5th ed. Tübingen, 1933. *The Quest of the Historical Jesus.* New York: Macmillan, 1968 (trans. W. Montgomery from 1st German ed., 1906).

Schweizer, E. *Jesus Christus im vielfältigen Zeugnis des Neuen Testaments.* 4th ed. Hamburg, 1976.

Sitta, H. *Geschichte und politischer Charakter der Deutschen: Ein Versuch.* Eigenverlag Friesoythe, 1980.

Smith, J. Z. "The Domestication of Sacrifice." In *Violent Origins: W. Burkert, R. Girard, and J. Z. Smith on Ritual Killing and Cultural Formation.* Ed. R. G. Hamerton-Kelly. Stanford, 1987, 191–235.

Steck, O. H. *Israel und das gewaltsame Geschick der Propheten: Untersuchungen zur Überlieferung des deuteronomistischen Geschichtsbildes im Alten Testament, Spätjudentum und Urchristentum.* Neukirchen-Vluyn, 1967.

Strecker, G., ed. *Jesus Christus in Historie und Theologie* (Conzelmann Festschrift). Tübingen, 1975.

Strobel, A. *Die moderne Jesusforschung.* Stuttgart, 1966.

————. *Kerygma und Apokalyptik: Ein religionsgeschichtlicher und theologischer Beitrag zur Christusfrage.* Göttingen, 1967.

Strube, G., ed. *Wer war Jesus von Nazareth? Die Erforschung einer historischen Gestalt.* Munich, 1972.

Stuhlmacher, P., ed. *Das Evangelium und die Evangelien.* Vorträge zum Tübinger Symposium 1982. Tübingen, 1983.

Theissen, G. *Soziologie der Jesusbewegung: Ein Beitrag zur Entstehungsgeschichte des Urchristentums.* Munich, 1977. *The First Followers of Jesus: A Sociological Analysis of the Earliest Christianity.* Philadelphia, 1978.

Tödt, H. E. *Der Menschensohn in der synoptischen Überlieferung.* Gütersloh, 1959.

Verdier, R., ed. *La Vengeance.* Études d'ethnologie, d'histoire et de philosophie (Coll. Échanges). Vols. 1 and 2.: *Vengeance et pouvoir dans quelques sociétés extra-occidentales,* ed. R. Verdier, Paris, 1980; Vol. 3.: *Vengeance, pouvoirs et idéologies dans quelques civilisations de l'Antiquité,* ed.

R. Verdier and J. P. Poly, Paris, 1984; Vol. 4.: *La vengeance dans la pensée occidentale,* ed. G. Courtois, Paris, 1984.

Vielhauer, P. *Aufsätze zum Neuen Testament.* Munich, 1965.

Vögtle, A. "Todesankündigungen und Todesverständnis Jesu." In *Der Tod Jesu: Deutungen im Neuen Testament.* Ed. K. Kertelge. Freiburg i. Br., 1976, 51–113.

Wengst, K. *Christologische Formeln und Lieder des Urchristentums.* Gütersloh, 1972.

Wenz, G. *Geschichte der Versöhnungslehre in der evangelischen Theologie der Neuzeit.* 2 vols. Munich, 1984, 1986.

Index

Acts of the Apostles
  arrest of Peter and John (Acts 4:1–22), 156
  regarding condemnation of Jesus, new elements in Acts, 157
  prayer of community after Peter and John's arrest, 156–57
Anselm of Canterbury, St.
  on eschatology, 34–35
  on God as "that which greater cannot be thought," 13, 197
  on method of showing divine goodness and greatness, 6, 197
  on natural theology and Christian reflection, 13
  point of departure of, in reconciling God's goodness and justice, 14
atonement
  Christ identified with all victims of sin, 192
  crucified one suffers with opponents and transforms, 187–88
  post-Easter ideas of, must come from Jesus himself, 103
  sins, distinction between intentional and unintentional in the Old Testament, 181–82
  and substitution, 191–92
Augustine of Hippo, St., on good and evil, 4–5

Balthasar, Hans Urs von
  drama, categories of, and Christian theology, 12
  God-drama and God's attributes, 8–9
  on person, theological or supernatural concept of, 219–20
  and "trinitarian inversion," 210
Barth, Karl
  on bringer of salvation brought to judgment, 82
  on Jesus' identification with sinners, 169, 172
  on predestination and God's goodness and anger, 7–8
  on self-revelation of God, 201–2
  on theology of the cross, 162–63

blasphemy, specific meaning of, in condemnation of Jesus, 85–87
Bultmann, R.
  on impossibility of knowing Jesus' understanding of his death, 155–56
  on Jesus' death as embarrassment, 50–51
  on Jesus' prophecies of suffering and resurrection, 74
  on kerygma of early church's lack of interest in history, 153
  suspicious of attempts to demonstrate credibility of Easter message by historical and rational means, 119
Burkert, W., sacrifice as derived from killing in hunter culture, 175–76
Butterfield, H., on historians and problem of aggression and projection, 131–32

Christian message, and the myths of the dying and rising deity, 127–30
christology, from above and from below, 210–11
Clement, on God's anger as educational, 3–4
Coffey, D.
  on christology from above and christology from below, 210–11
  on Holy Spirit as transcendental love of Son's human nature for the Father, 216
Corbin, M., on St. Anselm, 5–6
Council of Trent, Mass as sacrifice, defense of doctrine of, 225
covenant
  and prophetic proclamation, 155
  of Sinai, as great Old Testament theme, 154–55

drama
  Balthasar's *Theodramatik*, 8–9, 12
  dramatic point of view on present and future kingdom of God, 35–36
  freedom and commitment of the actor, 218
  of Jesus' experience of abandonment by the Father, 116